Snakes
in the Temple

Snakes in the Temple

*Unmasking Idolatry
in Today's Church and
Pointing the Way to
Spiritual Breakthrough*

David Orton

Sovereign World

Sovereign World Ltd
PO Box 777
Tonbridge
Kent TN11 0ZS
England

ISBN 1 85240 376 4

Cover design by CCD, www.ccdgroup.co.uk
Typeset by CRB Associates, Reepham, Norfolk
Printed in England by Clays Ltd, St Ives plc

To Jenny
A Covenant Woman
My truest friend and partner in all of life

Contents

Acknowledgments

We stand on the shoulders of those who have gone before us. While only I can be held responsible for what I have falteringly expressed in this book I am in debt to many who have inspired me over the years. Without their input my vision would, I think, be more limited than it presently is.

I want to thank my first pastors, Paul and Bunty Collins, church planters and missionary pioneers, for their big hearts and their model of faith and courage. To them, I owe my love for the larger body of Christ and my vision for the nations. To David Jackson, my pastor and early mentor, I owe my love for the Word of God, for revival, and for the prophetic. Thanks to Dean Sherman, pioneer of YWAM Australia, for a power encounter with God and for introducing me to a lifestyle of radical discipleship.

From more of a distance, I am indebted to men such as of Bob Mumford and Ern Baxter. They imparted, in our youth, an awesome vision for the kingdom. Bob's understanding of the ways and dealings of God has constantly pointed Jenny and me back to true north, helping us to make sense of our own lives. And sitting at Ern's feet as new Christians, listening to his experiences with William Branham and the healing revival was an awesome privilege. It has given us a hunger for this generation to see a greater day of God's power.

In bringing this book to fruition thanks must first go to Jenny, my wife, for her hours of dialogue and for patiently listening to every new insight and corner turned. She has checked and re-checked the manuscript many times, but more crucially she has borne in many private ways the high cost of its message. While men do not see, there is One who does see and will reward. Honey, I am in awe of you, and with the angels above I salute you.

Thanks must also go to Mark and Sue Whitby and the folk of Jubilee in Melbourne for their special friendship. Without them this book would not have been written. Thanks also to David and Helen Jamison for their constant encouragement to keep writing; and to friend and intercessor, Cathy Posterino, who has faithfully prayed with Jenny and me every week for the last three years during the writing of this book.

Thanks also to Dr Kevin Conner for so carefully checking through the manuscript and for his helpful and affirming words. Likewise, to Kevin Forlong and especially to Marc Dupont for believing in us and for seeing the importance of this message. Even so, these men cannot be held responsible for the text, the message, nor the inevitable imperfections of the writer. In this I stand alone.

And thank you to my father-in-law, Peter Matheson, for his unstinting support. Your understanding during this time of transition has meant more than you know.

Foreword

In the past decade I have had the privilege of writing endorsements for many new books. For the most part they have been books, which not only educate in the ways of God, but also encourage Christians to press on to a higher calling in Christ Jesus. Most have been very good, with a few being excellent. However, I must say this is one of the few books I have read in recent years which I believe to be a must-read for any Christian who is serious about seeing the kingdom of God increase on the face of the earth today.

A popular definition of insanity goes something like this: 'Insanity is doing the same thing you've always done, the same way you've always done it, and yet expecting a different result.' That has certainly been a truism for those who are serious about the increase of God's *reign* and *rain* on the face of the earth. We must come to grips with at least one essential truth – if we are to see a dramatic increase of the kingdom of God in our pagan Western culture, merely continuing to refine what is already established will not produce it. As David Orton highlights in *Snakes in the Temple*, what is desperately needed is not more of the same church growth *innovation*, but rather true biblical *reformation*.

It may come as a surprise that quite often God's breakthroughs are not a result of doing brand new things. Kingdom breakthroughs almost always come out of Holy Spirit inspired revelation that returns the church to the ways which God originally intended for His people. This is put into perspective when we recognise that true prophetic ministry is not simply about foretelling, but also about *restoration*. Jesus, in speaking about John the Baptist's ministry (the true forerunner), said that *'Elijah is coming and will **restore** all things'* (Matthew 17:11 NASB). The ministry of the prophet is not so much simply prophesying

11

future events as it is two things: Firstly, helping the contemporary church return to biblical foundations and ways; and secondly, helping the people of God to see Jesus more clearly (Revelation 19:10). Under the constant demand of *'anointed entertainment'* the church has almost lost a sense of need for true prophetic input. *Snakes in the Temple* is exactly that – solid and very necessary prophetic input to both restore the church into a more biblical relationship with God and to really know His glory!

Having said that, however, it must also be stated that David Orton is not merely writing as a prophet of truth, but as a representative of 'the Truth Himself'. He is communicating from the Father heart of God. Unfortunately, there are too many prophets who see a need for restoration and repentance but lack the balanced perspective of God's heart. Truth without love ends up killing rather than healing. God's heart, even when He chastises, is about love and restoration. *Snakes in the Temple* is powerful in the truth it gives us. Yet, it also fills us with faith, hope, and expectancy for the future as we grow in the knowledge of God's ways.

This book is a true gem. How the first two chapters sort out our confusion between the *goal* and the *prize* is worth the price of the book itself, while the chapters in section 2 on the Jezebel spirit and idolatry in ministry ought to be mandatory for all who are in ministry. And the book ends with a profound truth – there will be no openness in the heavens until God finds brokenness on earth.

I whole-heartedly recommend this book, especially to those in ministry who have a vision and hope for revival.

Marc A. Dupont
Ft. Wayne, Indiana, USA

Introduction

This book has emerged from my own spiritual quest.

I met the Lord as a teenage 'hippie'. Inhaling the uniquely heady atmosphere of the late 1960s I would swing from a hard-nosed radical Marxist on the one hand to a flower-smelling hippie nirvana on the other, and back again. This went on for several years, but neither won out.

Underneath, and animating both, was a hunger for reality – for some kind of ultimate meaning. Along with many at that time I rejected both the middle-class materialism and religious nominalism of our culture. I rebelled against the spiritual anaemia of institutional Christianity, but found myself possessed by an insatiable cry for truth. Little did I realise it was a thirst for God. Its intensity grew until finally His presence broke through in a powerful supernatural encounter.

I soon found myself in a growing church. The Lord began to strip away the junk, including the idols of a rebellious youth culture. I cut my hair, lost my beads, my Levis, my sandals, and very nearly my soul! But I was soon to discover that the idolatry of the religious system was far deeper and more insidious than the scene I had come from.

This book reflects my own personal quest for a true spirituality – a spirituality my generation initially cried out for and one the next generation, I believe, will possess. The stakes are the highest they have ever been – the final cosmic battle of the ages is upon us. The restoration of true apostolic Christianity is coming to this generation and Satan knows that his time is short. It is time to recognise the nature of the warfare and to rise up in holy rebellion against the spirits of darkness – spirits of religion and deception that have held the people of God in Babylon for virtually two millennia. The greatest spiritual breakout of history is imminent. Vast multitudes, held captive by the spirits of control and religion within the man-made systems of the church, are going to be set free to enjoy a new found intimacy with the Father. They will be a part of a currently underground but emerging church that will see the restoration of the presence and glory of God and the final transformation of the nations.

Snakes in the Temple is a book which casts a biblical vision of the church's awesome future and speaks to the hindrances of that future. Section 1 provides a prophetic forecast of that future – one of increasing revival and world-wide spiritual awakening; secondly, it provides an initial diagnosis of the core problem of idolatry in the church as the primary hindrance to revival. Section 2 continues with a more detailed diagnosis and description of that idolatry, and finally Section 3 gives the prescription for breaking its power and restoring the presence of God, accelerating world-wide spiritual awakening and the fullness of His kingdom on earth.

Be warned – this book is somewhat polemical.[1] It states its case with a measure of poetic and prophetic intensity. Therefore, while a solid biblical base is provided, it does not pretend to be a smooth, qualified, nor politically correct statement.

Now is the time for a revolutionary generation to arise, hungering and thirsting for God alone. If you want to be a part of that generation and discover the breakthrough that will see the glory of God flood the nations – read on!

SECTION 1

Revival Futures – The Dream

Envisioning World-wide Spiritual Awakening

Chapter 1

Receiving the Prize – World-wide Spiritual Awakening

'... straining towards what is ahead,
I press on towards the goal to win the prize
for which God has called me heavenwards in Christ Jesus.'
(Philippians 3:13–14 NIV)

The race has finally been won. In the wake of medal presentations and media coverage, the winning Olympians will soon enjoy the rewards of victory. Lucrative offers beyond their wildest dreams – endorsements, sponsorships and commercial opportunities will be theirs for the taking. Through their own unique 'vale of tears' they have finally reached the *goal* of Olympic victory and will now begin to receive the *prize* – the rewards of that victory. A new chapter begins.

It is a picture of this generation reaching the *goal* to win the *prize*. They have reached the goal of '... *the knowledge of the Son of God ... attaining to the **whole measure of the fulness of Christ***' (Ephesians 4:13 NIV). In other words – unhindered intimacy with Christ. And having reached the goal, they now receive the prize.

This generation will reach a point in history when they will receive, with Christ, the reward of His suffering – the prize of global revival and the harvest of the nations (Isaiah 53:11–12; Psalm 2:8).

Experiencing the fullness of Christ

Revival is not an event – it's a relationship!
The goal and the prize are joined at the hip. The prize of *world-wide revival* cannot be separated from the goal of the *fullness of Christ*. We have misunderstood revival, seeing it as either a church or an evangelistic event. Revival, however, cannot be

humanly organised – it is in essence, a meeting with God. It happens when the human bows to the divine – allowing heaven to invade earth. Revival is a relationship. It is an encountering of who God *is* – of His majesty and glory revealed in the person of Christ. And, when the church fully encounters Him, reaching the goal of *'the whole measure of Christ's fullness'*, she will receive the prize of a world-wide spiritual awakening. The whole earth will be filled with the glory of the Lord (Habakkuk 2:14) triggering the greatest 'ingathering' in all of history.

Through His Spirit in our inner being

The *fullness* of Christ, though, is indeed the *goal*. According to Paul it is something still to be reached: '... *until we all attain ... to the fulness of Christ'* (Ephesians 4:13 NASB).

But how will this happen? By being filled with His Spirit. Paul's apostolic burden for the Ephesians was that the Father

> '... *may strengthen* [them] *with power through His Spirit in* [their] *inner being, so that Christ may dwell in* [their] *hearts ... that* [they] *may be filled to the measure of all the fulness of God.'*   (Ephesians 3:16–17, 19 NIV)

To be filled with the *'fullness of God'* isn't just receiving a gift *from* God. It is receiving *God!* God Himself fills our inner-life, invading every hidden corner of heart and mind. He establishes His stronghold within from where He rules. Theological or biblical information alone, as good as that is, or even church activity, cannot bring the indwelling presence of Christ. It only comes by the Spirit.

'Fill ... more!'

When the current renewal hit, some of us joked among ourselves that every person prayed for in some large conferences seemed to have the same name – 'Phil Moore'. As the preacher prayed over those who came out in the ministry time he would lay hands on them and with an authoritative voice say, *'Fill!'* ... and a moment later in an equally powerful voice, *'More!'*

Despite our pathetic sense of humour the Holy Spirit is definitely emphasising in the present renewal our need to receive 'more' and to be 'filled!' (Ephesians 5:18).

Every Christian who is born of the Spirit has a *measure* of Christ living in their hearts already, but Paul teaches that there is an inner filling beyond this *'to the **measure of the fulness** of Christ'* (Ephesians 4:13). Jesus had received the Spirit *'without measure'* (John 3:34) but we have received Him *'in measure'*. There are therefore greater measures of the Holy Spirit to be received until we reach the measure of Christ's own *fullness*.

Christ – the fullness of God
To know Christ is to know God:

> *' . . . He is the radiance of His glory and the exact representation of His nature.'*   (Hebrews 1:3 NASB)

Jesus radiates the light and warmth of God's complete glory and nature. Paul says of Him,

> *' . . . God was pleased to have all his **fulness** dwell in him.'*
>   (Colossians 1:19 NIV)

When Jesus came as the Hebrew babe of Bethlehem, God came, enfolded in human form. All the fullness of the eternal God invaded human history in the body of a man. Veiled in human flesh the full force of God's glory was hidden from the naked eye.

> *'He had no beauty or majesty to attract us to him,*
> *nothing in his appearance that we should desire him.'*
>   (Isaiah 53:2 NIV)

If we were to judge Christ *'after the flesh'*, (John 8:15 KJV) all we would see is Joseph's son, the carpenter's boy from Nazareth.

But at the Mount of Transfiguration, divinity broke through humanity! The glory, which Jesus had enjoyed with the Father before the world began (John 17:5) shone through His physical body and became visible! The man from Nazareth, with whom the disciples ate and slept, was absolutely transfigured.

> *'His face shone like the sun, and his clothes became as white as the light.'*   (Matthew 17:2 NIV)

The church – the fullness of God
But this awesome display of the Father's glory was not meant to finish with Christ's physical body. As it was with His natural body, so also with the spiritual. Just as Jesus was *filled* with all the *fullness* of God He now becomes

> '... *head over everything for* **the church, which is his body, the**
> **fullness of him** ...'
> (Ephesians 1:22–23 NIV)

As *Jesus* was destined to manifest the *fullness* of the Father
individually, so the *church* is destined to manifest it *corporately*.
This is the *'mystery of Christ in you the hope of glory'* (Colossians
1:27). And so, *'as partakers of the divine nature'* (2 Peter 1:4), we are
destined to experience a greater dimension of the *'shekinah'* glory.

The transfiguration – 'Hey ... this is my boy!'

But this visible manifestation of God's glory will not come to an
immature Christ. The transfiguration was the Father's unquali-
fied approval of the *mature* Son – the *man* Christ Jesus. Jesus had
so developed in His humanity that the Father could proudly
declare from heaven,

> *'This is my Son, whom I love; with him I am well pleased. Listen
> to him!'*
> (Matthew 17:5 NIV)

The transfiguration was God the Father saying with paternal
pride, 'Hey ... check this out ... this is my boy!'

Likewise, when the church, the *corporate Christ*, reaches
maturity, all heaven and earth will resound with the Father's
pleasure. Creation's long travail will have finally realised the full
manifestation of the sons of God, as heaven comes to earth in a
world-transforming revival.

The goal-prize of Ephesians 4

When Christ ascended,

> *'He gave some as apostles, and some as prophets, and some as
> evangelists, and some as pastors and teachers for the equipping of
> the saints for the work of service, to the building up of the body
> of Christ; until we all attain to the unity of the faith, and of the
> knowledge of the Son of God, to a mature man, to the measure of
> the stature which belongs to the fulness of Christ.'*
> (Ephesians 4:11–13 NASB)

The ascension-gift ministries of apostles, prophets, evangelists,
pastors and teachers are given to bring the body of Christ to the
fullness of Christ's stature – to a corporate maturity, manifesting

all of Christ's character, authority, and power – culminating in the 'transfiguration' of redeemed humanity.

This is where God is heading. Therefore, the true measure of an Ephesians 4 ministry is the degree to which the *whole* church is being released towards the *whole* purpose of God – towards *'the full stature of Christ'* – towards maturity.

Paul breaks this maturity down to four elements:

- City-church catholicity (*unity of the faith*)
- Bridal intimacy (*knowledge of the Son of God*)
- Corporate maturity (*a mature man*), and
- Cataclysmic spirituality (*the fullness of Christ*)

City-church catholicity

> *'... until we all attain to the unity of the faith ...'*
>
> (Ephesians 4:13 NASB)

God is raising up a city-wide church for a city-wide revival – a global church for a global revival. True Ephesians 4 ascension-gift ministries are not given to a particular church or denomination for their own aggrandisement, but to the entire body of Christ for its edification. These people are called to the *universal* church – to the church of a city, region, nation or nations, according to their sphere of God's sovereign assignment and their measure of God-given grace (2 Corinthians 10:13–15). They are *catholic* in the true sense of the word, serving the whole church, *'preparing God's people'* (Ephesians 4:12 NIV), regardless of their denominational tag, *'until we **all** attain'* the four-fold goal of Ephesians 4:13 (see above). The reaching of the goal is reserved for the *whole* church, not just a *part*, or a spiritual elite. The coming world-wide awakening will be so extensive, and so intensive, that one group will not be able to handle it. In fact, it will demand a new wineskin – the emerging *city-church*.

So what will this look like? The emerging city-church will simultaneously become larger and smaller. It will not only gather for massive city-wide celebrations, filling the largest sports arenas and public parks, but will also gather from house to house where they will break bread and have fellowship. There will be a restoration of both *temple worship* and *house fellowship* (Acts 2:46). Vast urban populations will be harvested through 'a church without walls'.[1] Institutional and denominational definitions of the church will become obsolete and only geographical ones will stand. Civil and local government jurisdictions will determine the church's boundaries, not schismatic or sectarian ones.[2] This is already occurring, in an embryonic form, in many cities around the world as pastors and intercessors transcend denominational loyalties to pray and intercede for city-wide revival and transformation. In my city of Melbourne, for example, God is raising up a city-wide movement of pastors and intercessors committed to praying for an outpouring of the Spirit. With a population of 3.4 million the city is divided into 31 municipalities, in each of which, at the date of writing, there is a trans-denominational praying group of pastors. Through a process of prayer and relationship, facilitated through an annual prayer summit, a servant-leader team has been recognised and released to nurture the unity of the pastors and the emerging city-church.[3]

Paul exhorted the church of the city of Ephesus to both *maintain* and *attain* unity. First, to *'maintain the unity of the Spirit'* (Ephesians 4:3), and secondly, to *'attain the unity of the faith'* (Ephesians 4:13). In our pursuit of city-church catholicity it is important to distinguish between things that differ. In this case between two dimensions of unity – unity of the *faith* and unity of the *Spirit*.

Unity, first of all, is *of* the Spirit. It is both a sovereign and supernatural gift and therefore cannot be *attained* – it cannot be organised or manufactured. It can only be recognised and *maintained*. No city-wide strategy, event, or formula can produce it. It has already been given to the church and only a sovereign relational process led by the Spirit will bring the gift of unity to full expression. He will lead the church of a city on its own unique journey of learning to *live in love*.

We tend to forget that Paul's exhortation to maintain the unity of the Spirit is introduced by his exhortation to *'be completely humble and gentle ... bearing with one another in love'* (Ephesians 4:2).

True unity can only flow from a heart of humility – a heart conquered by the love of God. So when the gatekeepers of the city, the pastors and spiritual leaders, humble their hearts before the Lord and towards one another, human agendas will no longer matter. Their hearts will become one as God's *presence*, and therefore His *purpose*, invade not only the councils of the church but entire cities and nations. In the light of His glory our offences and opinions will fade into insignificance.

And with the *unity of the Spirit*, the way will be made for *unity of the faith* – for the emergence of a truly catholic and apostolic church. Through a revival of the love of God, of the unity of the Spirit, we will ultimately come to unity of the faith, to one apostolic church. Because of broken and purified hearts God will finally be able to entrust His people with the apostolic authority to pastor whole cities and nations.

God will not ignore a broken and contrite spirit (Psalm 51:17). When we embrace *brokenness on earth* God will release *openness in heaven*. Across our cities a new apostolic church will emerge. Just as Jesus prophesied, *'there shall be **one flock** and **one shepherd'*** (John 10:16 NIV). His high priestly prayer *'that all of them may be one'* (John 17:21) will be answered. There is only one reason we refuse to believe this – fear – *'Don't you know that it's been like this for 2,000 years! How do you think you're going to change the entrenched attitudes of millennia? Have you any idea what this will cost us? What about our programme . . . my ministry . . . my position . . . . my salary . . . I might even have to humble myself and be reconciled with Pastor . . . !'*

We are standing at our Kadesh-Barnea (see Deuteronomy 1:19–46). Will we face our giants and go into the Promised Land of Ephesians 4? Or will we withdraw for another circuit in the wilderness? Is there really a choice? The generation that will go in is now alive. A *post-sectarian era* is upon us when the church of each city will live in the reality that

> *'there is **one body** and one Spirit . . . one hope . . . one Lord, one faith, one baptism; one God and Father of all . . . '*
> (Ephesians 4:4–6 NIV)

Love will prevail. Sectarianism and denominationalism will become obsolete. A global and universal unity, born of the Spirit, will prevail in every part of the church. It will spread across whole cities and nations as the church is revived and restored.

Bridal intimacy

> *' . . . until we all attain to . . . the knowledge of the Son of God . . . '*
> (Ephesians 4:13)

The Spirit of God is calling out a bride for the Son. And as she responds her beauty will win His heart:

'You have stolen my heart, my sister, my bride;
you have stolen my heart
with one glance of your eyes . . .

How delightful is your love, my sister, my bride!'

(Song of Songs 4:9, 10 NIV)

The sheer beauty of her grace and form will completely capture Him.

Paul explains that Christ so loved His Bride that He,

*' . . . died for her, to make her holy and clean . . . so that he could give her to himself as a **glorious** church without a spot or wrinkle or any other blemish . . . holy and without a single fault.'*

(Ephesians 5:25–27 TLB)

The bride is so filled with God's glory that she radiates His presence and power. As Paul says, *'the woman is the glory of the man'* (1 Corinthians 11:7). The bride is without moral or spiritual blemish reflecting the image of Christ – a church of grace and beauty, endowed with every spiritual attribute, and prepared for her heavenly Bridegroom – for the great day, the wedding of the Lamb (Revelation 19:2; Matthew 22:2; 25:1–13).

But how is she prepared? She is prepared as the worshipping Bride. So close is the intimacy of Christ with His church that Paul describes it as *'one flesh'* (Ephesians 5:28) and Peter as *'participating in the divine nature'* (2 Peter 1:4). We are one with Jesus – our union is spirit to spirit, and as we spend time communing with Him we are *'changed into his image'* (2 Corinthians 3:18). One of the laws of human relationships is the law of replication – we become like the people with whom we socialise. So, if we spend time with Jesus, worshipping and loving Him, we become more like Him. And like the Shulamite, if we take time to rest in the shadow of His presence,

'I delight to sit in his shade,
and his fruit is sweet to my taste.'

(Song of Songs 2:3 NIV)

then we will taste the sweet fruit of love, joy, peace, patience, kindness, goodness, faithfulness, gentleness, and self-control (Galatians 5:22 NIV).

Bridal intimacy is the heart of the apostolic burden:

> *'I am jealous for you with a godly jealousy. I promised you to one husband, to Christ, so that I might present you as a pure virgin to him. But I am afraid that just as Eve was deceived by the serpent's cunning, your minds may somehow be led astray from your sincere and pure devotion to Christ.'*   (2 Corinthians 11:2–3 NIV)

And so, as the Father draws out a Bride for the Son, the Holy Spirit will increasingly confront those things that have led her astray from *'pure devotion to Christ'*. The prophetic spirit, the searchlight of truth, will increasingly unearth the issue of spiritual adultery. This is the historic controversy that God has had with His people – of pursuing other gods while maintaining the pretence of true worship. Therefore every false image to which the church has bowed will be brought down as she is restored to full bridal intimacy.

Corporate maturity

> *' . . . until we all attain to . . . a mature man . . . '*
> (Ephesians 4:13 NASB)

The word for 'mature' in Greek is *telios*. It means, 'that which has reached the set goal'.[4] Just as Christ's natural body reached the *goal* of normal physical maturity so it is with His spiritual body the church. Referring to His physical body, Hebrews declares, *' . . . a body you prepared me'* (Hebrews 10:5 NIV). Likewise, a spiritual body, the church, is being prepared for Him. As the body of Christ, it will reach an ultimate point of *spiritual maturity*. From the point of its supernatural conception Christ's human body was genetically encoded to go through all the normal processes of human maturation. In the same way the church, as the body of Christ, is spiritually encoded with the Father's DNA, which will, despite temporary sickness or disability, inevitably bring it to maturity – *'to a mature man . . . to the fullness of the stature of Christ'* (Ephesians 4:13).

Jesus said to the Pharisees and to Herod,

> *'Go tell that fox, "I will drive out demons and heal people today and tomorrow, and on the **third day** I will reach My **goal** [or, 'I will be perfected'].'' '*
> (Luke 13:32)

This word 'goal' in Greek is a similar word to 'mature' (*telios*) – it is *teleioo*, meaning 'to complete, finish, fulfil, or perfect'.

As it was for Jesus, so the 'third day' of the church (the third millennium) is a day of 'destiny purpose' – a day of fulfilment and perfection (Hosea 6:1–3). Just as Jesus pressed through the resistance of political (Herod) and religious (Pharisees) opposition, this 'third day church' will move forward to the goal.

This same word is used in Hebrews:

> *'In bringing many sons to glory, it was fitting that God ... should make the author of their salvation **perfect** ['teleioo'] through suffering.'*
> (Hebrews 2:10)

So the 'third day destiny' for Jesus, was to be perfected through suffering and *'bring many sons to glory'*. Through suffering he learned obedience, was perfected as a man, and enabled to raise up a new humanity in his image (Hebrews 5:8–9).

As the author (or the 'pioneer') of their salvation (Hebrews 2:10) He blazed a trail for this new humanity to experience all the fullness of God. This is a dimension of perfect union (and communion) with Jesus – what Peter describes as *'participating in the divine nature'* (2 Peter 1:4). And what Paul describes as the ultimate maturity of Christ's body (Ephesians 4:13, see also Hebrews 2:11).

In this 'third day' a new humanity will arise in the earth. It will stand in the full blaze of God's glory, enjoying without hindrance all the fullness of Christ. The church will be so 'full of God' they will reflect Paul's description of Christ's body, which is *'the fullness of him'* (Ephesians 1:23; 3:19).

Jesus was propelled on a journey into the 'third day' – to the cross – He had to keep going today, tomorrow and the next day. In the same way, there is an urgency – an imperative – coming from the Spirit to this present generation.

This new humanity will not be distracted from its 'destiny purpose' – from

> *'the fellowship of sharing in his sufferings, becoming like him in his death, and so, somehow, to attain to the resurrection from the dead.'*
> (Philippians 3:10–11 NIV)

And so, out of suffering and death a new humanity will arise. Paul says that

> *'His purpose was to create in himself one new man ... and in this*
> ***one body*** *to reconcile both of them to God through the cross.'*
>   (Ephesians 2:15–16 NIV)

He was talking about the reconciliation of Jew and Gentile.

> *'For he himself is our peace, who has made the two* [Jew and
> Gentile] *one and has destroyed the barrier, the dividing wall of*
> *hostility ... '*   (Ephesians 2:14 NIV)

The one new man is the body of Christ. And as the body reaches
spiritual adulthood it will become the most powerful reconciling
force in the world, not only bringing down sectarian and
denominational barriers within but racial, social, and religious
ones too. It will become a reconciling world-force. The church is
destined to display God's wisdom to a watching world

> *' ... to the intent that now the manifold wisdom of God might be*
> *made known* ***by the church*** *to the principalities and powers in*
> *the heavenly places.'*   (Ephesians 3:10 NKJV)

As Christ prayed for the church:

> *' ... that all of them may be one ...* ***so that the world may***
> ***believe that you have sent me.'***   (John 17:21 NIV)

The body of Christ is the only answer to the Palestinian–Israeli
conflict, the Catholic–Protestant division of Northern Ireland,
the global divide between the Islamic and Western worlds, and
the increasing divide between rich and poor. With the ministry
of reconciliation the mature, corporate Christ will salt the
nations with forgiveness, cleansing them from the curse of racial,
religious, or class hatred.

Cataclysmic spirituality

> *'until we all attain ... to the measure of the stature which belongs*
> *to the fulness of Christ.'*   (Ephesians 4:13 NASB)

Every maturing body experiences sudden growth spurts. When
our kids were younger we were sometimes woken at night by one
of them crying with aching legs – they were experiencing

growing pains! The body of Christ is no different. Throughout her history the church has periodically experienced seasons of sudden and sometimes painful growth – seasons of cataclysmic change.

The *Britannica World Language Dictionary* defines 'cataclysm' as 'an overwhelming flood . . . any violent and extensive subversion of the ordinary phenomena of nature . . . ' or 'any sudden over-whelming change or political or social upheaval'.[5]

A 'cataclysmic spirituality', therefore, is one that embraces *sudden* and sometimes *violent* spiritual phenomena. During seasons of revival the Holy Spirit floods the church with *spiritual growth hormones*. The power of God surges through the church's bloodstream triggering sudden and violent growth over and above the normal processes of spiritual life. These accelerated and intense operations of the Spirit usually provoke upheaval in both the church and in the world, producing *overwhelming change*.

We are rapidly approaching the *'fullness of time'* when the church, through seasons of unparalleled revival, will rise to *'the stature which belongs to the fulness of Christ'* (Ephesians 4:13). It will be a time of cataclysmic spiritual outpourings that will shake the world. Haggai prophesied concerning this time: *'Once more I will shake not only the earth but also the heavens'* (Haggai 2:6). The writer to the Hebrews explains,

> *'The words "once more" indicate the removing of what can be shaken – that is, created things – so that what cannot be shaken may remain.'* (Hebrews 12:27 NIV)

Every created thing – every idol and human institution – will suffer severe shakings and be removed *'so that what cannot be shaken may remain'* (Hebrews 12:27).

Idolatrous political, economic and religious systems will falter before they are either removed or renewed by the power of the gospel. The institutional church will suffer a major collapse. But, as it does so, massive outpourings of the Spirit across the earth will awaken the sleeping giant of the body of Christ. A corporate Christ, unfettered by human control, manifesting all the fullness of God, will decimate sin, disease and the powers of darkness. Through the shakings that are coming we will *'receive a kingdom that cannot be shaken'* (Hebrews 12:28) – the kingdom of Christ and His power. All that Christ purchased for His body will be possessed – He will divide the spoil among the strong. And the nations will be received as an inheritance (Isaiah 53:10–12; Psalm 2).

Clothed in Christ's ascension glory the church will displace demonic principalities and powers over cities and nations, triggering the greatest harvest in history. The entire world will be transformed, producing a season of unparalleled global peace and justice as all things in heaven and earth are brought together in Christ (Ephesians 1:10; Isaiah 2:1–5; Micah 4:1–3).

'The tide is coming in!'

So how does this work? Times of visitation and revival are like the surf. I live on the Pacific Coast of Australia where every surfer learns to read the ocean and the wind. Despite the fact that the swell produces both big and small 'sets' (a group of waves) the tide still increases. So it is with revival. Every wave of visitation, big or small, rides on the incoming tide of the kingdom. We might be tempted to think, *'This is only a small wave – it's not all that significant'*. Or we may think, *'Look, the wave has gone out – I knew it wouldn't last – the refreshing is over'*. But we forget that the next 'set' is coming. And whether it's bigger or smaller than the last, it will be driven further up the beach by the invisible, but inexorable force of the incoming tide. Likewise, every wave of revival, despite the lull between sets, increases the tide of Christ's presence and rule on the earth.

Get ready, because the full-tide is almost upon us!

The restoration of true worship and acceleration of the harvest
Amos foretold this day of visitation:

> *'In that day I will restore*
>   *David's fallen tent ...*
>
> *that the remnant of men may seek the Lord,*
>   *and all the Gentiles who bear my name ...*
> *The days are coming ...*
>   *when the reaper will be overtaken by the ploughman*
>   *and the planter by the one treading grapes.*
> *New wine will drip from the mountains*
>   *and flow from all the hills.'*
>
> (Amos 9:11, 13; Acts 15:16–18 NIV)

Two things will characterise the coming move of God: the *restoration of pure worship* – David's tabernacle – and the *acceleration of world evangelisation* – the ploughman overtaking the reaper.

The rebuilding of David's tent typifies the restoration of true and universal worship, embracing men of every tribe, nation, and tongue. The normal process of seedtime and harvest will be supernaturally accelerated. What has previously taken months and years, or even generations, in the reaching of the nations, will now take hours or days under an extraordinary impetus of the Spirit. What men have attempted to do, often in their own strength, will be accelerated supernaturally as they enter higher realms of worship. Worship always brings heaven to earth. But this is not why they worship. The people of God will be caught up with *who He is* more than with *what He does*. Enamoured with His person – with His nature – with His holiness and majesty, a spirit of adoration and love will ascend as sweet incense to heaven. The Lord will respond by pouring out more and more of His presence on the earth. The more worship is restored, the more the harvest will accelerate until it is totally out of control. With more people alive today than have previously lived in the whole of history, heaven can now be populated in one generation!

Jonathan Edwards and a future universal awakening

Jonathan Edwards, leader of the 18th-century great awakening and one of the greatest theologians of revival saw this coming day of visitation. He believed in a future universal awakening of such magnitude that Satan's kingdom would be completely demolished and Christ's kingdom established on its ruins.

> 'The Spirit of God shall be gloriously poured out for the wonderful revival and propagation of religion ... This pouring out of the Spirit when it is begun, shall soon bring great multitudes ... The work of conversion shall break forth, and go on in such a manner as never has been hitherto ... God, by pouring out his Holy Spirit, will furnish men to be glorious instruments ... for the promoting [of] the kingdom of Christ, and the salvation of souls ... The gospel shall begin to be preached with abundantly greater clearness and power than had heretofore been ... The work of conversion shall go on in a wonderful manner, and spread more and more ... The visible kingdom of Satan

shall be overthrown, and the kingdom of Christ set up on the ruins of it, everywhere throughout the whole habitable globe.'[6]

We stand on the edge of a great end-time revival. We have the whole force of prophetic testimony behind us, from both Scripture and from men and women of God through the ages. And we now have the evidence of the burgeoning renewal movement, the growing edge of Christianity, globally numbering over 500 million people. According to David Barrett, Professor for Missionmetrics at Regent University, Virginia Beach and publisher of the World Christian Encyclopaedia, the rise of the so-called 'neo-apostolics' is particularly marked, now numbering over 20,000 movements and networks with a total of 394 million church members. They are one of the fastest-growing church movements in the world and in Barrett's estimation, will have 581 million members by 2025 – 120 million more than all the Protestant movements. They reject historical denominationalism and restrictive or overbearing central authority, and seek a more effective missionary lifestyle.[7] We also have the exponential growth of Christianity in the third world. In the decade that just passed (1990–2000) Evangelicals have been the fastest growing major religious movement in the world, growing by 120 million, representing 4.7% per year with approximately 73% of them now found in Africa, Asia, and Latin America.[8] In addition pockets of renewal are breaking out sporadically in the West – all warning signs of the imminent global visitation – tremors before the big quake.

But the Western institutional church, even with signs of renewal, has been in negative growth – contracting in size despite its best attempts at church growth. While the third world is experiencing unprecedented harvest, the first world languishes. So why is this, and what are the roadblocks to full-blown revival? In the next chapter we will discover it is because we have confused the *goal* with the *prize*.

Chapter 2

Confusing the Goal with the Prize

'... let us run with endurance ... fixing our eyes on Jesus ...'
(Hebrews 12:1–2)

At last, victory is in sight! As the marathon runners enter the arena they are hit by the roar of the crowd. Adrenaline surges through their bodies and in one last effort they strain towards the goal.

As a spiritual Olympian the apostle declares,

> *'But one thing I do: Forgetting what is behind and straining towards what is ahead, I press on towards the **goal** to win the **prize** ...'* (Philippians 3:13–14)

A stirring analogy. It inspires us to press through our pain and achieve great things for God. But there is a difference between reaching the *goal*, and receiving the *prize*. Whoever reaches the goal, crossing the finish line as a winner, automatically receives the prize. As Paul said, *'I press on toward the **goal** to win the **prize**'*. On seeing the prize-winner's dais it is not a smart athlete who cuts out of the race, thinking, 'Wow – the prize, all I have to do is cut across the field – and go get it!' And yet, tragically, this is exactly what the church has done.

Let me explain. Because the Western church has lost sight of the *goal*, taking short cuts to get the *prize*, she has been disqualified. Paul warned,

> *'Run in such a way as to get the prize ... so that ... [you] will not be disqualified ...'* (1 Corinthians 9:24–27)

In fact, the Western church's goal has *become* the prize. We will discover, in a moment, what the true goal is. But before we do, let us briefly explore some of the goals that have replaced it.

Building the church

First, we have seen our goal as building the church. But Jesus said, 'You seek me and I'll build the church!' (Matthew 6:33; 16:18.) Because we have this wrong, vast human and financial resources have been poured into church growth programmes. We have raised up systems, personnel and facilities to achieve this goal. We say to ourselves, 'If we could only build a bigger congregation, or bigger buildings, or get on TV, or plant more churches. Then we'll be kicking some goals!' This might help to explain the anomaly that over a recent five-year period over $20 billion was spent, in the USA alone, for new church sanctuaries dedicated to the glory of the God who said, 'I do not live in temples made by human hands'![1]

In the first several centuries churches were planted and prospered without buildings, structures, or programmes. Christianity spread like a prairie fire across the entire Roman Empire and beyond. Men and woman by the thousands were won to Jesus, but only as they were invited to follow Jesus and surrender to His reign. The Holy Spirit presided over this fledgling movement, empowering and directing its expansion, often through the untrained and uneducated. They knew nothing of modern-day demographics, target-marketing, or communication techniques. But they knew the person of the Holy Spirit. Nor did they preach, 'Come to our *church*, and fill out a visitor's card'. What they did preach, was 'Come to *Jesus*, and experience His kingdom.'[2]

City-reaching and the great commission

Second, we have made a goal of the great commission. More often than not, an emphasis on church growth is subverted by our own selfishness, securing our own comfort as resources are poured into servicing religious consumers. World mission and city-reaching, on the other hand, focuses the church outward, to the challenge of the harvest. It turns the attention of a self-seeking Western mindset onto the missionary heart of God, and to the transformation of the world.

Before we go any further I want to stake my claim as one committed to world missions and city-reaching. But even here, if we focus exclusively on the *task* of mission, we can become spiritually short-sighted. Sometimes the great commission can be less threatening than the great commandment – to *'Love the*

Lord [our] *God with all* [our] *heart . . . soul and . . . mind'* (Matthew 22:37).

This great commandment probes the heart's deepest thoughts and affections. It uncovers things we prefer not to know. As Paul reflected,

> *'If I give all I have to the poor and even sacrifice my life, and do not have **love**, I have nothing.'*   (1 Corinthians 13:3)

All my sacrificial endeavours in the task of missions, even over a lifetime, without *love* do not, in God's estimation, amount to 'a hill of beans'! Paul, however, used far stronger language than this, comparing his own efforts and achievements to *dung* – literally *excrement*, or *refuse!* (Philippians 3:8).[3]

Revival

Third, many of us are pursuing full-scale revival as our goal. Take a moment to surf the net and you will soon discover a glut of websites offering books, conferences, churches, and ministries promoting revival. But there is untold confusion as to what revival actually is. The term has been reduced in meaning until, for many, it has become another humanly organised event – 'revival meetings' promoted and presided over by professional 'revivalists'. We think nothing of advertising our meetings and conferences as a 'revival', as if it were a commodity that could be produced at a scheduled time and place! Hollywood's caricature of this in Steve Martin's movie *Leap of Faith* cuts close to the bone. We have robbed the word 'revival' of its true content, commercialising and reducing it to a product that can be purchased over the counter by religious consumers. Before his death in 1963 Dr A.W. Tozer concluded that: 'A widespread revival of the kind of Christianity we know today ... might prove to be a moral tragedy from which we would not recover in a hundred years.'[4] While I am committed to revival, we must be clear what we mean by it and whether it is really the goal we should be pursuing.

We have confused church growth, the great commission, and revival as the real goals when, in fact, they are the prize. I believe that the Western church will only receive the *prize* when she rediscovers the *goal*. When she returns to the true goal we will reach a turning point in history – where revival will be poured out, the church will grow, and the great commission will be completed. I am firmly persuaded that the church will fulfil God's *goal* for her and she will receive the victory wreath – the *prize* of His manifest presence, signalling a time of unparalleled blessing and supernatural power. But first we need to get some things right.

The fallout – 'something is radically wrong!'

Our confusion between the *goal* and the *prize* has been deeply injurious. Why is it that, in the USA alone, up to '1,600 pastors per month are terminated or forced to resign'?[5] Surely, this screams out that there is something radically wrong! What is the cause of this incredible fallout? Research from the 1980s and 1990s has revealed that 'the leading cause of pastor fallout was the *"control and power factor"*. This is reflected by a lack of unity, or factions in the congregation. In addition, expectations on pastors are far different to a generation ago' (emphasis mine). The same researcher continues, 'Churches are doing more marketing now, there's more pressure to *perform* (emphasis mine) and entertain and succeed.'[6]

The twin virus of performance and power

A virus has invaded the body of Christ – and, it's systemic. It infects the whole Christian community – pastors, congregations, denominations and para-church ministries. It is the twin virus of *performance* and *power*. And, we've contracted it from the surrounding culture. In a goal-oriented, task driven Western world we are programmed from childhood to kick goals – to achieve for reward and approval. Consequently, productivity and performance determine self-worth. Therefore achieving goals – increased attendance, more 'tithing units', more church plants, more conversions, more healings, more product sold, more staff and more money all feed our sense of value. The route to *power* in the corporate world is determined by achieving a set of *performance* criteria. Consequently, with the contemporary corporatisation of the church, all its activity is geared toward performance.

'So? What's so wrong with that?' you ask. Empirical *performance* criteria may have its place, but it is not the criteria of the kingdom! We must remember that Satan put it into David's mind to number Israel (1 Chronicles 21:1). Measuring their strength by their size was not God's idea. In fact, He was so angered by it He brought a plague upon them, killing seventy-thousand men. Rather than increasing their forces, God reduced them! He is not looking at the size of our budget, our church or our mailing list – He does not need them! He can save by *many*, or by *few* (1 Samuel 14:6). The issue is where we place our trust – in the strength of man or of God.

Nor is God impressed by the icons of human *power*: by ministry titles or position, church buildings, our clothing, technology or the car we drive. Neither, as we shall discover, do our spiritual gifts, education, or achievements impress Him!

Idolatry – worshipping created things

These are all created things. They will all pass away when the perfect comes. Even the gifts of the Spirit, such as prophecy, knowledge and tongues will, one day, cease! (1 Corinthians 13:8–10).

By pursuing the *prize* instead of the *goal* we have unwittingly *'worshipped and served created things'* (Romans 1:25). Through replacing the true *goal* with church growth, the great commission, and revival, we have inadvertently made these things *idols*. And consequently, we have sacrificed at the altars of false gods – the gods of Western culture – of *performance* and *power*.

My argument is this: that the *sin of idolatry* lies at the heart of the Western church's malaise. This is the reason, I believe, Western cities and nations are not experiencing the breakthroughs that Africa and Asia are now seeing. It explains why when we import the leading apostles of strategic city-reaching, adopt their models, and implement their plans, we find them stalling after a period. It is why our best efforts are stillborn. And why vast regions of the third world are experiencing revival while the first world, on the whole, languishes in a spiritual wasteland.

The idolatry of technique

If it is true that we have taken on the dominant gods of our culture, performance and power, it will inevitably result in the ascendancy of the *utilitarian* – of technique and method. The pursuit of growth-goals demands new strategies to achieve them. Church leaders ask each other – *'What model do you follow – G12 or houses of prayer – seeker sensitive or cell church – house church or no church?'*

We therefore pursue *programme* over *presence*, and *activity* over *adoration*. Even prayer and spiritual warfare become just another means to an end – the engine of a church growth or city-reaching strategy. It is something we have to do to get the results – *'If we want revival – if we want to reach our city, we've got to pray!'*

The Western church, like a passive smoker, has inhaled the toxic fumes of its culture. Like Israel of old, she has bowed at the altars of the surrounding nations. And, like Israel, she has inevitably come under a discipline of God. Unlike Asia and large regions of Africa, the West is apostate. Having embraced the Creator-God as her Bridegroom, in the first several centuries she turned to other lovers – to false gods. But to whom much is given much is required (Luke 12:48). Because of the light she received in those first several centuries her judgments will be that much more intense. Therefore, until the Western church falls on the Rock, the Rock will continue to fall on her (Matthew 21:44). The reason we are not seeing the breakthrough in the West, in my view, is simply because God is resisting it!

The kingdom of God either works for us or against us. If we persist in our pursuit of other gods we will continue to be resisted. The idolatry of technique and the frenetic pursuit of new and better models of doing church will only continue to provoke His displeasure. Even spiritual warfare will fail if the underlying sin is not dealt with. Our controversy is not so much with principalities and powers as it is with God! As the Creator of the earth, He is the ultimate 'Territorial Spirit'. The earth is His and if we return to Him as the one true and living God He will give it to us – He will bring down every proud demonic stronghold over cities and nations, because those strongholds have first been brought down in us. Our warfare is, therefore, the warfare of brokenness and pure devotion. It is one that pursues the *goal* over the *prize*.

So, what is the goal?

Personal intimacy

For Paul the goal, was personal intimacy with Christ. It was, *'to know him ...'* (Philippians 3:10), not just to master the theology of His person and work, but to actually have an experiential association with Him. Although Paul had walked with the Lord for many years and had known Him intimately when he penned these words, he knew there was still more to experience. This 'knowledge' is far more than accumulating information *about* God. Rather, it is the knowledge *of* God. Through Paul's use of the

Greek word *ginosko* (to know), the Holy Spirit has breathed into the sacred text something of the passion and intimacy of truly knowing Jesus.[7] It is the word Scripture uses for the most intimate human experience – the sexual union of a man and a woman (Matthew 1:25). Throughout redemptive history God has related to His people, under both the old and new covenant, as a lover, using the analogy of sexual intimacy to convey the passionate covenant bond that He has with those He loves (Jeremiah 2:1–3; 3:1; 6–13; Ezekiel 16; Hosea 2:1–8, 19–20; 4:10–13; 5:4; Ephesians 5:25–33). This experiential intimacy with Christ was Paul's life-purpose. It was his finishing line – his goal.

Journey into intimacy – the way of the cross

I have a running love affair with books! I not only enjoy reading them, but I love smelling them! I am sure I have a serious addiction to bookbinder's glue! As a young newly married man God spoke to me, and said, *'Invest yourself in Jenny (my wife), she will open you up more than books ever will!'* God knew my weakness. But He also knew that *information* doesn't guarantee *transformation*. And that real change only comes through *intimacy*.

The route to relational intimacy, though, is through making an investment – there is a cost. It is an act of *self*-giving, in vulnerability, to another. It is a *powerless place* – a place of transparency and weakness. It is what we call *the way of the cross* – the self-emptying of Christ (see Philippians 2).

The cross is the terminal point for human strength. It's where we come to the end of ourselves and fall into the hands of God. It means dying to the strength of our self-life – to our ability to deliver ourselves from the *people* or the *places* of His choosing. This is what it means to be conformed to His death. As I humble myself under his hand I discover, in due time, His faithfulness to raise me up (1 Peter 5:6). In the *'fellowship of his sufferings'* we discover Him as our resurrection and life (Philippians 3:10–11; Luke 9:24). Paul, glorying in his weaknesses, knew this when he declared, *'it is no longer I that live, but Christ that lives in me'* (Galatians 2:20).

Knowing Jesus intimately then, as a person, entering His death and resurrection, is our life-purpose – our goal. For Western Christians this will require a fundamental shift. In a society where a person's worth is either determined by their economic output, their physical approximation to a Hollywood ideal of beauty or conformity to a sacred mantra of political correctness it will take Herculean strength to break free. We have been deceived into believing that 'success' is the goal when all the while Jesus only desires the intimacy of our fellowship. He is set on being the centre and circumference of our lives – the beginning, the end and everything in between.

Destiny, distortion, or destruction

As an enthusiastic young potter, in my High School art room, I discovered the importance of 'centring'. If the clay was not centred on the wheel disaster would strike. As the speed of the wheel increased the centrifugal forces would eventually fling the emerging pot to its destruction, usually against the nearest wall! Or at best, if it managed to cling on, the finished product was greatly distorted.

As a potter, the Father's moulding impress is designed to *centre* us. We feel the pressure of His centring hand through our circumstances. God often allows things in His wisdom that He could change by His power. Situations are sent to mould and to change us – to build within us the stronghold of His own character – to *centre* us in Him so that He becomes our peace and a place of inner refuge. The result is *destiny* – Christ-likeness – a life moulded for the master's use (2 Timothy 2:21). But if we resist, the alternatives are either *distortion* or *destruction*. Areas of our life are distorted – they are not conformed to Christ's image and our spiritual usefulness is therefore limited. In addition, by completely refusing the correction to be centred at all, we can be delivered over to our own lusts and destroyed.

DeVern Fromke, the author of the classic book, *The Ultimate Intention* says:

> 'Believers may not often realise it, but even *as believers we are either centred in man, or centred in God*. There is no alternative. Either God is the centre of our universe or we have made ourselves the centre and are attempting to make all else orbit around us and for us. When the truth dawns, we are amazed to discover how the snare of making all things to revolve around man has become the bane of most of our preaching and teaching'[8] (emphasis mine).

In fact, we have built a religious system that places man at the centre. God and the church exist to save *me*, heal *me*, pastor *me*, comfort *me*, help *me* and deliver *me*.

'. . . from him . . . through him . . . to him . . . '

My message is summed up in Paul's doxology: *'for from him and through him and to him are all things'* (Romans 11:36).

The three prepositions *from, through* and *to* explain the essence of our relationship with God. Our walk with Him is a process of realignment until He experientially becomes the *source, sustainer,* and *centre* of all things. It is completely experiential – not theological nor an article of faith. Unless my self-worth – my sense of being – my identity as a person comes *from* Him, is energised *through* Him, and directed back *to* Him we will take a created thing and make it our god. We will look for identity within ourselves or in a position, a title, a career, possessions, a church movement, a ministry or even a theology. Or perhaps in activity and service – in productivity and success. This is what the Bible calls idolatry. In Section 2, we will discover what idolatry is and how it works in the church.

Beginnings determine endings

God's creation is built on a seed-principle (Genesis 1:11–12, 21, 24–25). We all know Biology 101[9] teaches that humans reproduce humans. Why is it, though, that when it comes to spiritual things we are suddenly rendered ignorant? The same principle applies. The seed determines the harvest. The Bible calls it sowing and reaping. Or, alternatively, *beginnings determine endings.* Recent surveys in the UK and Australia show a rapid decline in church attendance. Between 1982 and 1998 Australia had a 12% decline in weekly attendance and the UK a 26% decline, representing 272,000 and 1,027,400 people respectively. Peter Brierley, author of *The Tide is Running Out,* points out that if this rate of decline continues, less than 1% of the population will be attending church on a typical Sunday in the UK by 2016![10] We have planted bad seed and we are reaping the harvest. It is time to rediscover the good seed of the kingdom – to find a new starting point.

Chapter 3

Finding a New Starting Point

'yet for us there is but one God, the Father,
from whom all things came and for whom we live ...'
(1 Corinthians 8:6 NIV)

I was recently meeting with a group of fellow pastors. In the course of discussion the following statement was made, *'Of course the church is for people, we exist for the world'*. 'Beep, beep, beep!' Something immediately went off, and it wasn't my mobile phone! Now, on the surface, what was said sounded fine and appealed to most of the group but something inside told me it was wrong. 'Surely', I thought, 'the church exists for God.' It is *His* house, *His* temple, *His* bride, *His* garden and *His* body. Jesus called it, *'His* church' (Matthew 16:18). In fact He is jealous with a holy jealousy for her – as a husband is for his bride (Exodus 20:5; 2 Corinthians 11:2). We are *His* possession and have been bought with a price – we are not our own! (1 Corinthians 6:20; 7:23.) We exist for Him.

Why would such a statement be made, particularly in a pastors' group, and be so acceptable? Because our *starting point* has been wrong. Remember that beginnings determine endings. We have started with man and therefore we end with man. We have bought the line that goes something like this, 'Jesus came to die for our sins; therefore our mission as the church is to get this message out to the world'. You say, 'Sounds fine to me, what's wrong with that?' The problem is, it's the *part* and not the *whole*.

Paul in his farewell message to the elders of the church in Ephesus declared that he had not neglected to teach them *'the whole purpose of God'* (Acts 20:27). As we will see in a moment, rescuing man from the Fall and its horrific effects is *part* of God's purpose and not the *whole*. Even so, experience of contemporary church life tells us the *part* has become the *whole*. We have taken the Fall of man, and his resulting condition, as God's starting point. God, therefore, sent His Son to save man. Consequently, He and the church exist to help our recovery. God Himself is domesticated – He is repackaged as the 'heavenly therapist', whose main assignment is to help us on the road to recovery. Therefore man, and his rescue from the damage and dysfunction of sin, becomes central to God's purpose in history. But is this true apostolic Christianity? Is it really God's starting point?

The Father's heart – our new starting point!

Paul provides the answer when he describes God as *'the Father, from whom all things came ...'* (1 Corinthians 8:6). Our starting point is not found in the Fall, in the human condition, but in *God the Father*, from whom all things come. This is borne out in Paul's letter to the Ephesians:

> *'Praise be to the **God and Father** of our Lord Jesus Christ ... For **he** [the Father] **chose us** in him [Christ] **before the creation** of the world ... **In love he predestined us to be adopted as his sons** through Jesus Christ, in accordance with his pleasure and will ... In him we were also chosen, having been predestined according to the plan of him [the Father] who works out everything in conformity with the purpose of his will ...'*
>
> (Ephesians 1:3–5, 11 NIV)

Regardless of what our stance may be on predestination one thing is clear – God's saving intent did not begin at the *Fall*, but in the *Father* before time began – *'before the creation of the world'* (Ephesians 1:4). This makes the Father the determining factor of history, not the Fall. God begins in Himself – in His own nature and will, not in the human situation: *'In the beginning God ...'* (Genesis 1:1).

This then begs the question, 'If man had not fallen, would Jesus still have come?' A definite, 'Yes!' Why? Because the Father was looking for sons, a family, with whom He could share His nature and enjoy relationship. Regardless of sin's intervention Jesus would still have come as man to be the first-born of a new humanity. Therefore the Father's purpose is for us to be *'conformed to the image of his Son, that he* [Jesus] *might be the firstborn among many brothers'* (Romans 8:29).

As the *'last Adam'* and the *'second man'* (1 Corinthians 15:45, 47) Christ came to terminate the old humanity and raise up a new one created in His own image. Why? Because it is the Father's nature to reproduce Himself in a *family*. The purpose of the cross, therefore, was not so much to rescue man but to bring forth mature sons – a family who would bring pleasure to the Father's heart and who as fellow-heirs with their elder brother, Christ, would share both His suffering and glory (Romans 8:17). Consequently, rescue from sin and its dysfunction is only necessary to restore us to the Father's original purpose to have mature sons.

Beginning in man – ending in man – man becomes as God

What begins in the Father also ends in Him. But the opposite is equally true – what begins in man ends in man. This is why the church has become another *human* institution – a religious country club geared for every human comfort. By viewing salvation as a rescue from our fallen state we have produced a religious system with man at the centre. Intimacy with the Father is shouldered to the circumference. And with ourselves at the centre we have, in effect, created a God in our own image. The essence of the original satanic seduction now occupies centre stage in the church – we have become as God (Genesis 3:5).

'You shall have no other gods'

'What – me, worship another god? – Not me!' It escapes our attention, though, that the first commandment was not issued to pagans but to the people of God. The implication is clear: God's people are prone to worshipping other gods. However, the way this works in practice is more subtle than any overt rejection of God. This subtlety was pre-empted in the prohibition of making any gods to be *alongside* Yahweh (Exodus 20:23).

Idolatry was Israel's besetting sin. But they engaged in it while maintaining the external ritual worship of Yahweh. While continuing in the form of religion they took other gods and placed them *alongside* the Lord. Bowing down to the *'idols of the heart'* (Ezekiel 14:3) they lost their internal purity while maintaining an external orthodoxy. To put it colloquially they were *two-timing* God. Idolatry therefore, became a covert *spiritual adultery*.

Spiritual adultery

In Chapter 2 we saw that Paul's life-pursuit, his *finish line* – his *goal*, was to *'know'* Christ. Paul, in referring to the sexual intimacy of marriage explains that it *'is a deep secret truth ... which I understand to be applying to Christ and the church'* (Ephesians 5:31 GNB).

Marriage is a *physical symbol* of a *spiritual reality*. The apostle uses the same analogy when addressing the church in the city of Corinth:

> *'I am jealous for you with a godly jealousy. I promised you to one husband, to Christ, so that I might present you as a pure virgin to him.'*
>
> (2 Corinthians 11:2 NIV)

God's nature demonstrated through marriage

The Bible, therefore, treats very seriously the issue of physical adultery. It was so serious under the old covenant that the civil law sanctioned it with the death penalty (Leviticus 20:10). Because marriage reflects both the nature of God and His relationship with His people, it was protected by the ultimate penalty. In the beginning God created man in His own image – *male and female*, with whom He could fellowship and through whom He could demonstrate His glory – His covenant nature – to the earth. Any violation of the marriage covenant, therefore, does violence to God Himself and damages its symbolic significance.

The divine romance

The relationship, therefore, between a man and a woman is designed to bring heaven to earth. It is a parable of the glory to be revealed through the covenant romance of Christ and His church.

This divine romance with man, first reflected in Adam and Eve, was continued through Israel, the old covenant church. The Lord said to them through Hosea:

> *'And I will betroth you to Me forever;*
> *Yes, I will betroth you to Me in righteousness and in justice,*
> *In lovingkindness and in compassion,*
> *And I will betroth you to Me in faithfulness.*
> *Then you will know the LORD.'* (Hosea 2:19–20 NASB)

Israel's adultery – breaking the heart of God

But Israel was unfaithful, pursuing other lovers:

> *' "But you have lived as a prostitute with many lovers –*
> *would you now return to me?"*
>
> declares the LORD*

> ... *the* Lord *said to me, "Have you seen what faithless Israel has done? She has gone up on every high hill and under every spreading tree and has committed adultery there. I thought that after she had done all this she would return to me but she did not ... she defiled the land and committed adultery with stone and wood ... " '*   (Jeremiah 3:1, 6–7, 9 NIV)

Israel committed spiritual adultery at the altars of foreign gods. If the covenant nature of God is affronted by the physical act of adultery, then how much more by spiritual adultery! If the breach of trust and the betrayal of affections between a man and a woman are deeply injurious, how much more when we betray our heavenly Bridegroom! Through our spiritual wanderings we can break the heart of God. In his book, *The Church at the End of the Twentieth Century*, Dr Francis Schaeffer underscores this when he asks,

> 'What does God say to our generation? Exactly the same thing that he said to Israel two thousand five hundred years ago when he said through Ezekiel, "I am broken with their whorish heart, which hath departed from me, and with their eyes, which go a whoring after their idols." I believe that this is how God looks at much of the modern church, and on our Western culture ... above everything else this is the way he looks into the churches ... God is saddened. Should *we* not be moved?'[1]

Unconscious blindness
But the Western church is not moved – indeed it is blind to its true condition. We say,

> ' "*I am rich; I have acquired wealth and do not need a thing." But you do not realise that you are wretched, pitiful, poor, blind and naked.*'   (Revelation 3:17 NIV)

Our problem is unconscious blindness. We are living in spiritual adultery but we don't know it.

Jesus had just healed a man of physical blindness and used it to underscore a principle of divine visitation. Speaking into this, Jesus said,

> '*For judgment I have come into this world, so that the blind will see and those who see will become blind.*'   (John 9:39 NIV)

When God comes He comes in mercy and judgment – judgment to those who claim to see but cannot, and mercy to those who know they are blind. In seasons of divine visitation those who presume they can see are shown as being blind, and those who admit they can't see are shown as seeing!

Seeing with the eyes of the heart

How does this work? Spiritual sight is conditioned by the heart:

> *'Blessed are the pure in **heart**,*
>   *for they will **see** God.'*
>
>   (Matthew 5:8)

It was because of their *hardness of heart* that Jesus taught in parables:

> *'This is why I speak to them in parables:*
>
> *"Though seeing, they do not see;*
>   *though hearing, they do not hear or understand."*
>
> *In them is fulfilled the prophecy of Isaiah:*
>
> *"You will be ever hearing but never understanding;*
>   *you will be ever seeing but never perceiving.*
> *For this people's heart has become calloused ... "'*
>
>   (Matthew 13:13–15)

Humility of heart is the soil of spiritual sight. But the converse applies: a proud heart is the soil of spiritual blindness.

The Pharisees responded, *'What? Are we blind too?'* (John 9:40) – it is the exclamation of *unconscious blindness* – of a proud heart. How do I respond to the suggestion that I might be guilty of idol worship? – *'Who, me? – No way – I don't see that!'* Well, that's the problem – the religious person or system does not question for a moment its ability to see. The Pharisees were convinced that they had cornered the market on the things of God – they were the guardians of orthodoxy, believing their interpretation of the Word of God was the only true one and that their group was the one God would use. And yet they were living in spiritual adultery. Jesus said to them,

> *'If you were blind, you would not be guilty of sin; but now that you claim you see, your guilt remains.'*   (John 9:41 NIV)

Their self-proclaimed ability to see, coming out of a hardened heart, became the measure of their judgment.

The implications of this are frightening. The Western church, blind to its true spiritual condition, is entering a season of judgment. Presuming to see, it will, like the Pharisees, be *judicially blinded* –

> *'God gave them a spirit of stupor, eyes so that they could not see and ears so that they could not hear.'*   (Romans 11:8 NIV)

Preparing the way of the Lord – a voice crying in the wilderness
Whenever God determines to move on the earth He raises up a prophetic voice to prepare the way. John the Baptist came as

> *'A voice of one calling in the wilderness,*
> *"Prepare the way of the Lord,*
>   *make his paths straight."'*   (Matthew 3:3)

John confronted a religious generation, demanding they *'produce fruit in keeping with repentance'* and that they stop relying on Abraham as their father (Matthew 3:7–9). His message was clear – *'turn to God and stop depending on your religious pedigree'*. But the religious leaders could not hear. Because of their *triumphalism* they were deaf to the prophetic voice. They were *'of Abraham!'* (Matthew 3:9) – the elect. If God were to do anything, it would be through them. Filled with their own self-belief they presumed to be the 'cutting edge' – to have the franchise on the things of God.

Let us learn the lesson – whether we are Anglican/Episcopalian, Catholic, Assemblies of God, Baptist or the latest renewal movement! God is not impressed by our theological pedigree, denominational heritage or renewal connections. While we may value the history of past movements, the heritage of sound theology or the pioneering and networking of new movements, pride in these things is offensive to God. What man considers as *valuable*, God views as *vanity* – as empty and meaningless. Because of this, there is no guarantee that He will use our group.

Triumphalism and *elitism* interfere with our receptivity to the things of the Spirit. Our *heart* conditions our *hearing*. Just because we denominate ourselves as Evangelical, Pentecostal or Renewal does not guarantee we will hear what the Spirit is saying to the church. Only a broken and contrite heart will open our eyes and ears, empowering us as prophetic forerunners of the next move of God.

Forerunners

Forerunners of the Reformation

God always sends forerunners before a major visitation. They are what I would call 'idol-busters'. In the spirit of John the Baptist they break open the spiritual atmosphere of the church, of cities and nations, and prepare the way for the Lord to come. They fearlessly call their generation back to a *new starting point* – back to the Lord, confronting the idols of religion and culture. They lay aside their own reputations, often forsaking worldly advantage to boldly confront the compromised religious systems of the day. They are men such as John Wycliffe (d. 1384) – the Oxford scholar and translator of the English Bible, and his contemporary John Huss of Bohemia (d. 1415). They are men who prepared the way in their bold rejection of church corruption and control, for the Reformation and the great reformers such as Luther and Calvin.

For a century and a half from 1350 to 1500 Western Europe was marked on the one hand by an attitude of cynical nominalism toward Christianity as it gave itself to Renaissance humanism. On the other hand it was marked by fresh movements of renewal which proved to be the forerunners of the Reformation. By all appearances Western Europe had been radically de-Christianised, from outside the church by humanism and from within by formalism and corruption. However, this was contrasted by fresh stirrings of dissent and renewal. Various voices – mystics and reformers – sought a greater approximation to apostolic Christianity. Mystics such as Catherine of Sienna (d. 1380) in Italy, Joan of Arc (d. 1431) in France, Walter Hilton (d. 1396) and Julian of Norwich in England, and Thomas à Kempis in Germany, to name a few, led a resurgence of prayer and a call to a deeper devotional life. The monasteries began processes of reform and the voices of Wycliffe and Huss began to be heard with great impact. In fact, Wycliffe became widely recognised as 'the morning star of the Reformation'. But these tremors of renewal were merely warnings of the coming quake.

On the 31st October 1517 an obscure Augustinian monk by the name of Martin Luther, in protest of church corruption, nailed 95 theses to the church door of Wittenburg, Germany.

And then it hit. The Reformation shook the Western world. With a convergence of virulent social, political and religious currents the Spirit of God shed fresh light on the truth of justification by faith. Entrenched power structures and belief systems that had held Western Europe in darkness for centuries were shaken and a new day began to dawn.

The hinge of a new age – preparing the way for global revival

There are transition or hinge-times in history on which the destinies of nations swing. As the Middle Ages passed, the Reformation Age (also called the Early Modern Era, 1500–1750) dawned, ushered in by a transitional generation – by prophetic forerunners such as Wycliffe and Huss. In the fullness of time, however, God visited the earth through the Reformation itself and shaped the Western world as we now know it. It not only began a restoration of apostolic Christianity but also a reshaping of society, producing many of the institutions and freedoms that the West now enjoys.

Like the epicentre of an earthquake the Reformation sent out shock waves of revival into the next age – the Modern Age (1750–1950). The transition into this was marked by the Great Awakening in North America and the Wesleyan Evangelical Revival in Great Britain. Both began in the 1730s, opening the door into the modern era in which successive outpourings of the Spirit have occurred, increasing right through to the twentieth century.

However, the sun is now setting on the Modern Era and the so-called post-modern age is beginning to dawn. *The 1950s through to 2025 will prove to be the hinge of this new age.* It is significant that this period began with the Latter Rain and Healing Revivals of the 1950s, flowing over into the more publicised Charismatic Renewal of the 1960s–1970s, and on to the 'Third Wave' of the 1980s and the 'Toronto Blessing' of the 1990s.[2] These moves of God have experienced a strong prophetic element as the fore-runners of what, I believe, will prove to be the greatest spiritual conflagration of history, heralding an end-time era of God's glory filling the earth.

Like the forerunners of the Reformation, this generation is witnessing a sovereign convergence of social and spiritual factors preparing the way for a new era, for an unprecedented increase of the kingdom.

While *church power* dominated the Middle Ages and *human*

power the Modern Age, manifesting in 'enlightenment human-ism' and 'statist tyranny', it remains for history to record what will dominate the post-modern age. As the idols of the previous ages (of the *church* and of *man*) fall, the generation is now alive that will usher in the next age – an age of *God's power* on the earth.

The 'Elijah Generation'
Just as he did before the Reformation, God is raising up an 'Elijah Generation' – a spiritual *avant-garde* – trail-blazers who, through a prophetic lifestyle, will bring down the Baals of religion and prepare the way for the new era of God's power as heaven invades earth.

The Elijah Generation will be used of God to restore the *apostolic foundations* of the church – they will return to a *new starting point* – to the Father's heart. With the current emphasis on the apostolic we do not need the implementation of *apostolic strategies* so much as a return to an *apostolic spirit* – in fact, a return to *'the Father of spirits'* (Hebrews 12:9). The forerunner anointing is a call to *move on* by *going back* – to pursue *destiny* by returning to *deity* – to the Father-heart of God.

The axe laid to the root
Jesus prophesied that *'everything the Father has not planted will be uprooted'* (Matthew 15:13). Every programme, structure, system, or mindset that does not originate in the Father will be uprooted. Every hindrance to full-scale revival will be removed.

Forerunners like Josiah and John the Baptist are *radical* (coming from the Latin *radix* meaning 'root'). And as radicals they deal with root causes. They go to the foundations. In fact they will *'raise up the age-old foundations'* (Isaiah 58:12 NIV). But to do so, like John, they will prophetically declare to the religious system that:

> *'The axe is already at the root of the trees, and every tree that does not produce good fruit will be cut down and thrown into the fire.'*
> (Matthew 3:10 NIV)

In Section 1 I have sought to give both a foretaste of the church's future and a preliminary diagnosis of idolatry as the hindrance to that future. And so as we turn to Section 2 we will now explore a more detailed description of idolatry as the roadblock to full-scale revival.

SECTION 2

Present Realities – the Diagnosis

Idolatry in the Church

Chapter 4

New Paradigms, Old Problems – Pouring Old Wine into New Wineskins!

The law of congruity

For several years I had the pleasure of driving a BMW. It came time to sell it, and in preparation I replaced the windscreen and wipers because of some minor damage. Then, to assure the prospective buyer of its good condition, a detailed inspection was performed on the vehicle by a BMW specialist. The written report came back. Everything seemed to be fine except for one thing. In bold print across the top of the page I read, *'Windscreen wipers – non-genuine parts.'* I couldn't believe what I was reading. What a minor detail! Safety was not compromised and the wipers were brand new. But they were not *genuine* BMW parts!

I had broken the *law of congruity*. You do not put non-genuine parts on a BMW! In the same way Jesus said,

> *'No-one sews a patch of unshrunk cloth on an old garment ...*
> *Neither do men pour new wine into old wineskins.'*
>
> (Matthew 9:16–17 NIV)

Ford parts go with Fords and BMW parts with BMWs. Oil and water do not mix. Some things are just incongruous.

Jesus is effectively saying, 'Don't attach the new onto the old!' He is answering a complaint from the disciples of the Pharisees and of John the Baptist about His own disciples. They were not fasting, as was the habit of the older groups. Without discussing the issue of fasting His response teaches us a deeper principle of *incongruity between the old and new order*. The 'Jesus-thing' is totally new and completely different from the 'Pharisee-thing' or the 'John the Baptist-thing'. It cannot be patched onto the old ways and old attitudes. In its purest form the old covenant, and even John the Baptist, were at best merely forerunners for the *'new thing'* (Isaiah 43:19) God was now doing.

New patches on the old thing

For several years, there has been a strong emphasis on developing new paradigms for the 21st-century church. We have been attempting to discover new models of doing church to give relevance and success in the shifting trends of contemporary culture. Every day promotional brochures pass across the desks of pastors, advertising one conference or seminar after another. Each one sells the advantages and successes of their model of doing ministry. We have the cell church model, G-12, megachurch, the meta-church, the city church, the house church, seeker sensitive and the new apostolic model. We import them to our cities and churches, thinking all we need to do is implement their strategies and we'll have success. *But all we are doing is patching-up the old thing.*

God is doing a new thing

Through the coming of Jesus God drew a line in the sand. The old order was finished and Jesus was the beginning of the new. The religious spirit and structures of the day were challenged to cross the line, but refused. Every season of renewal and revival is similar. The majority of us though do not reject 'the new thing' outright. We edge right up to the line, stop, lean over into it, grab a part that's working, pull it back over onto our side, and patch it onto the old.

Superimposing new paradigms on old problems

I can hear some say: 'But, you don't understand – we're not just patching the old thing up – it's a whole new thing – we're rebuilding the church from the bottom up – this is a reformation!'

My question is this, 'Is it possible to actually *superimpose new paradigms over old problems*, and not realise it?' Absolutely!

> *'See, I am doing a new thing!*
> *Now it springs up, **do you not perceive it?***'*
> (Isaiah 43:19 NIV)

Just as I took a new part and bolted it onto the BMW, oblivious to their incompatibility, the church bolts on new parts to an old machine.

Reformation or innovation?

We can talk *reformation*, while actually doing *innovation*. To innovate means to make changes or alterations in anything established; to bring in new ideas or methods;[1] whereas to reform means to make better by removing abuses, to alter; to restore to a better condition; to put an end to; to stop (an abuse, malpractice, etc.).[2] Innovation merely introduces new methods to the existing order. But reformation carries with it moral and spiritual overtones that demand a finish to the old, and a new beginning.

An example of this is the addition of small groups to programme-based churches. Observing the dramatic growth of the Korean church through cell groups, the Western church during the 1980s pursued a wholesale adoption of small group programmes, adding them to a plethora of other programmes. And when it did not produce growth we wondered why, not realising that God wasn't interested in innovation – the addition of a new small group programme – but wanted the total reformation of the church. He wanted the revolutionary recasting of the church, from the inside out, into the image of His own Son, the corporate Christ.

When disease or illnesses occur in the human body there are four options: treat the symptoms, cut out the problem, give a transplant, or die. Much of what we do in the church is to treat the symptoms. Someone complains – so we innovate – we change the colour of the carpet and cut the sermon by twenty minutes. We aim to please – to keep them happy at all costs. Or, if it is a major problem we innovate yet again. We might get radical and do an organ transplant – bring in a new programme or ministry to keep the church alive.

But we run the risk of *recipient rejection*. The new organ proves to be incompatible and is rejected by the host body. If the *new practice* doesn't conform to the *old values* it will eventually tear apart.

> *'No-one sows a patch of unshrunk cloth on an old garment, for the patch will pull away from the garment, making the tear worse.'*   (Matthew 9:16 NIV)

It is significant that the word used here for 'tear' is *schisma* from which we derive our word *schism* or *division*. The history of revivals shows that every time God moves there is division – a tearing of the new from the old. Old mindsets, attitudes and values cannot adjust to the new thing God is doing. Strongholds of power and religious control are threatened and ultimately the new is rejected. The Greek word used for 'patch' is *pleroma* meaning 'fullness'. It is the same word used for 'the fullness of Christ'. Our patch may even be a fuller experience of the Holy Spirit but if it's stitched onto the old order it will inevitably create tension until it pulls apart.

If we are not diagnosing the disease then we are only addressing symptoms. And we presume that our part – our model, our strategy, our 'patch' will change the whole. But all we are doing is putting band-aids on melanomas. They are deep-rooted and potentially terminal.

Sometimes the old just has to die. Any death causes pain and it causes grief but if we let the old go we run the risk of a resurrection – the raising up of a new thing!

Pouring old wine into new wineskins

Jesus said, *'You don't put new wine into old wineskins'* (Matthew 9:17). But what we are doing is putting *old wine* into *new wineskins!* Let me explain. The issue is one of spirit and of structure. The wineskin exists for the wine – not the other way around! Therefore new wineskins should only be created for new wine – *new paradigms*, therefore, should come out of a *new spirit*. So very simple! But we get it all wrong. We put all our energy into producing new *wineskins*, new *models* and new *structures*. We import the latest church growth and leadership formulas, thinking they will produce the new wine of life and growth when all-the-while, according to Jesus, *new structures* come out of a *new spirit*.

As we have seen, a lot of what is happening today is an emphasis on new paradigms of ministry. The contemporary church landscape is littered with a multiplicity of conferences and books on new apostolic structures, cell structures and so on. We think all we need to do is change the system. With frenetic energy pastors scurry from one conference to the next trying to find the secret to growth. They are bombarded with the message that all they have to do is *structure* for growth. 'All you have to do is plug into an apostolic network and you'll be on the growing edge.' Or, 'You need to structure your services to be seeker-sensitive – and hey, they'll come!' Or, 'Structure for cells – do G12^3 and you'll experience multiplication.'

'Praxis' and 'ethos'

A city-reaching friend recently gave me a brilliant 'reading' on the current church scene. He drew my attention to two words *praxis* and *ethos*. He commented,

> 'We are hell-bent on salvation through *"praxis"*! There has to be a system, a process, a strategy, someone or something we can import to knock the socks off our city. So, we have moved in western culture from ineffective to more effective to most effective praxis. We are eaten up with *praxis* – "Are you purpose driven? Or seeker sensitive? What model or method are you using? G-12 for your groups? Or some other model?" I am not opposed to more effective *praxis* – *but what we have ignored is "ethos"* – that is, the texture, the intangible, that element which is almost indefinable, that which is difficult to quantify, but arguably impacting. It has to do with "how" to do *"praxis"* – the atmosphere, the attitude, the interior.
>
> We are attempting to engage praxis – more and better praxis – in an atmosphere which is blatantly unhealthy. Unless the church moves from unhealthy ethos, to healthy ethos, to vibrantly healthy ethos, anything we do will be sabotaged. It is not a matter of ethos over praxis. It is rather that *we must see effective praxis intersect with healthy ethos*. And we have ignored ethos altogether.
>
> I don't see anything that keeps us more centred, that forces us to do introspection, that moves us to holiness of heart and purity in relationships, than does prayer. It is the fountainhead of healthy ethos. But if prayer is only an engine where God is engaged as a power supplier for our purposes on His behalf – if we continue to say, "You have to pray!" as if it was some necessary evil we know we would rather not do but must if we are going to accomplish our purposes, then the question comes, "How little can we talk with Him and get the same result?" It is clear that we are more in love with our work, our mission, and the fulfilment it gives us than we are with God Himself.
>
> The ethos of the church must change or we will only

continue to simulate renewal. *And simulated renewal can no more produce a genuine revival than can a simulated pregnancy produce a live birth.*'[4]

We pursue better praxis but refuse to address ethos. We build bigger buildings and promote better programmes but fail to make a dent on the spiritual atmosphere of the church, let alone the city. We almost pride ourselves as innovative entrepreneurs, when God has called us to blaze new trails as reforming pioneers. And so, rather than travail in birth as spiritual parents for a new move of God and a new generation we prefer to simulate renewal as religious technicians.

So, what is the old wine?

We know that new wine is a symbol of the Holy Spirit (Acts 2:13 and Ephesians 5:18). So what about old wine? Surely it is the opposite – symbolising the spirit of the world?

Paul says,

> '*We have not received the* **spirit of the world** *but the Spirit who is from God, that we may understand what God has freely given us.*' (1 Corinthians 2:12 NIV)

If drinking the new wine of the Spirit enables us to '*understand what God has freely given us*', then the old wine of the *world's spirit* does the opposite. It numbs our spiritual understanding and highlights only what the world can give. It is an anti-Christ spirit, setting up value systems that displace God, putting confidence only in human ability.

It manifests as the following.

Utilitarianism

Utilitarianism has become one of the prevailing philosophical constructs of Western culture. It can be defined as 'a system that holds *usefulness* to be the end ... of action; the ... doctrine that actions derive their moral quality from their *usefulness* ...'[5] The saying, 'The end justifies the means', is the popular rendering of it. Value is afforded an action, person, or thing according to its usefulness in reaching the goal.

Therefore, prayer, unity or any aspect of a biblical lifestyle is not embraced because it is right or because it brings pleasure to the heart of God but as a *means* to reach our goal. Scant regard is paid to the fact that some things have value because God says so, or that certain actions have value because God commands them. For example, why do I pray? 'To make me more spiritual of course!' It sounds right – but using prayer as a *means* to an end, even if it is a good end, is utilitarian. I pray because God commands it.

Utilitarianism pays no heed to motive. An action or behaviour is judged not by its moral value but by its effectiveness in producing results. So, in a utilitarian system, if prayer makes me more spiritual it has value. Praying, therefore, becomes just another means to either increase my spirituality, bless my ministry, or reach my city.

Pragmatism
The slogan, *'Truth is what works'*, captures the meaning of pragmatism. It is related to utilitarianism but is used as a construct to arrive at what is true. The sole test of truth is whether it *works*. If the practical consequences are positive, it must be true. For example, if a particular programme increases revenue and church attendance it must be right. Or if a ministry is attested to supernaturally what they're saying has to be true. In other words, the beneficial results authenticate the particular model, message or ministry. Pragmatism says, 'By their *results* you shall know them'. Absolutes are lost, truth becomes relative, and spiritual discernment goes out the window.

Consumerism
When the goals of a society are reduced to personal peace and affluence it becomes not only utilitarian and pragmatic but also consumerist. The church is reduced to a middle-class club for religious consumers and is programmed not to make them *holy*, but to keep them *happy*.

Political correctness
The spirit of the world produces a culture of conformity. Real issues of truth and justice no longer exist. Because values are only relative to our goals of personal peace and affluence right and wrong become cosmetic. Semantics and protocol take over. We dare not offend or break faith with the popular morality of the day and we lose the clarity or the courage to speak the truth. In the church this gives way to the spirit of Pharisaism – to religion and politics.

Utilitarianism and pragmatism are products of the 'world-spirit'. They have provided major philosophical constructs, along with social-Darwinism, for Western culture, legitimising the human abuses of statist tyrannies, of economic rationalism and the Industrial and Info-Tech revolutions. Within the dictates of political correctness virtually any policy that produces economic results is legitimate.

What are the effects of all this on the church? It means the church becomes corporatist, market driven and streetwise. The presidency of the Spirit is usurped by human skill and politics. True men and women of the Spirit are marginalised –

> *'the prophet is considered a fool,*
> *the inspired man a maniac.'*
>
> (Hosea 9:7 NIV)

Churches become goal-oriented, programme-based and politically correct. People are viewed as 'tithing units' and are valued for their economic worth to the church 'vision'. Pastors are driven in this cultural milieu by their own need for self-worth, empowered by boards, congregations and denominations to produce results with their success primarily measured, to put it crudely, by backsides on seats and bucks in the plate. Like the world, any programme or model that delivers these kind of measurable results is legitimised and pursued with zeal.

'I am rich . . . and have need of nothing'

But, what delights man often displeases God. Through seasons of renewal the Bridegroom comes to disturb the status quo. Our own carnality and the spirit of the age have lulled us to sleep:

> *'I sleep, but my heart is awake;*
> *It is the voice of my beloved!*
> *He knocks, saying,*
> *"Open for me, my sister, my love,*
> *My dove, my perfect one."'*
>
> (Song of Songs 5:2 NKJV)

Although our heart, in some measure, is wakened, it is not enough to change us. We respond,

> *'I have taken off my robe –*
> *must I put it on again?*
> *I have washed my feet –*
> *must I soil them again?'*
>
> (Song of Songs 5:3 NIV)

It is inconvenient – we are too secure to move from our bed of material ease. Our inner condition echoes the words of the Laodicean church: *'I am rich; I have acquired wealth and do not need a thing'* (Revelation 3:17).

The words of Amos speak to a people seduced by comfort and success:

> *'Woe to you who are **complacent** in Zion,*
> * and to you who **feel secure** ...*
> *you **notable men** of the **foremost nation**,*
> * to whom the people of Israel come! ...*
> * Is their land **larger** than yours? ...*
> *You **lie on beds** inlaid with ivory*
> * and **lounge on your couches**.*
> *You **dine on choice lambs***
> * and fattened calves.*
> *You **strum away on your harps like David***
> * and improvise on musical instruments.*
> *You **drink wine by the bowlful***
> * and use the finest lotions,*
> * **but you do not grieve over the ruin of Joseph**.*
>
> *... the* LORD *God almighty declares:*
>
> *"**I abhor the pride of Jacob***
> * and **detest his fortresses**;*
> *I **will deliver up the city***
> * and **everything in it**."'*   (Amos 6:1–8 NIV)

Their leaders triumphantly boasted of their success and prosperity. But as they luxuriated in their material wealth, an internal decay ate at the heart of the people. While increasing in prosperity and power they worshipped at the altars of foreign gods. Of course, they still worshipped Jehovah. They celebrated their Sabbaths and feast days. They gathered in their assemblies, they sang and made music. But all-the-while they were paying homage to the Canaanite god of Baal, looking to him as the source of their fertility.

> *'She* [Israel] *has not acknowledged that I was the one*
> * who gave her the grain, the new wine and oil,*
> *who lavished on her the silver and the gold –*
> * which they used for Baal.'*   (Hosea 2:8 NIV)

Worshipping the gods of this age

What a parallel to the Western church worshipping the gods of this age! We have bowed to the Baals of *productivity and power*. Seduced, we have pursued our plans for growth – to be the largest or fastest growing denomination – to build the largest buildings, the biggest congregations and the most successful programmes. Of course we say, 'It's for the kingdom'. But we are self-deceived. We come near to the Lord with our mouth but our hearts are far from him (Matthew 15:8). We hold our worship events, our conferences, celebrations and services – but He says,

> *'I hate, I reject your festivals,*
> *Nor do I delight in your solemn assemblies ...*
> *Away with the noise of your songs!*
> *I will not listen to the music of your harps.'*
>
> (Amos 5:21 NASB, 23 NIV)

God sees through the volume of words and music to the heart. We say, *'I am rich ... and do not need a thing'* (Revelation 3:17 NIV).

But, Jesus says we are deceived,

> *' ... you do not realise that you are wretched, pitiful, poor, blind, and naked.'*
>
> (Revelation 3:17 NIV)

The sin of pride

Behind idolatry lies the sin of pride. The Lord declared through Amos,

> *'I abhor the pride of Jacob*
> *and detest his fortresses;*
> *I will deliver up the city ... '*
>
> (Amos 6:8 NIV)

Our fortresses of pride – of *self-sufficiency* and *independence* do not impress Him. The Western church has come under a dealing of God because of its spirit of pride. Our cities have been delivered up. And more importantly, the *city of God* itself – the church, has been overrun. The wall has been breached and we have been occupied. Many have a vision for city-reaching – but how can we deliver the city when the *city of God* itself is captive?

Idolatry – the root cause of decline and renewal

Joshua's generation served the Lord. But when he died the next generation, *'who knew neither the Lord, nor what he had done for Israel'*, pursued other gods (Judges 2:10–19). As a remedial discipline they were handed over to their enemies – to captivity. And in their desperation they called on the Lord and He answered by pouring out His Spirit on deliverers who set them free. But secure in their new-found freedom they soon turned back, prostituting themselves again to other gods. The cycle of decline, captivity and deliverance was repeated.

This, too, is the story of revival history.

The Western church – drinking the old wine of idolatry
The historic failure of God's people has been idolatry – their worship of other gods. This was the single cause of their chronic cycle of revival and decline from Moses' time onwards:

> *'... they rebelled against the Spirit of God ...*
>
> *They did not destroy the peoples*
>   *as the Lord had commanded them,*
> *but they mingled with the nations*
>   *and adopted their customs.*
> *They worshipped their idols,*
>   *which became a snare to them ...*
>
> *Therefore the Lord was angry with his people ...*
> *He handed them over to the nations,*
>   *and their foes ruled over them.*
> *Their enemies oppressed them*
>   *and subjected them to their power.*
> *Many times he delivered them,*
>   *but they were bent on rebellion ...*
> *But he took note of their distress*
>   *when he heard their cry ...*
>   *and out of his great love he relented.'*
>
> (Psalm 106:32–36, 40–45 NIV)

The Christian West has not been an exception to this. Early on in the vigorous missionary expansion of the Christian era the church was seduced by the spirit of the age and led into captivity from at least as early as the 4th century. This flowed on into

Renaissance and Enlightenment humanism, culminating in the utilitarian consumerism of the 20th century. Western humanity has, in the last century, witnessed the full bloom of the idolatry of *self*. Just as Narcissus fell in love with his own reflection, Western humanity, made after its own image, has become its own god.

But it has not been without flashpoints of revival. Just as prophets and kings were raised up by God to warn and deliver His old covenant church, He has sent times of refreshing under the new covenant too. First through the often misunderstood and maligned Montanists – the first revival and prophetic movement of Christian history (circa 175 AD). From this to the monastic movement through to the forerunners of the Reformation, to the Reformers themselves including the Anabaptists; Puritans, down to the Evangelical Revival under Wesley and Whitfield in England; to the Prayer Revival of 1859 and the Second Great Awakening. These were followed by the 20th century outpourings of the Spirit in the Welsh revival of 1904; the Los Angeles Pentecostal revival of 1906; the Latter Rain and Healing revivals of the 1950s; and the Charismatic Renewal of the 1960s–70s which included the Jesus Revolution (the move of God amongst the hippies of the 1960s–70s). More recently the 'Third Wave' signs and wonders revival through the Vineyard movement and the Toronto outpouring of 1994.

Every one of these revivals has been the voice of the Bridegroom calling to His beloved to turn from the gods of the nations back to intimacy with Him – to turn from the god of self and find a new centre in Him. Tragically, each new visitation of the Spirit is eventually compromised by the next generation turning to other gods. And as they lose their *internal integrity* a religious and *external orthodoxy* creates a spiritual vacuum, sucking the old wine of idolatry into the new wineskins.

New paradigms or new hearts

The new covenant, though, is not a promise of *new paradigms* but of *new hearts* (Ezekiel 36:26). While there are certainly paradigms of church life that more adequately facilitate spiritual life, heaven's priority is on the *wine* not the *wineskin* – on the *spirit* not the *structure*. No amount of superimposing new paradigms – new methods, techniques or programs – onto the old problem of idolatry, will produce revival. It will *simulate renewal* for a short while but it will never *stimulate revival*.

Only a return to the 'heart of David' will produce the revival we are longing for. Like David, God give this generation a cry for a 'new spirit' (Psalm 51) – for a clean heart – a heart that will not bow to another god (Psalm 16:4–11)!

With the root problem of idolatry diagnosed let us now explore what it is to bow to false images.

Chapter 5

Snakes in the Temple – Confronting the Enemy Within

'But I am afraid that just as Eve was deceived by the serpent's cunning, your minds may somehow be led astray from your sincere and pure devotion to Christ.'
(2 Corinthians 11:3 NIV)

False self-image

As a teenage 'hippie' I experienced a powerful conversion and received a clear call to preach. I went into ministry training, got married and at the age of twenty found myself serving the Lord full-time in one of the fastest growing churches in our city and one of the leading catalysts for renewal. I was passionately in love with Jesus and the world lay at my feet. God was moving – and so was I!

But little did I know what was around the corner. I was not only riding the wave of a move of God in my own life and in the renewal but I was filled with all kinds of 'stuff' that He saw and was committed to changing. He saw my deep feelings of inferiority and insecurity, which I was too ashamed to own. He saw, mixed with my hunger for God, my impatience and determination to fulfil the call of God in my own strength. He saw through my 'image-building' right into my need for identity. He knew who I really was and was committed to a process that would set me free to be true to His design.

So two things happened – I heard from God and I found myself out of the ministry.

I heard from God

First the Lord spoke to me and said, 'David, I'm wanting to draw you aside and satisfy you in deeper realms ... I'm wanting to have a union with you and a fellowship. Don't try and be like others that you might see going here and there and doing this or that ... *don't try and force an image on yourself.* What I want is your fellowship – it will take many, many hours just soaking in my presence.'

With shame I recall my reaction to this word from God. I effectively said, *'Send it back – don't like it – another one thanks!'* I groaned within myself, and complained not only to my pastors but also to God. What I wanted was something fitting for the nation-shaking ministry I was destined to be! I wanted the earth to move! I wanted the works – trumpet blast, thunder, lightning, the heavens opening – God saying, *'Hey, this is my servant, my anointed – apostle to the nations extraordinaire – watch out!'* Come on! What did I want with a word like the one I got – hour upon of hour of just soaking in His presence? Sure, I had a passion for the presence of God and had already committed myself to a lifestyle of prayer. But I was a young man of twenty filled with spiritual testosterone. I had been captured by a vision of God impacting the nations and we were on track to do it. Our church was breaking new ground in worship and intercession. It was engaged successfully in publishing, renewal conferences, ministry training and strategic church planting in major centres of South East Asia. Why would I want anything to do with a word suggesting I wasn't going that track? Soaking in His presence just sounded all a bit effeminate – I wanted the lightning and thunder – I wanted action. But God had other ideas.

Out of ministry – 'God blew on our church like a pack of cards'

The second thing that happened was that God blew on our church like a pack of cards. Whatever else may be said about bad choices or enemy activity, the fact is, God is still in control and uses all things for our good (Romans 8:28). We had purchased an office building to facilitate all the things that were happening. It proved to be a flawed decision and the church hit the rocks financially. The enemy had a field day. He had infiltrated our team with what can only be described as 'false-brothers', who rose up against the founder with false accusations. He was wrongfully accused of fraud, of being a 'wolf in sheep's clothing' and forced, not only out of the church, but also out of the country. The church survived, but being a junior team member I found myself without a job and without a ministry.

Talk about being unplugged. All my youthful dreams lay in the smouldering wreck of a church crash and I found myself selling life insurance to survive. Dazed and wondering, 'What was that all about?' I tried to make sense of it. Fortunately God had already spoken, showing me that what He wanted to do in my life was not like others. That I was not to look at those who were *'going here and there and doing this and that'*, and seemingly achieving things in ministry. He had also shown me that I was going to be hidden in the *'cleft of the rock'* (Exodus 33:22) even as I watched my peers progressing and gaining visibility in the work of God.

False images or Christ's image

But what was the purpose of these dealings of God? Put very simply – to expose *'false images'* and conform me further to *'the image of Christ'*:

> *'And we know that **God causes all things to work together for good** to those who love God, to those who are called according to His purpose ... **to become conformed to the image of His Son ...** '*   (Romans 8:28–29 NASB)

God's design through life's circumstances, including ministry deprivation, is to conform us to the image of His Son. He is infinitely more committed to our *character* than our *career*! The Lord had warned me not to force an 'image' on myself. Looking at men of God in ministry I admired, I wanted to be like them – to be doing the sorts of things they did. I found myself unconsciously imitating them.

Emulating maturity or imitating ministry

But I was to discover that there is a difference between *emulating maturity*, and *imitating ministry*. To be inspired to live closer to Jesus through the example of another is one thing. But to imitate someone else's anointing, style or personality is another. With the outbreak of the current renewal it has been interesting to observe ministries imitate the style and anointing of some of the high-profile leaders. All of a sudden we had Rodney Howard-Browne look-alikes running around the countryside doing their thing. Or alternatively we have had pastors imitating the church growth gurus producing 'cookie-cutter' churches. *Emulating maturity* develops within us *Christ's image* – *imitating ministry* only fabricates *false images*. One *simulates renewal* and the other *stimulates revival*.

Ezekiel's vision of snakes in the temple

A prophetic-intercessor friend recently visited a respected church in a particular city. It belonged to a reputable Pentecostal denomination, but during the worship her eyes were opened and she saw, in the Spirit, a large serpent along the length of one whole wall. And as they left the service the car park was swarming with writhing baby serpents.

What was the significance of this? And how could a 'Spirit-filled' church, looking respectable by man's estimation, become a habitation for serpents – for demons?

In Ezekiel chapter 8, the prophet saw a vision of Israel's idolatry. He was taken, in the Spirit, to Jerusalem, right into the inner recesses of the temple:

> '*And he said to me, "Son of man, **do you see what they are doing** – the utterly detestable things the house of Israel is doing here, **things that will drive me far from my sanctuary?** ..." Then he brought me to the entrance to the court. I looked, and I saw a hole in the wall. He said to me, "Son of man, now dig into the wall." So I dug into the wall and saw a doorway there. And he said to me, "Go in and see the wicked and detestable things they are doing here." So I went in and looked, and I saw portrayed all over the walls all kinds of crawling things and detestable animals and all the idols of the house of Israel. In front of them stood seventy elders of the house of Israel ... Each had a censer in his hand, and a fragrant cloud of incense was rising. He said to me, "Son of man, **have you seen what the elders of the house of Israel are doing in the darkness, each at the shrine of his own idol?** They say, 'The* LORD *does not see us; the* LORD *has forsaken the land.'"*' (Ezekiel 8:6–12 NIV)

'*I saw portrayed all over the walls all kinds of crawling things*' (Ezekiel 8:10)

Hidden deep within the walls of the temple, in a dark and secret room, the elders worshipped false images. The KJV describes the room as, '*the chambers of his own imagery*' or the NIV as '*the shrine of his own idol*' (Ezekiel 8:12). Every private home at this time had a room or closet dedicated to the secret worship of images. This room in the temple was so secret though, that the prophet was instructed to dig through a small hole in the wall to discover it (Ezekiel 8:7–9). Without any correspondence to the design of

Solomon's temple, it appears to have been purpose built for their secret and idolatrous practices.

Snakes on the wall!

Inside the room Ezekiel saw images covering the walls of *'crawling things, detestable animals and all the idols of Israel'* (Ezekiel 8:10). The Hebrew term for 'crawling things' (*remes*) refers to all small animals such as rodents and especially reptiles. Ezekiel, like my intercessor friend, saw, among other creatures, snakes on the wall of this hidden room.[1]

Though what Ezekiel saw was hidden, it was a blatant rejection of the Lord's covenant which prohibited idolatry of *'creatures that move along the ground'* (Deuteronomy 4:15–18).[2] This text uses the noun form of *'crawling things'* which also carries the meaning of animals that *glide* along the ground – i.e. snakes. Although the outward ceremony of the temple was maintained, the secret worship of snakes and other creatures was, in fact, an out-and-out rejection of the Lord's covenant love.

However, despite the hidden practice of snake worship, from the outside nothing had changed. The temple looked the same. To the naked eye it was still the holy place of God's presence. This is the very essence of deception – an external appearance of spirituality, but an altogether different reality within.

Deceived by the serpent's cunning

What does all this signify? The snakes in the temple symbolise for us the activity of *deceiving spirits*. Paul, in addressing the Corinthian church, declared:

> *'I am jealous for you with a godly jealousy.* **I promised you to one husband, to Christ, so that I might present you as a pure virgin to him.** *But I am afraid that just as Eve* **was deceived by the serpent's cunning,** *your minds may somehow be led astray from your sincere and pure devotion to Christ.'*
>
> (2 Corinthians 11:2–3 NIV)

More subtle than false doctrine

We usually think of the spirit of deception as corrupting doctrine. However, it is far more subtle than that. Symbolic of Satan (Revelation 12:9), the serpent's design is to draw the Bride away from the heart-purity of her devotion to Christ. Through deceiving spirits he seeks to draw her heart after other gods – into spiritually adulterous liaisons.

While preserving the appearance of doctrinal orthodoxy and even spirituality, another spirit seduces the affections of the heart.

Seduced through 'super-apostles'

We conform to an appearance of spirituality but live out of a wrong spirit. Paul was concerned that the serpent's cunning would seduce the Corinthians into receiving a different spirit (2 Corinthians 11:4).

But how? Through a breed of *'super-apostles'* (2 Corinthians 11:5) who were competing among themselves and with Paul, presenting an image of success and spirituality:

> *'We do not dare to classify or compare ourselves with some who commend themselves. When they measure themselves by themselves and compare themselves with themselves, they are not wise.'*   (2 Corinthians 10:12 NIV)

This underscores the whole Corinthian correspondence. Paul was confronted by a mindset which *'looked only at the surface of things'* (2 Corinthians 10:7) and compared him with others, saying, *'in person he is unimpressive and his speaking amounts to nothing'* (2 Corinthians 10:10).

Paul – the only apostle with one eyebrow!

The Corinthians were viewing Paul through the eyes of the world. Coming out of the Greek idolatry of beauty – of mind and body – they looked at Paul's appearance and drew their conclusions. A second-century description tells us he was small, bow-legged, beetle-browed (in fact, the description says 'meeting eyebrows'), beak-nosed and bald![3] Wow! The only apostle in the world with one eyebrow! Hardly your average six-foot-four 'all-American' tele-evangelist. Compared to the physical appearance and eloquence of the Corinthian 'super-apostles' and the itinerant orators of the day Paul was not in the race. He would have been a nightmare for even today's 'image-makers'.

The image of external things

And so Paul concluded that the Corinthians were, *'taking pride in what is seen rather than what is in the heart'* (2 Corinthians 5:12 NIV). In so doing they were, *'led astray from their sincere and pure devotion to Christ'* (2 Corinthians 11:3). They had, in effect, bowed to a worldly and idolatrous image of external things – of success, glamour and power. Using these things, including self-promotion, the so-called *'super-apostles'* had enslaved and exploited the Corinthians. Exposing their tactics Paul declared,

> *'many are boasting in the way the world does ... you even put up with anyone who enslaves you or exploits you or takes advantage of you or pushes himself forward or slaps you in the face.'*
>
> (2 Corinthians 11:18, 20)

Through their self-promotional ways and false value system they had resorted to *'secret and shameful ways'* – to *'deception'* and *'distorting the word of God'* (2 Corinthians 4:2).

While to the Corinthians they are their self-proclaimed 'super-apostles', to Paul they are false apostles and *'deceitful workmen, masquerading as apostles of Christ'* (2 Corinthians 11:13).

The Corinthians were led astray by appearances. And because they were worshipping a visible image of success and spirituality (1 Corinthians 14:37; 2:15 – 3:1) they lost their ability to discern the invisible. They looked at the surface of things only, informed by their five senses but not by the Spirit. Blinded by impressive appearances and worldly success they were unable to discern the true character behind the image.

Imaginations of the heart

Paul, being aware of the schemes of the devil (2 Corinthians 2:11) warned them

> *'that just as Eve was deceived by the serpent's cunning, your* **minds** *may somehow be led astray ...'*   (2 Corinthians 11:3)

The idolatry of the elders in Ezekiel 8 is only symptomatic of a far deeper spiritual condition. The 'chambers of one's own imagery' (Ezekiel 8:12) in which they worshipped, alludes to the imaginations of the heart. The same Hebrew word for 'image' (*maskit*) can be used figuratively for the imagination: *'The imaginations* [maskit] *of their heart run riot'* (Psalm 73:7b NASB), or *'the evil conceits* [maskit] *of their minds know no limits'* (Psalm 73:7b NIV).

Ezekiel is not seeing actual happenings in the temple but rather, through vision and symbolically, he is seeing into the spiritual condition of Israel's leadership. He is seeing into the temple of their hearts. Just as idolatry was hidden deep within the inner recesses of the physical temple, so it is with the human heart. The leaders of Israel were, in fact, mesmerised by the idolatrous images of their own minds. Idolatry is, therefore, far more than ritual worship. Rather it is a bowing of the heart to its own imaginations.

Strongholds of self-justification

Ezekiel was asked,

> *'do you see what the elders of the house of Israel are committing in the dark, each man in the room of his carved images? For they say, "The LORD does not see us; the LORD has forsaken the land."'*
> (Ezekiel 8:12 NASB)

The only way the elders could continue in their secret sin was to play mind games. They justified themselves by blame-shifting. They rationalised: 'God has let us down ... he has forsaken the land ... he has not fulfilled his side of the covenant ... why should we fulfil ours?' (Ezekiel 8:12). They were now free to turn to other gods for their protection.

The mind – the battlefield of the enemy

Paul knew that the mind is the battlefield of the enemy:

> *'But I am afraid that just as Eve was **deceived by the serpent's cunning**, your **minds** may somehow be led astray from your sincere and pure devotion to Christ.'*   (2 Corinthians 11:3)

It is the place where the serpent's cunning leads the child of God astray. Through deceitful mental processes Satan takes ground and establishes strongholds. Consequently he explains to the Corinthians,

> *'The weapons we fight with are not the weapons of the world* [flesh]. *On the contrary, they have divine power to demolish **strongholds**. We demolish arguments and every pretension* [every deceptive fantasy and every imposing defence, J.B. Phillips] *that sets itself up against the knowledge of God, and we take captive every thought to make it obedient to Christ.'*
> (2 Corinthians 10:4–5 NIV)

Strongholds – a defensive position

A stronghold, in warfare, is a *defensive position*. It is where we dig in and build a fortress to defend ourselves. Therefore strongholds of the heart and mind usually consist of defensive arguments. This usually works through blame-shifting and self-justification, as with the elders in Ezekiel's vision. It was God's fault that Israel was in this mess. They were only in Babylonian captivity because God had forsaken them, and so they were justified in looking for help elsewhere.

Self-defence is the essence of idolatry. In indigenous cultures idols are worshipped solely for the protection they promise either from enemies, the forces of nature, or the spirit world. And so our self-justifying thoughts become a source of protection and security – and therefore an idol – a stronghold. Our proud imagination, which we raise up for our own protection, hinders us from resting in Christ's justifying work. We consequently trust in our own righteousness and thus become like the Pharisees.

The weapons of our warfare

But Paul has an answer. He talks of weapons that are mighty through God to the pulling down of idol-strongholds (2 Corinthians 10:3–5). They are not of the flesh – they are not found in our own strength, or in self-justifying arguments. The Corinthians and their 'super-apostles' had been boasting in their own accomplishments – in fact, in their own spirituality (remember this church was the Charismatic/Pentecostal church of the New Testament). But Paul, coming out of the opposite spirit, said, *'If I must boast, I will boast of the things that show my weakness'* (2 Corinthians 11:30 NIV).

This was the genius of his message:

> *'For the message of the cross is foolishness ... but to us ... it is the power of God ... For the foolishness of God is wiser than man's wisdom, and the weakness of God is stronger than man's strength.'*   (1 Corinthians 1:18, 25 NIV)

This is why he explains,

> *'Not many of you were wise by human standards; not many were influential; not many were of noble birth. But God chose the foolish things of the world to shame the wise; God chose the weak*

*things of the world to shame the strong. He chose the lowly things
of this world and the despised things – and the things that are not
– to nullify the things that are, so that no-one may boast before
him.'*   (1 Corinthians 1:26–29 NIV)

The weapon, therefore, that brings down idolatry – that destroys
every proud self-justifying attitude – is the humility of the cross.
The mind that bows to its own self-justifying arguments considers the cross as weakness. But when in repentance and
humility we confess our sins the serpent's cunning is destroyed.
Through the humility of depending on Christ's righteousness
alone we are justified and the spirit of the anti-Christ is brought
down.

The image of God

So, what exactly was the image that I was forcing on myself; and,
was I sinning against the commandment: *'You shall not make for
yourself a carved image . . . '* (Exodus 20: 4–5 NKJV)?

God has made us in His own image (Genesis 1:26–27). To
make ourselves into another image is, therefore, to reject the
image of God. It is rebellion and idolatry. We are told not to
make an image of anything, either in heaven or on earth. Paul, in
describing the dynamics of idolatry, explains how we exchange
*'the glory of the immortal God for images made to look like mortal
man . . . '* (Romans 1:23 NIV).

But, we might respond, 'I'm not bowing down to some idol of
wood or stone!' We have already discovered through Ezekiel's
vision that idolatry is a thing of the heart. On another occasion
the Lord showed Ezekiel that the leaders, *' . . . have set up idols in
their hearts . . . '* (Ezekiel 14:3 NIV).

Covetousness and idolatry

Paul described *covetousness* or *greed* as idolatry:

> *' . . . put to death your members which are on the earth: fornica-
> tion, uncleaness, passion, evil desire, and **covetousness, which
> is idolatry.'***   (Colossians 3:5 NKJV)

In another place he describes the covetous person as an idolater:

> *'no . . . unclean person, nor **covetous man, who is an idolater**,
> has any inheritance in the kingdom . . . '* (Ephesians 5:5 NKJV)

In both references the same Greek word *pleonexia* is used to convey the inordinate and selfish desire to possess more, especially that which belongs to someone else and is included in the list that Jesus gives of the evils that come from the heart (Mark 7:21–23).

In both these instances Paul is addressing the church. Unlike some sins, covetousness or idolatry is not always obvious, particularly in a materialistic success-oriented culture. While Paul speaks to the church in general, Peter, more specifically, points to *false ministries*, describing them as having *'a heart trained in covetous practices'* (2 Peter 2:14 NKJV).

This is heavy duty! God was putting His finger on something in my life, as a man and as a minister, that He considered important. It may not have been very visible or obvious to others but God sees through appearances to the heart. To force an image on myself, other than the image of Christ, was to covet the gifts and attributes of another person. Whether it was their anointing, ministry, or even their style, it was idolatrous to imitate it. Sure, it is healthy to *emulate* those who are more mature in God, as Paul encouraged the Corinthians, *'Follow my example, as I follow the example of Christ'* (1 Corinthians 11:1 NIV; see also 1 Corinthians 4:16; 1 Thessalonians 1:6).

But to *imitate* another person's ministry is idolatry. I had made an idol of mortal man – not a literal idol – but I coveted what belonged to another and presented to the world a false image.

Once we have created an image for ourselves, we must inevitably 'serve it'. When we build reputations that are not based on the character of Christ, but on the imitation of a ministry model or style – or an image of success, popularity or perhaps spirituality, then the lie must be maintained, resulting in a deep spiritual dissonance. We experience a lack of inner harmony with God and with others, making it very difficult to be real or vulnerable.

Today's church

The parallel between Ezekiel 8 and today's church is clear. As the elders in Ezekiel's day secretly practised idolatry, so we do today. There is a crisis in the leadership of the Western church. But it is not a crisis for lack of skills or better techniques – it is a crisis for lack of true men and women of the Spirit. Those who, in the secret recesses of the heart, have refused to bow to foreign gods and the systems of men.

Satan's schemes are never obvious. Like snakes, silently and surreptitiously, spirits of religion and deception have entered the temple. Under the cover of serving the church of God, mixed and unclean motives have infiltrated ministry. As leaders, we have become *ministers of the church* rather than *ministers of God*. We have worshipped false images – images of success, spirituality and power. We import into our churches and cities the latest models and formulas that guarantee success. Looking at them from afar – from another city or country – they look so tantalising, so promising. But like a mirage, the hoped for explosion of church growth or of city transformation vanishes the moment we move forward. Why? Because we have refused to pay the price of humbling ourselves – of having our strength broken – our programmes and planning – our eloquence and speaking – our music and talent – reduced to nothing. If what we are doing is not conceived in the womb of *our* weakness, we will never give birth to the wonder of *His* power. There are only two options: *it is either born of God, or of man*. Without experiencing brokenness, every new model produces more dependence on our organising abilities, our communication and networking skills, our financial resources, or our musical creativity. If we import the latest success model to our city without embracing the humility of the cross we will only be bowing to empty images. Like the super-apostles of Corinth we will be taking *'pride in what is seen rather than what is in the heart'* (2 Corinthians 5:12 NIV).

We have in reality deceived ourselves, thinking we advocate the latest models of church growth, city transformation or revival for the sake of our city and for the kingdom. If the wraps were taken off and we could see into our own hearts, we would be on our faces. We are like the ministries Peter describes, who have *'a heart trained in covetous practices'* (2 Peter 2:14 NKJV). We look on the success of others and long to have it for ourselves – Oops, I'm sorry, I should have said, 'for the kingdom'. If we were honest we would see that much of the push to grow our church or denomination comes from competition:

> *'And I saw that all labour and all achievement spring from man's envy of his neighbour ...'*   (Ecclesiastes 4:4 NIV)

For a number of years I was a pastor in a church movement which, at one point, was the fastest growing of its kind in the nation. But with the loss of its founder momentum waned and they were overtaken by another movement. Much of its planning for growth is now, sadly, spurred by the intimidation of the other movement's success.

The spirit of the world in the church

The spirit of the world has seduced us. We used to joke that 'Jesus saves – and Jesus shaves!' But many actually believe that the spirit of the world *is* Rock and Roll, spiked hair and nose rings. Come on – let's get real! Do you think the devil really cares where you wear your jewellery or what hairstyle you have? What he, as a master strategist, is after, is the thing that controls it all – the heart. This is why the wisdom-writer exhorts us to,

> *'Watch over [our] heart with all diligence,*
> *for from it flow the springs of life.'*   (Proverbs 4:23 NASB)

It is the citadel of God's presence – the spring from which flow the sweet waters of the Spirit or the bitter waters of covetousness, competition and pride. Where better for Satan to set up shop than in the temple of God itself – in our hearts! But because the serpent is silent we are unaware of his entry.

The spirit of the world enters in three ways: through *'the lust of the flesh and the lust of the eyes and the boastful pride of life'* (1 John 2:16 NASB).

▶ **The lust of the flesh**. The lust of the flesh is not so much sexual sin but the strength of our human nature. It fills the church with human organisation, programmes and agendas. Do not get me wrong – excellence in management and creativity is basic to our service for God. But it has become the head rather than the tail. The spirit of man has taken control.

▶ **The lust of the eyes**. The lust of the flesh is fed through the eyes. We are captured by the 'outward show of things without enquiring into their real values'.[4] Mesmerised by the outward display of success or spirituality we lose our discernment. Our five senses govern our approach to the things of God and determine our values. We are easily persuaded by the pragmatism of results, without inquiring into their true values or motivation.

▶ **The pride of life**. The final step is the boastful pride of life. The lust of the flesh and the lust of the eyes have been sated. And so now a smug self-satisfaction in our external circumstances – in our wealth, prestige or position sets in. It boasts in our achievements and the rewards gained by them. It can come through in an air of triumphalism when we experience some growth and success. This boasting proud spirit can operate through the work of God when we advertise and promote the size of our movement and churches, our budget, our mailing lists or our ministry. When success comes we reward ourselves with the trappings of prestige and power. With a bigger office or a more prestigious motor vehicle. Or with bigger and better titles – senior minister, bishop, overseer, president and in many cases now, 'apostle'. This is despite the fact that Jesus said,

> *'But you are not to be called "Rabbi", for you have only one Master and you are all brothers ... The greatest among you will be your servant. For whoever exalts himself will be humbled, and whoever humbles himself will be exalted.'*   (Matthew 23:8–12 NIV)

The glory of God lifts

Ezekiel saw the manifest presence of God:

> *'And there before me was the glory of the God of Israel, as in the vision I had seen in the plain.'*   (Ezekiel 8:4 NIV)

As a seer Ezekiel not only saw the splendour of the *shekinah* glory but also the secret depths of Israel's idolatry. What a roller coaster! One minute the full radiance of the glory of God, the next the hidden depths of Israel's idolatrous heart. The prophetic ministry always moves between these two polarities. It stands before the light of God's glory to call an adulterous people back to faithfulness and truth. The temple was holy – set apart as the sole preserve of God's presence – His dwelling place. But it had been invaded by the idol of jealousy and God's presence had no option but to lift:

> *'Now the glory of the God of Israel went up from above the cherubim ... and moved to the threshold of the temple.'*
>   (Ezekiel 9:3 NIV)

And in time, not only from the temple but from the city as well (Ezekiel 10:4, 18; 11:23). Just as in Samuel's day the glory departed and *Ichabod* was written over the house of God (1 Samuel 4:21). The Lord had warned that their idolatry would 'drive him far from his sanctuary ...' (Ezekiel 8:6). It had now happened.

Understanding the root cause of spiritual decline is not difficult: *when the people of God shift the glory of God lifts.*

Our worship of other images – of success and spirituality – moves us from a place of covenant faithfulness and opens the temple of God to another spirit – to the spirits of deception and pride. The experience of previous generations is equally true today:

> *'For although they knew God, they neither glorified him as God nor gave thanks to him, but their thinking became futile and their foolish hearts were darkened. Although they claimed to be wise, they became fools and exchanged the glory of the immortal God for images made to look like mortal man and birds and animals and reptiles.'*
> (Romans 1:21–23 NIV)

In the next chapter we will define idolatry and see how it works in the life of a Christian.

Chapter 6

Idols of Power

'... make us gods who will go before us ...'
(Exodus 32:1 NIV)

So, what is idolatry?

They had just seen the awesome power of God destroy the most powerful army on earth. As if they'd stepped into a Spielberg movie they had experienced unbelievable signs and wonders – at Moses' command rivers had turned to blood – frogs, locusts, flies, darkness and death had covered the land. Not to mention the split-second timing of the Red Sea opening before their eyes, providing a miraculous way of escape, then closing over the mightiest army on earth, just as the last Israelite straggler scrambled to safety.

But there was more. God staged the ultimate 'light show', complete with smoke. They arrived at Sinai and were enveloped by a cacophony of blaring trumpets, thunder, lightning, clouds and billowing smoke. The earth itself quaked under their feet as God descended from heaven and spoke – audibly!

Talk about sensory overload – their circuits were blown! What an awesome introduction to Signs and Wonders 101! Until this point their faith had been sustained by their five senses. They had seen, heard and felt all these awesome manifestations of God. Moses had been visibly out front cutting a heroic figure as their deliverer. But suddenly he was drawn into the swirling cauldron of thick darkness as he vanished up Mount Sinai. Their visible leader was gone. And he didn't seem to be coming back in a hurry.

Scripture records that,

> *'When the people **saw** that Moses was **so long** in coming down from the mountain, they gathered around Aaron and said,*

> *"Come, **make us gods who will go before us**. As for this fellow Moses who brought us up out of Egypt, we don't know what has happened to him." '*
> (Exodus 32:1 NIV)

They couldn't handle two things: *sensory-deprivation* and *delay*. Moses couldn't be seen and he was too long.

Sensory-deprivation

If our faith in God is sustained by sense-knowledge, even if that is by signs and wonders, then we falter when the evidence of His presence subsides or stops. God tests us. This is when we are vulnerable and look to other sources for a sense of protection and well-being.

Hezekiah was faced with a dilemma – the forces of the Assyrian army were breathing down his neck. But in his moment of crisis, *'God withdrew from him, in order to test him, that He might know all that was in his heart'* (2 Chronicles 32:31 NKJV). God withdrew to see whether Hezekiah would resort to military alliances – whether he would depend on the strength of man or on God – on the visible or the invisible.

Perhaps the manifestations of renewal have subsided. God is testing us to see what is in our hearts. Will we continue to press into Him – in humility, seeking His face – waiting in His presence – hungering and thirsting for more of Him? Or will we resort to the latest and hottest church growth programmes and to business as usual?

Divine delay

God may have given us a promise concerning the future. But the fulfilment is delayed – it just doesn't seem to be happening – it's not becoming visible, not even on the distant horizon. And I'm thinking, *'Maybe, it was me – I just imagined it'*. So what do we do? Do we wean our souls from human things – from impatience – from the nervous energy of the flesh – from the ways of this world which depend on human ingenuity, and wait for God? Or do we, like Abraham, short-circuit the ways of God by depending on a visible means and produce an Ishmael?

As a young minister I'd been invited to preach in a small struggling Pentecostal church on the other side of our city. The pastor had recently died and his widow, temporarily holding the fort, was looking for a senior pastor. I'd heard the call of God to serve Him and was chaffing at the bit. In my zeal I ignored the timing of God and kept pressing in and accepting their invitations to preach. They were really warming to me and it was a happening thing until one fateful Sunday. I told the story of a lady who asked Billy Graham, *'Dr Graham, Dr Graham, should I wear makeup?'* The response, inevitably, being, *'Lady, if the barn door needs painting, paint it!'* Well that did it. I hadn't noticed – not one woman in that church wore makeup! The honeymoon was over – in fact we never made it to the altar. I never received another invitation. And, thankfully, an Ishmael was terminated.

We were another four years in our home church before God opened the door on the next phase. But in my impatience the ministry I could see was better than the one I couldn't see. What was visible looked so good to the natural eye. But God had something further down the track that was of His choosing.

Israel under Moses had already depended on the visible – on their own sensory perception of God's activity through Moses *'who brought them up out of Egypt'* (Exodus 32:1). They were too dull to discern the invisible – that behind Moses the man, was an awesome, supernatural but invisible God. It was very easy then to turn more fully to the visible – to created things – to idols for their security – *'they will go before us'* (Exodus 32:1).

This was Israel's test case. Not out of Egypt five minutes, with the impact of the Sinai manifestations hardly subsiding and the disappearance of Moses just occurring, they turned to idols. God allowed them to experience sensory-deprivation and divine delay to test their hearts – to see whether they would walk by faith or by sight.

For the child of God these two lessons determine everything. Failing them provides the entry point for idolatry, consigning us to the wilderness until we die – die to our flesh and to the idols of power.

Idols of power

The precedent

What were the false gods that Israel turned to? The Sinai test case became the precedent they were to follow throughout their history. Five hundred years later Aaron's Sinai speech was echoed by Jeroboam when unveiling the golden calves: *'These are your gods, O Israel, who brought you up out of Egypt'* (Exodus 32:4; 1 Kings 12:28)

The golden calf became the pattern for Israel's continuing

idolatry. By Jeroboam's time two golden calves were officially instituted as the focus of Israel's worship. Calf-worship became the enduring idolatry of God's people so that Hosea, another two hundred years later, was still confronting it.

> 'Now they sin more and more;
>   they make idols for themselves . . .
> cleverly fashioned images . . .
> It is said of these people,
>   "They offer human sacrifice
>   and kiss the calf-idols." '
>
> (Hosea 13:2 NIV)

Baal – the worship of power

The calf-idol was, in fact, a young bull – the symbol of *virile power*. The bull was an object of worship throughout the ancient world, including the Egyptians, Babylonians and the Phoenicians. More importantly it became for the Canaanites the symbol of Baal, a fertility deity, and chief of their gods. As the most active and supreme of the Canaanite pantheon Baal was the god of rain and vegetation and therefore responsible for *productivity*.[1] As Professor R.K. Harrison indicates, 'the primary concern of Canaanite worship was that of insuring the fertility of the land, of flocks and herds, and of the human populace.'[2] While Baal worship had been pursued in Israel since the time of the Judges (Judges 2:13; 6:25) it was not fully instituted until Ahab's marriage to the Phoenician princess, Jezebel, daughter of the high priest of Baal (1 Kings 16:29–33). This opened the door to a demonic influx of error and deception which we will explore in Chapter 8 – 'The Spirit of Jezebel'.

The problem of power

God's people, from the beginning, were called to be *idol-busters*. Moses commissioned them before entering the land:

> 'When the LORD your God brings you into the land you are entering to possess and drives out before you many nations . . . nations larger and stronger than you . . . Break down their altars, smash their sacred stones, cut down their Asherah poles and burn their idols in the fire. For you are a people holy to the LORD your God.'
>
> (Deuteronomy 7:1, 5–6 NIV)

But what happened? Why did they fall prey to the gods of the

nations? Because they stumbled over the problem of power.
Moses pre-empted this:

> 'You may say to yourselves, "These nations are stronger than we
> are. How can we drive them out?"'　　　　(Deuteronomy 7:17)

With human thinking and natural eyes they looked on the *power*
of the nations, concluding that the mandate to extirpate pagan
worship and to serve the world as a prophetic kingdom of priests
was impossible. Even so, they were encouraged,

> 'But do not be afraid of them; remember well what the LORD your
> God did to Pharaoh and to all Egypt. **You saw with your own
> eyes** the great trials, the miraculous **signs and wonders**, the
> mighty hand and outstretched arm, with which the LORD your
> God brought you out. The LORD your God will do the same to all
> the peoples you now fear ... Do not be terrified by them, for the
> LORD your God, who is among you, is a great and awesome God.'
> 　　　　　　　　　　　　　　　　　　　(Deuteronomy 7:18–21)

But they had already flunked *Idol-Busting 101* at Sinai! Sometimes
seeing is not believing. Israel had seen the *acts of God* but did not
know the *ways of God* (Psalm 103:7). A senior man of God by the
name of Bill Hawkins had a significant impact on us in our early
years. He was trained by William Cathcart, the founder of the
Apostolic Church in Australia. Bill possessed a wonderful revelation of the ways of God and drilled into us that the *acts* of God
are known by *observation*, but the *ways of God* by *association*.
Learning the ways of God only comes with the experience of
sensory-deprivation and *divine delay* – where we either trust the
invisible God for His power; or turn to the *visible* gods of power –
to created things.

As with the pagan nations Israel turned to idols to secure
protection and power. Protection from the elemental forces of
nature and power over their enemies. The pagan gods promised
to deliver. And they could be *seen* – and so could the enemy
nations.

In the new covenant church

'OK', you may say, 'All very informative – that was back then –
but how does this relate to me?' Paul, in addressing the new
covenant church, applies the lesson:

> *'Now **these things occurred as examples** to keep **us** from setting **our hearts** on evil things as they did. **Do not be idolaters**, as some of them were ... These things happened to them as examples and were written down as **warnings for us**, on whom the fulfilment of the ages has come. So, **if you think you are standing firm, be careful** that you don't fall! ... Therefore, my dear friends, flee from idolatry.'*

> (1 Corinthians 10:6–7, 11–12, 14 NIV)

What things are *'these things'*? The text refers to the *idolatry* of old covenant Israel! Paul is saying that their genetic disposition towards idolatry is just as real for us today. Indeed these 'testings' that Paul refers to are examples or 'types', warning the end-time generation, *'on whom the fulfilment of the ages has come.'* If God's end-time purpose of world-wide awakening and revival is to be fulfilled the issue of idolatry cannot be side-stepped! It is historically the number one roadblock to spiritual breakthrough.

Our working definition of idolatry

We cannot assume that we are *'standing firm'* any longer. Perhaps we've already fallen into idolatry but don't realise it. Let's explore how this works.

For our purpose, we will use this working definition of idolatry:

> ▶ *Idolatry is the feeling of well-being gained from my relationship to a created thing, either material or non-material.*

From where do I draw my sense of well-being?

Asking ourselves this question is the one sure way to expose idolatry. It means anything has the potential to be an idol – a person, possession, position or even a perception – our own self-image – even a thought-process through which we rationalise or justify ourselves. Anything that gives us a sense of identity, a feeling of significance in the world – and therefore a feeling of power.

Just as ancient Israel turned from the Lord to idols for protection and power, we too are drawn away for the same reasons. God is spirit, and invisible. Israel lost their visible leader. Even the manifestation of God's presence seemed to leave them – they were on their own in the world and needed to feel safe. Rather than live out of the revelation-knowledge of God, by faith, they opted to live by sight and serve a god they could see and feel. They turned to Baal, represented by the bull, a symbol of virility and power. As a fertility god he would give them fruitful wombs and crops. The Lord's appeal through Hosea underscores this:

> *'O Ephraim, what more have I to do with idols?*
> *I will answer him and care for him.*
> *I am like a green pine tree;*
> *your fruitfulness comes from me.'* (Hosea 14:8 NIV)

Fruitfulness was the issue – it meant productivity leading to economic prosperity, and therefore also to power. Only then could the people truly feel secure. Baal was in reality a god of *productivity* and *power*.

Idols of productivity and power

Throughout the church's history the false gods of productivity and power have seduced leaders and people alike. Concepts of power and authority very quickly shifted from the lifestyle and values of Jesus and the apostles. I will discuss the church's historical roots of idolatry and human authority in Chapter 9. Suffice to say at this point that by the middle of the second century human power structures emerged which stopped the move of the Holy Spirit. By the fourth century they totally dominated. Despite the Reformation, the same value system and many of the structures have been inherited by the contemporary church. Just as the old covenant church institutionalised the gods of the nations, so too, the church of the new covenant. We have, enshrined in many of our institutional structures, the spirit of the world – values that are, in fact, antagonistic to the Spirit of Christ and therefore to apostolic Christianity.

Our whole society is infected with this idolatry. It begins in the education system's preparation for economic survival. The purpose of life is to maximise our earning power for the accumulation of things – designer clothing, split-level four bedroom homes with pool and jacuzzi, luxury cars, boats, membership at the fitness club, and don't forget the annual overseas holiday. I worked in the insurance industry for many years and one of the tactics to increase sales targets was to encourage agents to increase their lifestyle and stay in debt. Advertising screams at us from billboards, TVs, radios and glossy magazines that we deserve more, more, more and more!

Don't get me wrong. Paul could say,

> *'I have learned to be content in whatever circumstances I am. I know how to get along with humble means, and I also know how to live in prosperity; in any and every circumstance I have learned the secret of being filled and going hungry, both of having abundance and suffering need.'* (Philippians 4:11–12 NASB)

I am the first person to enjoy the aesthetic quality and convenience of good things. But for the apostle, and for us, the issue is one of *contentment* verses *covetousness*. The absence of the former opens us to the latter, and therefore to idolatry.

Buildings, budgets and badges

The same virus plagues the church. Whole denominations, ministries and churches bow to the Baals of productivity and power. We want bigger *buildings*, bigger *budgets* and bigger *badges* – all for the kingdom of course. Historically, though, these have been the church's icons of power and wealth.

It's not very different from my experience in the corporate world. Achievement was not only rewarded with the status of an increased lifestyle – bigger and better homes and motor vehicles, but with the badges of status and recognition by the industry and the adulation of peers. Apart from times of praise and worship, some pastors' conferences are not a lot different from those I experienced in the corporate world. The corporation's achievements, product and image are hyped until, in a triumphal frenzy of self-belief, our invincible team is ready to take on the world. We want more members, more programmes, more services, more dollars in the offering, more ministries, more leaders, more buildings and more churches. And when we have more, we have success – and success is power. Denominational pastors' conferences shout loud the praises of those that are kicking goals in the numbers game. We are shouting from our conference platforms and through our glossy magazines, 'Well done, good and *successful* servant!'

The idol of success

Every pastor knows the pressure of showing measurable achievement each year in new members and increased giving. They are forced into playing a numbers game. Some are more obvious about it than others. I was training in North America where my wife and I attended a conservative evangelical church of about 3,000 people. I can still recall our first visit. After the service we exited through the foyer where we were stunned by a large flashing sign – *'2,942 people attended our service this morning!'* Compared to back home, this sure was different! Perhaps we were just more dishonest about it. I know of a pastor who when the church was in decline would delay months or years in updating the church membership records and decline lodging them for denominational publication. We are tyrannised by the god of success. On the one hand being pressured into triumphalism, on the other being pressured into shame. J.I. Packer, powerfully exposes the idolatry of success when he says,

> '... the passion for success constantly becomes a spiritual problem – really, a lapse into idolatry – in the lives of God's servants today ... to feel that one must at all costs be able to project oneself to others as a success is an almost demonised state of mind, from which deliverance is needed ... Christ's agents in building His church now feel they have to have track records that show them as successes in everything to which they ever put their hand. So the imposters have a field day: anything that in the short term looks like triumph (opposition overcome, obstacles surmounted, expansion encompassed) is equated with personal success, and anything that in the short term looks like disaster (loss of money, status, job, support, or whatever) is seen as failure. Successful looking performance at all costs becomes the goal, and unreality creeps into people's view of themselves as a result.'[3]

We measure success through a broken lens. Our perspective is not God's – man looks at the outward appearance of things but God sees the heart. Isaiah prophesied that Christ,

> '... will not judge by what he sees with his eyes,
>   or decide by what he hears with his ears.'   (Isaiah 11:3 NIV)

Our measure of success is based on natural criteria and by the appearance of things.

What guarantee is there though, that once we are successful by human standards we will rate in heaven. We may plant a record number of churches, grow the largest church in the city, preach to more people than Billy Graham, heal more people than Kathryn Kuhlman and feed more people than World Vision but what if God never told us to do it?

> *'Many will say to Me on that day, "Lord, Lord, did we not prophesy in Your name, and in Your name cast out demons, and in Your name perform many miracles?" And then I will declare to them, "I never knew you; DEPART FROM ME, YOU WHO PRACTICE LAWLESSNESS."'* (Matthew 7:22–23 NASB)

'I never knew you ... depart from Me' – what a horrific obituary to echo through all eternity, particularly after a lifetime of service! The issue from where God sits is whether He *knew* us. Obviously God has all-knowledge and knows everybody. The issue is rather one of *intimacy*, of knowing Jesus and being known by Him, and of doing the will of the Father:

> *'Not everyone who says to Me, "Lord, Lord," will enter the kingdom of heaven;* **but he who does the will of My Father ...** *'* (Matthew 7:21 NASB)

We all know about doing *bad* things outside of the will of God. But we're not so familiar with doing *good* things outside His will. According to Jesus it is possible to do ministry, even operating in the supernatural, in disobedience to the Father. As Saul discovered, *'To obey is better than sacrifice'* (1 Samuel 15:22). Like him, we can offer the sacrifice of ministry but do it in rebellion, operating outside of the Father's express wish for that moment. In fact these ministries are described by Jesus as those who *'practice lawlessness'* (Matthew 7:23 NASB). Their ambition for success has driven them beyond the Father's will to habitually *practice* ministry in rebellion against God.

The idol of church

Jesus is the reign of God. He is absolute over all that is, making all else relative, including the church. But we have, instead, viewed the church as God's reign on the earth so that what was designed to be a *part* has become the *whole*. We have said, *'If you want God, plug into the church'*. So the church, by default, has become God. Richard Rohr, the director of the Center for Action and Contemplation in Albuquerque, New Mexico, picks this up:

'the Church – just like the people of Israel – has continually been tempted to idolise itself ... The proclamation of the Reign of God means that only *one* thing is absolute – everything else is relative. Everything else is a means to the end. That includes the Church ... The first image of an idol was made by the first priest, Aaron. As soon as Moses came down from the mountain ... his brother Aaron quickly produced religion by making the golden calf. That way you have God at your disposal, you have God in hand, we're in control. The temptation of religion always consists in turning the tables so that we ourselves take charge of the situation. Thus the first mistake consists in confusing the Reign of God with the Church.'[4]

We have forgotten that Jesus said, '*You* seek the kingdom' and '*I'll* build the church' (Matthew 6:33; 16:18). Reversing the roles, we build the church and forsake the kingdom. If we truly understood this, it would spark a revolution. We now understand why pastors can live prayerless, spiritually barren lives but still succeed in the church system. And why, for many pastors, the church is more important than their wives and families, their health and even their spiritual life. We can now understand how institutionalised religion can be abusive and controlling. I know of a church that doesn't give a moment's thought to the appropriateness of automatically deducting a tithe from staff salaries. A small thing you may think, but a presumption coming out of the institutionalising of the reign of God in the church. It completely ignores the New Testament teaching on giving as an issue of individual freedom (2 Corinthians 8:8, 12; 9:5, 7).

It now makes sense that the religious system can be actually antagonistic to true spirituality. When we cut off God's people from the true reign of God by idolising the church, the reign of man – of power, prestige and possessions, takes over.[5] Strip back the religious veneer and at its core the church, the *city of God*, becomes instead the *city of man*.

In Jeremiah's day the temple had become an idol. He cried out, warning,

> '*Do not trust in deceptive words and say, "This is the temple of the* LORD, *the temple of the* LORD, *the temple of the* LORD!" ... Will you ... burn incense to Baal and follow other gods you have not known, and then come and stand before me in this house ...*

and say, "We are safe" – safe to do all these detestable things?
Has this house, which bears my Name, become a den of robbers to
*you? But I have been watching! declares the L*ORD*.'*

(Jeremiah 7:4–11 NIV)

It reminds me of a game we used to play as kids called 'twister'.
Instead of twisting limbs though, we twist words and the truth to
win our religious power games. But no amount of spin and high
sounding phrases can make our particular institution the house
of God. Our claims of being 'Evangelically orthodox', or 'capital
P Pentecostal', or 'apostolic', or 'cutting edge' will not impress
Him. We can cry, *'This is the temple of the L*ORD*, the temple of the*
L*ORD*, the temple of the L*ORD*!'* (Jeremiah 7:4) until Jesus comes
again, but it will never move God if all the while we are living in
idolatry. The fact is that in Jeremiah's day it had ceased being the
temple of the Lord and had instead become an idol.

And because God destroys idols, the fate of the temple was
sealed. In 586 BC it was finally destroyed and the people went
into captivity until the times of restoration arrived. And so today
God is destroying what we have called 'church', making way for
a restored people true to the reign of God in the person of Jesus.

The idol of self

We have looked at a working definition of idolatry and explored
some of its expressions in the church. But what is at the core of
idolatry, what is its internal motivating force?

The sociologist Emile Durkheim,[6] in his research of indigenous religious culture uncovered this. He discovered three
stages in the development of religion: first, the culture develops
various traits and values; second, it uses an animal to symbolise
those traits or values; and third, it worships the animal in the
form of a totem or idol. And if the totem or animal represents
the traits of their own people-group then who, in effect, are they
worshipping? You guessed it – themselves!

The Western Evangelical/Pentecostal Church is no exception.
It has created an image of God based on its dominant traits and
values. We bow to the totems of productivity and power. But
these are the traits of our own people-group, of Western civilisa-
tion. We are therefore worshipping ourselves and have created a
god in our own image (Romans 1:18–23).

Self is the ultimate idol of power. It places man in the driver's
seat. Remember idolatry is a problem of power. Because God

cannot be seen, in a moment of need we turn to created things – to gods that can be seen and used for power and protection. And who better than ourselves?

This explains why the therapy of *self* is endemic in the Evangelical Church. Take a quick glance over the shelves of any Christian bookstore. Books on personal wholeness, emotional recovery, personal relationships, sexual enjoyment, prosperity and physical fitness abound.

Both God and the church exist for *my* recovery, *my* therapy and *my* support – they are there to bring *me* into personal fulfilment and to make *me* feel good about myself. In fact, God is a kind of heavenly *Dr Feel-good* – even worship becomes a *feel-good* experience. Sunday morning worship is a time for *me* to feel exhilarated and uplifted. Heaven help anything that gets in the way of that – particularly the volume or music style! As a pastor I've seen so many people become decidedly *un*-Christian about worship – some like it slow – some like it fast – some like it contemporary – some like it traditional – some like it electric – some like it acoustic – some like it loud – some like it quiet. And some will kill to get what *they* like!

Pastors, rather than serve as men and women of God who, in a spirit of gentleness, exhort, rebuke and correct, become *personal therapists* and *counsellors* (1 Timothy 5:2; 2 Timothy 4:2). The church, instead of being the temple of God becomes the temple of man – a country club, or perhaps a night club, depending on that particular church's speciality. We pay membership fees – tithes and offerings – for club privileges, and in return we expect service. And above all else, as discerning consumers, we look for choice – 8.30 or 10 am service – traditional or contemporary – small group or large group – seeker-sensitive or purpose driven – conversational or inspirational – Sunday or mid-week – morning or evening.

In the idolatry of success and of self the church has created a 'beast'! It devours pastors and people alike. And when it has sucked them dry it spits them out. The following three chapters (Chapters 7, 8, 9) uncover the nature and tactics of that beast – of the religious spirit and system.

Chapter 7

The Beast –
Idolatry, Division and Unity

'Come, let us build ourselves a city,
with a tower that reaches to the heavens,
so that we may make a name for ourselves . . . '
(Genesis 11:4 NIV)

After the second brutal slaying in broad daylight, our normally peaceful community was in panic. It was obvious that a serial killer was on the loose and to allay fear a community meeting was called. Invitations went out to all our community leaders, except to one group – the pastors. At this moment of crisis they were obviously viewed by our civic leaders as irrelevant. In response, one of the pastors called about twelve of us together. History was in the making: for the first time ever we were together to pray.

It was a Monday morning as we stood hand-in-hand agreeing in unity and asking God to intervene. On Friday a third murder occurred – *'So much for unity and the power of prayer!'* But, the very next day the homicide detectives from police headquarters picked up two people and brought them in to the local police station: one was a suspect and the other an off-duty local detective who had, coincidentally, become a Christian several weeks before.

The homicide detectives proceeded with the interrogation during which the suspect broke off pointing to the Christian detective, silently sitting in the corner, and said, *'Get that man out of here – he's fussing with my brain!'* The battle was on. Eventually, when the homicide detectives couldn't get any further, he asked if he could interrogate the suspect himself. They left him to it.

Eyeballing the suspect he said, *'It's evil within you, isn't it, that causes you to do these things – and I bind that evil now in the name of Jesus!'* Not your standard police practice, in our city at least! The suspect broke, confessing to all three murders.

Case solved. The community breathed a collective sigh of relief. And the pastors came together confessing their attitudes and suspicions of one another, catalysing a weekly prayer meeting and over time, various city-wide celebrations.

God is interested in our unity. Jesus said, *'I have given them the glory ... that they may be one as we are one'* (John 17:22 NIV). But it's not just any kind of unity. It comes out of His *'glory'*, that is, from His presence and holiness. It is a supernatural unity born of His Spirit.

Recently a prophetic word was given to our city. Although it came through a mature ministry I initially had difficulty believing it. It warned that a wall of *false unity* was being built in our city that could ultimately resist a move of the Spirit. I couldn't believe it. How could our unity, brought to birth by a miracle, become a wall that could resist the move of God? That's what we're about to discover in this chapter.

Origins of false unity

At the very beginning of history the world saw a move toward unity – it was called the tower of Babel. It became the foundation for Babylon. 'But, surely,' you say, 'Babel is the Ecumenical Movement and the United Nations – we're not falling for that kind of unity!' The enemy trades in caricatures, using them as a diversion, then comes at us more subtly. Aware of this, let's examine some of the more subtle characteristics of false unity.

Re-creating Eden without God – the right vision, but the wrong spirit

> *'They said to each other, "Come let's make bricks ... " Then they said, "Come, let us build ourselves a city, with a tower that reaches to the heavens ... "'* (Genesis 11:3–4)

Babel is a counterfeit city of God. Abraham, however, was called out of the counterfeit to search, not for an earthly city, but for a city whose architect and builder is God (Hebrews 11:10). We likewise, as the seed of Abraham, are called to a quest for the city of God, the true church – *'the holy city, the new Jerusalem which comes down out of heaven from God, prepared as a Bride'* (Revelation 21:2). When the Holy Spirit was poured out on the day of Pentecost all heaven and earth resounded with the cry, *'Now the dwelling of God is with men . . . '* (Revelation 21:3) – the true church, as the dwelling of God's presence, had arrived.

But from its beginning the satanic strategy was to *seduce* and *reduce* the church until it became a pale counterfeit of the real. The *city* and *tower* of Babel therefore represent two expressions that Satan seeks to compromise. The city represents the *city-church* and the tower, *city-wide prayer*. I need to qualify what I am about to say with a statement: I am totally committed to both! I believe the *city-church* will be one of the most dominant paradigms the Holy Spirit restores to the 21st-century church. In fact I believe the city-church together with unified intercessory prayer are integral to the full recovery of the apostolic unity of Christ's body. But there is a lesson to be learned.

Babel had a *city vision* – but it was animated by a *human spirit*. It is possible to have unity in external things – in a city-reaching vision, as well as strategy, but to be internally at discord with God. The people at Babel had a unity of *purpose* but not a unity of the *spirit*. In fact they had moved beyond *toleration* to *collaboration* but were withheld by God from *visitation*. Why? Because while they had the right vision they had the wrong spirit. Over time the seeds of human independence, planted in the garden through Adam's disobedience, had come to maturity in Babel's attempt to *re-create Eden without God*.

Babel was a restoration and revival movement. It symbolises our aspirations to re-build the city of God – to restore the garden of the Lord, the true apostolic city-church, independently of God. Their declaration *'let us make'* and *'let us build'* reveal *self* as the motivation and means *'to reach heaven'* (Genesis 11:3–4).

The contemporary institutional church[1] has become a city whose builder and maker is *man*. We develop our own plans and implement them independently of God. Some of us believe we have the *apostolic blueprint* for the reformation of the church but through the deceitfulness of sin we run with it in our own strength. And instead of heaven coming down to earth we place one more brick in yet another religious tower built to the glory of man.

Visitation and judgment

> *'But the* LORD *came down to see the city and the tower that the*
> *men were building.'*   (Genesis 11:5 NIV)

We are all praying for God to *'come down'* in revival, but do we
really understand what we're asking? When God comes in
visitation, He not only comes to bless but to *check us out!* The
meaning of the word 'visitation' in Greek (*episkope*) is *inspection*.
It refers to the function of an elder to *look-over, oversee,* or *inspect*
the flock (1 Timothy 3:1). Consequently, seasons of divine
visitation are not only seasons of mercy, but of judgment, as
God *inspects* His people.

Jerusalem – Babylon the Great!

So, when Jesus wept over Jerusalem, the rebellious city of God,
warning of imminent judgment, it was because they did not
recognise the time of their visitation (or 'inspection') (Luke
19:44). God had come down in the person of His Son to inspect
His people. What He discovered was the mature fruit of their
idolatrous ways. Beginning with Aaron's golden calf, and continuing with the Baals of Canaan, the people's idolatry ripened
in its Pharisaic rejection of Messiah Himself. Because of their
spiritual adulteries they were unable to respond to the Bridegroom and transition to the new thing that God was doing. They
had so imbibed the spirit of pride by the time of Christ that John
identified Israel as the *'great city, Babylon, the city of power'*
(Revelation 18:10)! The *great city* of Babylon, the *great harlot*,
was none other than Jerusalem herself![2] She was so drunk with
the world-spirit – so enamoured with the work of human hands,
that she had become the *city of man* – Babylon itself.

The spirit of the world and the spirit of pride

Jerusalem, now identified as Babylon, shows the frightening
potential for the redeemed community's illicit liaison with the
world-spirit. Babylon represents man organising himself apart
from God and as such is animated by a spirit of pride and
independence. This is the ruling principle of the world. And is
the same spirit that seduced our first parents in Eden, which their
progeny gave free reign to at Babel, and that the church
continues to do battle with at this end of the age. Isaiah's inspired
proclamation against the king of Babylon shows Satan himself as

the animating spirit behind her proud spiritual aspirations. Satan's five *'I wills'* are identical, in spirit, to the aspirations expressed at Babel.

> *'You said in your heart,*
>   *"***I will*** ascend to heaven;*
> ***I will*** *raise my throne*
>   *above the stars of God;*
> ***I will*** *sit enthroned on the mount of assembly,*
>   *on the utmost heights of the sacred mountain.*
> ***I will*** *ascend above the tops of the clouds;*
>   ***I will*** *make myself like the Most High."'*

(Isaiah 14:13–14 NIV)[3]

Each one of these *'I wills'* represents a spiritual aspiration. Pursuing spiritual ends out of *self-will* is the most subtle satanic temptation. It is the spirit of Babylon and it chronically infects the Christian ministry, corrupting the church with the spirit of pride and an alien value system.

The harlot and the beast!

John represents the people of God, breached by the spirit of the world, as seductive and vicious – as *harlot*[4] and *beast*. In Revelation chapter 13 two beasts appear. One emerges from the sea, the other from the land. The first beast represents *world powers* and their beast-like nature as they emerge from the tumultuous *sea of peoples*. For John's audience this was personified in Rome and its despotic power. We will give our attention, though, to the second beast – the land-beast (Revelation 13:11–18). But first, we need to identify *'the land'*. Chilton points out that, 'John uses the expression *"those who dwell on the Land"* twelve times in Revelation (once for each of the twelve tribes) to refer to *apostate Israel* (3:10; 6:10; 8:13; 11:10 [twice]; 13:8, 12, 14 [twice]; 14:6; 17:2, 8).'[5] 'The Land', therefore, is the Promised Land of Canaan – possessed, or alternatively, dispossessed, under the terms of covenant blessing or cursing. And the 'beast', the religious animal, which emerged from *'the land'*, is none other than the back-slidden old covenant church!

The church becomes a false prophet

The *land-beast* (the back-slidden Old Testament church) is also identified as the *false prophet* (Revelation 16:13; 19:20) whose role is to operate as the agent and advocate of the *sea-beast* (the world).

> *'And he* [the land-beast] *exercises all the authority of the first beast* [the sea-beast] *in his presence.'*
>
> (Revelation 13:12 NASB)

The land-beast stood *'in his presence'* (i.e. in the presence of the sea-beast). This is in contrast to the true prophet who *'stands before the LORD'* (Jeremiah 23:18, 22; Deuteronomy 10:8), under whose authority he serves and whom he represents. The Old Testament church literally became the prophet and press-agent for the world-spirit!

Who really is the beast?

A warning to the end-time church
Surely, 'the beast' is the antichrist! That is exactly what Satan would want us to believe. As a liar and deceiver he diverts attention from the true nature of the anti-Christ spirit. In fact, the term 'Antichrist' does not appear at all in the book of Revelation. However, John does use it in his epistles:

> *'Dear children, this is the last hour; and as you have heard that the antichrist is coming, even now many antichrists have come. This is how we know it is the last hour. They went out* **from us** *... the spirit of the antichrist, which ... even now is already in the world.'*   (1 John 2:18–19; 4:3 NIV)

We are so busy looking across the world-scene for some future or contemporary political super-leader as the antichrist that we are completely unaware that the anti-Christ spirit is operating right under our noses in the church! John said that many anti-Christs have gone *'out from us'*. Forget about the world for the moment – the church has been the breeding-ground for the anti-Christ!

Israel's idolatry for our warning
As Israel, the old covenant church, had been so led astray by the time of Christ and the apostles that she could be described as *'the beast'* and *'the false prophet'* so it is too with the new covenant church.

Paul understood this, explaining that the history of Israel's idolatry was recorded for *our* warning – for the end-time church upon whom the climax of the ages had come (1 Corinthians 10:11). A warning implies a danger – the potential for a fall. This occurred within the first several centuries with the church succumbing to the *spirit of the world* in the form of state patronage, hierarchical leadership structures, doctrinal schisms, wealth, and the pursuit of position, prestige and power. This was the prophesied great *'falling away'* (2 Thessalonians 2:3; Matthew 24:10). Despite reforming movements throughout her history, climaxing in the breakthrough of the Reformation and counter-Reformation of the 16th and 17th centuries, the same spirit of idolatry has continued. John calls it the love of the world:

> *'If anyone loves the world, the love of the Father is not in him.'*
> (1 John 2:15 NIV)

In the same breath John describes how the love of the world manifests – as *'the lust of the flesh* [craving for sensual gratification], *and the lust of the eyes* [greedy longings of the mind], *and the pride of* life [assurance in one's own resources or in the stability of earthly things]' (1 John 2:16 AMP).

The church-system – a mirror image of the world-system

To the degree that the *lust of the flesh*, the *lust of the eyes* and the *pride of life* operate in the church, the church serves the god of this age. And as such the church is animated by a predatory nature and can accurately be described as 'the beast'. The beast-nature of the church-system is merely the mirror-image of the world-system. And as the *'false prophet'*, it serves as the world's press-agent by setting up the world's image, in the church, for all to worship:

> *'He* [the land-beast/back-slidden church] *ordered them to set up an image in honour of the beast* [the sea-beast/the world] ... *He was given power to give breath to the image of the first beast, so that it could speak and cause all who refused to worship the image to be killed.'*   (Revelation 13:14–15)

Corporate McChurch

A spiritually compromised church becomes an idolatrous image of the world. The church's image has the appearance of substance

– it has the breath of life so that it can speak – it is very articulate, and persuasive.

> *'He was given power to give breath to the image . . . so that it could speak . . . '*   (Revelation 13:15)

The church's glorification of the world can be seen in corporate models of governance and image making, in the professional-ising of the ministry which reduces it to successful programme management, in the commercialising of worship as an industry and in the cult of celebrity amongst ministers and musicians. It has produced the hybrid senior pastor – half CEO and half entertainer, who on Sunday 'brings the house down' and on Monday presides over corporate 'McChurch'.

Conflict of flesh and spirit
Her idolatrous worship of the world-spirit and its values is so ravenous and beast-like that it attempts to devour and destroy all those who refuse to bow:

> *'He was given power to . . . cause all who refuse to worship the image to be killed.'*   (Revelation 13:15)

The flesh always conflicts with the Spirit:

> *'But as at that time he who was born according to the flesh persecuted him who was born according to the Spirit, so it is now also.'*   (Galatians 4:29 NASB)

Ishmael, the son of the flesh, persecuted Isaac, the son of promise by *mocking* him (Genesis 21:9). The scribes and Pharisees *mocked* Jesus as he hung on the cross (Matthew 27:41). The disciples were *mocked* on the day of Pentecost when they were filled with the Spirit (Acts 2:13). And Peter prophesied that in the last days *mockers* would come following their own lusts (2 Peter 3:3). A mocking spirit is often disguised by humour. The Hebrew word for 'mocker' comes from a root 'to play, to sport, to laugh'.[6] Even 'friendly' jesting can be a deceitful and cowardly form of mocking:

> *'The words of his mouth were smoother than butter, but war was in his heart: his words were softer than oil, yet were they drawn swords.'*   (Psalm 55:21 KJV)

As the age comes to a climax men and women of the Spirit will find themselves increasingly coming under attacks from false brothers (2 Corinthians 11:26; Galatians 2:4), from those who have bowed to the world's image and who will increasingly manifest the beast-nature of religion. The last great end-time move of God will bring a final divide between flesh and Spirit – between false brothers and true when the Son of Man will weed out of the kingdom everything that offends (Matthew 13:41).

Judgment and division

Why is there so much disunity?

Despite our human attempts to build unity, we now have 22,000 denominations! Maybe the 144,000 in the book of Revelation really refers to the final number of denominations – only 122,000 to go! If it wasn't so tragic it would almost be humorous. However, we have to ask ourselves why, in the face of John 17 and Ephesians 4, which so clearly present a church living in unity, is there so much disunity?

The answer is found in Babylon's beginnings (Genesis 11). When the Lord *'came down'* to check out what man was building, He said,

> *'If as one people speaking the same language they have begun to do this, then nothing they plan to do will be impossible for them.'*
> (Genesis 11:6)

Seemingly the potential for human strength unified in one spiritual purpose is unlimited. But God stepped in and declared, *'Come, let us go down ...'* (Genesis 11:7), as a parody of man's own proud declaration, *'Come, let us build'* (Genesis 11:4). This satirical echo of man's own proud power-talk gives God the last word – and the last laugh. Putting it colloquially God is saying, *'In your face!'* He alone is God and He will fulfil His plan for humanity in His way. From this point man was scattered over the whole earth and man's language confused.

Division – judgment on the spirit of pride

Division, therefore, is the judgment of God on the spirit of pride. Because their hearts were already divided from God, He divided them from each other. Even the disciples' first response at the transfiguration was to *institutionalise* the experience by building three shelters for Moses, Elijah, and Jesus (Matthew 17:4). The human propensity to build and to control is at the heart of division. Unrepented of, it ultimately calls down God's judgment. He comes down in times of visitation to resist human attempts to recreate Eden. He always resists the proud and gives grace to the humble (James 4:6).

God brings division. Jesus said,

> *'Do you think I came to bring peace on earth? No, I tell you, but division.'* (Luke 12:51 NIV)

When God comes down He divides between flesh and Spirit. He judges the spirit of pride and man's independence. Paul acknowledged that God uses division in His end-time purpose to expose the false and approve the true:

> *'For there must also be factions among you, in order that those who are approved may have become evident among you.'* (1 Corinthians 11:19 NASB)

Seasons of refreshing and revival inevitably shake and sift human structures and hearts to move the church closer to the image of Christ. He disciplines and humbles us that we may share His holiness (Hebrews 12:10).

God is, consequently, not looking for our so-called 'apostolic strategies' of unity or city-reaching, so much as for a restoration of a true apostolic spirit. This is one of humility and brokenness where we have finally learned to be *'completely humble and gentle ... bearing with one another in love'* (Ephesians 4:2 NIV).

He is not interested in our apostolic blueprints, grounded in human pride, planning or promotion. He is looking for those who are *'humble and contrite of spirit and who tremble at his word'* (Isaiah 66:2).

He is searching for a 'safe-place' where He can come and dwell – where His presence will not be humanly manipulated or merchandised.

Therefore any attempt at unity, without the breaking of our spirit of pride, will only result in more division.

The genesis of the church

In the very next chapter of Genesis (ch. 12) God did exactly that – He brought further division. He called Abraham out of Ur of the Chaldees, from Babylon, to separate himself for the regaining of Eden by the *obedience of faith*. In contrast to Babel and its proud human ways God took the initiative in calling forth a pilgrim people who, like their father, were looking for a city whose builder and maker is God (Hebrews 11:10). As the seed of Abraham (Galatians 3:7) this is the genesis of the church – in God's judgment on human pride. And as the *ecclesia – the called out ones*, we are called out of Babylon – out of the spiritually adulterous world-city – out of liaisons with the gods of this age and alliances with the flesh (Revelation 18:4; Isaiah 48:20; 52:11; 2 Corinthians 6:17). We are called to be holy even as He is holy.

As we saw in the previous chapter, the hidden core of idolatry is the worship of *self*. It is our attempt to reach spiritual heights through *self*-will and *self*-reliance. Babel was merely the corporate manifestation of it. We may *talk* unity, but with pride in our hearts we only succeed in attracting God's judgment and more division. He frustrates our plans and strategies for unity sending us division and confusion of tongues until we learn true brokenness where our boast is in nothing but the cross of Christ. Only then will the church discover God's kind of unity – becoming one, just as the Father and the Son are one (John 17:21).

We will now discover, in the next chapter, how the church is seduced and controlled by 'the spirit of Jezebel'.

Chapter 8

The Spirit of Jezebel –
Idolatry, Deception and Control

'I have this against you: You tolerate that woman Jezebel, who calls herself a prophetess. By her teaching she misleads my servants . . .'
(Revelation 2:20 NIV)

It was 6 am on a Thursday morning. I was praying with a small group of young men from our church when one of them started to take authority over what was felt to be a 'spirit of control' operating in the life of the fellowship. He only managed to pray a few words before he was physically hit by an invisible force. Little did we realise the intensity of the warfare we were stepping into.

Paul tells us that,

> *'we do not wrestle against flesh and blood, but against principalities, against powers, against the rulers of the darkness of this age, against spiritual hosts of wickedness in the heavenly places.'*
> (Ephesians 6:12 NKJV)

Behind flesh and blood people and circumstances lie demonic principalities and powers. We were embarking on a life-and-death struggle, experiencing first-hand the subtle deception of 'control'. If we are unaware of Satan's devices it is very easy to be outwitted by his sleight-of-hand (2 Corinthians 2:11; Ephesians 6:11; 4:27).

In this chapter we'll explore, both from the Bible and personal experience, some of the 'devices' employed by the spirit of control. As we've just seen from the above quote, the New Testament teaches that the believer is engaged in warfare against the cosmic rulers of spiritual darkness (Ephesians 1:21; 2:2; 3:10; 6)[1] In my view the most subtle, deceptive and pervasive spiritual force historically confronting the church is the spirit of control. It is a 'principality' with global designs over the entire church.

This spirit is personified in the Old Testament by Jezebel, a Phoenician princess married to Ahab, king of Israel. Just as Jezebel, as a foreign princess, exercised control over the Old Testament church through a marriage of political convenience, this spiritual prince-power has designs of cosmic proportions to control the New Testament church through its leaders.

First we will discover who Jezebel was, her character and how she operates; and second we will look at Ahab. Without Ahab Jezebel cannot function. He represents the kind of leader through whom the spirit of Jezebel operates.

The spirit of Jezebel

John, the writer of Revelation, prophetically confronted the spirit of Jezebel in his message to the church of Thyatira (Revelation 2:18–29). As with each of the messages to the seven churches Christ reveals Himself appropriate to their need. To this church He is manifested as *'the Son of God, whose eyes are like blazing fire and whose feet are like burnished bronze'* (Revelation 2:18 NIV). This is the only description of Christ in the Revelation as *'Son of God'* which underscores for them the awesome deity and power of His person in contrast to the idolatrous and puny pretensions of Jezebel. Christ is revealed as the true God over and above Jezebel's false gods.

Discerning the spirit of Jezebel

His eyes are as *'blazing fire'*, searching *'hearts and minds'* (Revelation 2:23). Satan specialises in painting caricatures to divert us from the subtlety of his schemes. The caricature of a dominating woman (and sometimes man) who seeks to control the pastor is one of them. It's easy to recognise. But Satan's devices are not always so obvious. The spirit of Jezebel is insidious – it disguises itself, deceiving and manoeuvring to infiltrate the inner life of the leader himself. One of our problems is that we are on the lookout for an external enemy, when all the while the enemy is within! Christ reveals Himself as having *'eyes of fire'* (Revelation 2:18), searching the hidden motives and thoughts of the heart, which is the source of deception (Jeremiah 17:9). The real 'depths of Satan' (Revelation 2:24) are only exposed when we are shown our own hearts. The Holy Spirit

> *'judges the thoughts and attitudes of the heart. Nothing in all creation is hidden from God's sight. Everything is uncovered and laid bare before the eyes of him to whom we must give account.'*
> (Hebrews 4:12–13 NIV)

Apart from a spirit of revelation, the inner workings of Jezebel, especially in ourselves or in those around us, cannot be discerned. They are not recognisable to the natural eye. Isaiah said of Jesus:

> *'The Spirit of the LORD will rest on him –*
> *the Spirit of wisdom and of understanding . . .*
> *the Spirit of knowledge and of the fear of the LORD . . .*
> ***He will not judge by what he sees with his eyes,***
> ***or decide by what he hears with his ears.'***
> (Isaiah 11:2–3 NIV)

We are blind to Jezebel if we judge by what we see and hear – by our natural senses. When this spirit is in operation, what you see is not what you get.

The church today is desperately in need of discernment to recognise the subtle workings of this 'prince-power'.

Let's explore some of its characteristics.

A spirit that targets leaders

The spirit seeks to operate through leaders and authority structures: ' . . . *she misleads my servants . . .* ' (Revelation 2:20 NIV). She is a leader of leaders. The spirit does not set itself up in open opposition to them; but finds access through seduction, attaching itself to the leader, and especially to those who oversee other leaders. It usually happens through the inner life of the leader or through people that surround them. Remembering that the book of Revelation is prophetic and symbolic, the Jezebel of Revelation is not necessarily a literal person, but rather a *spirit*. Therefore if the spirit can find ground in the life of the leader it will operate through them. In a moment we will look at that ground in the life of Ahab. But first we'll consider the origins and activities of Jezebel.

Her family and religious connections are significant. As we've already noticed she was the daughter of the king of Phoenicia who also served as high-priest of Ashtoreth. Ashtoreth is described by Jeremiah as the Queen of Heaven (Jeremiah 7:18), originating as Ishtar of Babylon where she was the goddess of love and war and the mother and creator of mankind. In Canaanite worship (Phoenicia – i.e. Tyre and Sidon – being a Canaanite nation) she became the moon goddess and consort of Baal.

Married to Ahab, king of Israel, to cement an alliance between Phoenicia and Israel, Jezebel introduced the worship of Ashtoreth and Baal into the life of the Old Testament church (1 Kings 16:31). When we focus on Ahab we'll explore the significance of political alliances in more detail.

At this point it's only necessary to underline that the spirit of Jezebel establishes liaisons with leadership. It operates under the aegis of legitimate authority structures – under the king. Therefore pastors and ministry leaders become targets and, often unwittingly, the agencies of its operation.

A spirit of sensuality and seduction

Jezebel is a spirit of sensuality and seduction. She presents herself as the voice of God:

> *'. . . who calls herself a prophetess* [and] *misleads my servants into sexual immorality and the eating of food sacrificed to idols.'*
> (Revelation 2:20 NIV)

She claims to be the voice of God to leaders (*'my servants'*), taking them into *spiritual* fornication and idolatry. The point here is not so much *literal* sexual promiscuity and idolatry but the *spiritual* promiscuity of playing around with other gods. While pagan idolatries are usually immoral in their practice, the act of idolatry is viewed by the Old Testament prophets as being *spiritually* adulterous. Therefore the teaching of Jezebel does not necessarily advocate or practice immorality. Satan is not usually that obvious. Although as a spirit of sensuality, if not dealt with, it can lead to immorality and in my view is the root cause for the current epidemic of immorality in the leadership of the Western church.

Even so, it primarily seduces leaders from intimacy with the Lord into a sensuous liaison with the god of this world – with the idols of success and power. And as with idolatrous Israel the appearance of spirituality is maintained, furthering the deception. It infiltrates our worship causing it to gradually become more appealing to the five senses. As a seductress (2 Kings 9:30) the Jezebel spirit, using her beauty, seduces through the senses. Rooted in our idolatry, it leavens much of contemporary worship with a spirit of sensuality. Not only looking beautiful but, as a prophetess, sounding like God. Jezebel manifests through worship as a *religious spirit*.

The spirit of religion is smooth and persuasive:

> *'For the lips of an adulteress drip honey,*
> *   and her speech is smoother than oil.'*   (Proverbs 5:3 NIV)

> *'With persuasive words she led him astray;*
> *   she seduced him with her smooth talk.'*   (Proverbs 7:21 NIV)

It is beautiful and promises immediate gratification – results that feed the senses – satisfying the lust of the flesh, the lust of the eyes, and the pride of life. This manifests in pragmatism.[2] Leaders refuse to deal with sin-issues and root problems in their personal lives or in the flock. They prefer cosmetic 'makeovers' to preserve image and maintain control. Sin realities are swept under the carpet – the religious machinery must be kept moving – and the outside of the cup is washed clean but the inside remains *'full of greed and self-indulgence'* (Matthew 23:25).

A spirit that kills the prophetic
Jezebel kills the prophets (1 Kings 18:4).

A personal story
During the 1970s and 80s I related to an international movement that grew out of the Charismatic Renewal. As a young leader with a prophetic call I was invited to relocate from my city to be trained by one of the movement's apostles. A year after relocating I was appointed by him to serve as the national co-ordinator of our publishing and conference ministry. I was ecstatic, believing that my expanding responsibilities were the fulfilment of God's call. However, on assuming the role I found my hands were tied. I was unable to exercise any initiative or leadership in fulfilling the assignment.

After eighteen months of marking time I found myself out in the cold without a job, without a relationship, and without an explanation. What began as a 'high', with a warm invitation and promises of dreams fulfilled, ended with disappointment in a cold and controlling system. I was confused and disoriented. How had I missed God and failed Him? With the help of those over me in the authority structure I began to question myself, looking for the fatal flaw that caused it. We sought to be faithful to where the Lord had placed us and remained in relationship with the movement for another eight years. What became increasingly apparent, however, over that time was the marginalising of prophetic people and the almost exclusive promotion of administrators and pastoral carers. I began to see what I increasingly felt were the dynamics of a sect. People with a heart for God and for the kingdom were subtly manipulated to do the bidding of the leader through the fear of missing God or of being rebellious. Fear became a powerful manipulative force – fear of rejection, fear of leadership or fear of the outside secular-humanist world. Leadership was increasingly elitist and removed from the people. While not advocated in the teaching of the movement, in pastoral practice people were denied the freedom to hear from God and make their own decisions. Also, a messianic and triumphalist belief in the movement slowly isolated it from the rest of the body of Christ. By this time I was selling life insurance to support a young family and had either been promoted or demoted in my leadership roles no less than five times, including a number of false promises relating to ministry support. The cold comfort was that it wasn't just me. Several others had the same tale to tell – of promotion and demotion, of the undermining of their character and call, of control and manipulation. Most of them were somewhat prophetic.

After a total of ten years under this leader, and twenty years with the movement, God spoke to me from Ezekiel,

> '*pack your belongings ... set out and go from where you are to another place ... While they watch, dig through the wall and take your belongings out through it ...*'   (Ezekiel 12:3, 5)

I made an appointment with one of the senior leaders to share what we felt the Lord was calling us to do. Many of us had walked together from our late teens when we first came to the Lord – they were our friends – we were family. I had no idea where we would go or what we would do. All we knew was that God had spoken and that He was leading us out. Within a matter of weeks He spoke again from Isaiah,

> *'Depart, depart, go out from there,*
> *Touch nothing unclean;*
> *Go out of the midst of her, purify yourselves,*
> *You who carry the vessels of the* LORD.
> ***But you will not go out in haste,***
> ***Nor will you go as fugitives;***
> ***For the*** LORD ***will go before you,***
> *And the God of Israel will be your rear guard.'*
>
> (Isaiah 52:11–12 NASB)

We were not to *'go out in haste'*, but to sit tight and wait for God.

Two months later it all broke. The senior leader returned from a ministry trip to the USA and I sensed something was up. By the end of that week I felt the Lord had shown me what it was and so I called one of the leadership team. I said, 'He's resigned hasn't he? And, it's over a moral issue isn't it?' The rest is history. What had come to light was a twenty-year lifestyle of adultery and immorality. That leader, almost one year to the day from being stood down, was taken out of this life with seven tumours on the brain. We received an unsolicited telephone call that October, only two months after the Lord had told us not to go *'in haste'*. It was an invitation to relocate to another city. We packed our bags and went through the *'hole in the wall'*, but not *'in haste or in flight'*, just as the Lord had said! He had gone before us and we were free.

Fear of exposure

I share this experience to show firstly how the spirit of control fears exposure from the prophetic and secondly how it will attempt to neutralise it. But thirdly – God will ultimately deliver. A spirit of control always has something to hide. If it is not sexual compromise it will be, at best, hidden agendas to secure personal advantage – our prestige, position or possessions. And these are usually advanced through a veneer of 'spiritual speak', i.e. 'for the sake of the church' or 'for the kingdom'. Smooth words clothe hidden motives in high-sounding phrases.

Jesus warned us to *'Watch out for false prophets'* (Matthew 7:15 NIV). He then described how they operate:

> *'They come to you in sheep's clothing, but inwardly they are ferocious wolves.'* (Matthew 7:15 NIV)

I always imagined the false prophets were Mormons and Moonies but that is too obvious. What Jesus was warning about was the *spirit of religion* – the thing that looks sheep, smells sheep, and feels like sheep. Externally it looks and sounds spiritual – it is totally orthodox and plausible. The deceptive cover of the sheep's clothing is, in fact, the spirit of religion.

But the wolf is the *spirit of control*. It operates under the cover of religion. It is a predatory animal driven by hunger and fear and it will kill to survive. It lives in fear of being exposed – in fear of the sheepskin being peeled back. The spirit of control operating through a spirit of religion becomes a false prophetic anointing and its greatest fear is the true *spirit of prophecy*. Consequently, it will attempt to shut down the prophetic, usually by killing the prophet. The spirit of control, operating through a spirit of religion, becomes a *spirit of murder*. Jezebel, in fact, pursued a systematic slaughter of the prophets (1 Kings 18:4, 13), and also vowed to kill Elijah after his Mount Carmel victory (1 Kings 19:2).

Symptoms of fear and intimidation

Jezebel works through *fear* and *intimidation*. The most common fear is the fear of man. Elijah, the great prophet of fire, had just come from his mighty victory over the prophets of Baal on Mount Carmel. Jezebel was so enraged that she attacked him with vehement death-threats:

> '*May the gods deal with me, be it ever so severely, if by this time tomorrow I do not make your life like that of one of them.*'
> (1 Kings 19:2 NIV)

Scripture records that Elijah, the mighty prophet, '*... was afraid and ran for his life*' (1 Kings 19:3). And unfortunately, when the door is opened to the spirit of fear, depression and despair quickly follow:

> '*... he went a day's journey into the wilderness ... and sat down ... and prayed that he might die.*'
> (1 Kings 19:4)

What happened? One moment a spiritual superman, slaying the prophets of Baal and calling down fire from heaven – the next, driven by an irrational fear and running for his life! How can this, and his subsequent depression, be explained except that he had confronted a significant supernatural force – a world ruler of this present darkness of sufficient strength to deceive not only a whole nation, but intimidate one of the greatest prophets of Israel's history! Confronted by its full force Elijah felt over-whelmed and ran in fear of his life. While not literally killed, he was silenced. The prophetic mantle on Elijah was successfully neutralised and soon passed to Elisha.

The spirit of Ahab

Giving ground to the devil

The spirit of Jezebel can only operate where it has been given authority. Paul exhorts the Ephesians not to *'give the devil a foothold'* (Ephesians 4:27 NIV). Drawing on his analogy of *wrestling* against principalities and powers (Ephesians 6:12) a secure foothold is crucial to victory. Without it the wrestler loses balance and is brought down. And so the devil is ever watchful to gain a foothold, looking for a space in our lives that he can claim – a shadow of sin where he can dwell – a hold on our lives through which he can throw us off balance and gain victory.

Ahab gave that foothold to the enemy. The Jezebel spirit cannot work without legal permission. She looks for an authority figure through whom she gains access to the church.

Let us have a look at that figure.

A successful builder

Ahab was a builder. He undertook large building programmes in Samaria, constructing a temple for Baal and a palace for himself inlaid with ivory (1 Kings 16:32; 22:39). Jericho was also rebuilt under his reign in addition to works in many other cities (1 Kings 16:34; 22:39).

A military leader who used the prophetic

Ahab was not only ambitious in his building programmes but a great military leader. He fortified the cities of Israel (1 Kings 22:39) but was quickly besieged by the king of Syria. Heeding the direction of a prophet, he inflicted a crushing defeat (1 Kings 20:1–21). Syria attacked again the following year, but fore-warned by a prophet Ahab inflicted yet another resounding defeat in spite of the enemy's overwhelming superiority (1 Kings 20:22–30). He eventually died a hero's death in battle (2 Chronicles 18:28–34).

A skilful politician

In spite of his military prowess, Ahab was conciliatory in his foreign relations as shown by his treaty with the freshly defeated king of Syria (1 Kings 20:31–34). Similarly, his marriage to Jezebel sealed a pact with the king of Phoenicia. He also restored unity between Israel and Judah for the first time since the division of the kingdom. This alliance was also sealed with a marriage – between Ahab's daughter and the crown prince of Judah (2 Chronicles 18:1; 21:6). No doubt Ahab believed these alliances would not only enhance national security but also increase prosperity through trade.

From our brief sketch we see a man who was capable and industrious in his administration of the kingdom. He strengthened his position through large building programmes, led his army in victory and negotiated alliances with potential enemies. He demonstrated management ability, a high degree of political pragmatism and even gave room for the prophetic in his battle plans.

The flip-side – a fatal spiritual blind spot

However, what looked good on a resume had a flip-side – Ahab had a fatal spiritual blind spot. His alliances with foreign nations and particularly his marriage to Jezebel were in direct disobedience to the command of God (Exodus 34:15–16). Although astute political moves they were also a disastrous spiritual dislocation:

> '*Ahab . . . did more evil in the eyes of the* Lord *than any of those before him. He not only considered it trivial to commit the sins of Jeroboam son of Nebat, but he also married Jezebel daughter of Ethbaal king of the Sidonians, and began to serve Baal and worship him . . . Ahab . . . did more to provoke the* Lord, *the God of Israel, to anger than did all the kings of Israel before him.*'
>
> (1 Kings 16:30–33 NIV)

How to Identify an Ahab-leader

What characterises the kind of leader open to the spirit of Jezebel?

A human spirit

An Ahab-leader pursues *programme* over *presence*. Ambitious and successful building programmes require native human ability and organisation. They depend on human skill to secure prosperity and prestige through the operation of successful programmes and political alliances. We do not find any record of Ahab seeking the Lord or leading the nation in revival or reformation. He was not a spiritual man. Churches and ministries become dependent on the hand of man – on human strength and energy rather than the hand of God. Even Pentecostal or renewal churches can resort to human methodologies for growth. Corporate models of management and marketing replace a dependence on the presence of God and ministries or churches that may have begun in the Spirit continue in the flesh.

We might respond, 'But, he was open to the prophetic!' Even so, it was to advance his military strategy. An Ahab-leader will *accommodate* the prophetic and thereby *domesticate* it, as long as it enhances their leadership. They will eagerly embrace the gift of prophecy for edification, exhortation and comfort (1 Corinthians 14:3) but reject the ministry of a true prophet who comes to teach, rebuke and correct (2 Timothy 3:16). Rather than receive Elijah's prophetic correction for the trouble he brought on Israel Ahab instead viewed the prophet as the 'troubler of Israel' (1 Kings 18:17).

A political spirit

Ahab-leaders depend on astute political alliances to secure their position. But they pursue them in disobedience to the Word of God. For the Ahab-leader it is more important to have man on his side than for him to be on God's side. The fear of man and the possibility of being overwhelmed by competitors will drive him into prohibited alliances. It becomes imperative to buy man's favour. But in reality they sell their own soul.

The political spirit is always a *spirit of betrayal*. Jesus was betrayed through the combination of a political alliance and a financial advantage. It behoves us to remember that the student is not above the master. Need we be surprised when these things come against the work of God in our day?

In my view, a political spirit is the most significant cause of demonic access to the church. The Scripture says that Satan *entered* Judas (Luke 22:3) when he negotiated his deal with the religious power brokers of the day. Likewise, Ahab's astute political alliance with Pheonicia, a wealthy maritime power, cemented by his marriage to Jezebel, provided an open door to Satan. Through this alliance there was an inrush of idolatry and a demonic principality was established over the kingdom. The *spirit of anti-Christ* enters the church through the door of political compromise.

A political spirit is not always easy to recognise. It is not openly antagonistic until the trap is sprung. But until then, as a deceiving spirit, it seduces – it woos through smooth words and feigned friendship. It usually operates through people close to an anointed leader, most probably from within their leadership team:

> *'If an enemy were insulting me,*
> *   I could endure it;*
> *If a foe were raising himself against me,*
> *   I could hide from him.*
> *But it is you, a man like myself,*
> *   my companion, my close friend . . .*
> *My companion attacks his friends;*
> *   he violates his covenant.*
> *His speech is smooth as butter,*
> *   yet war is in his heart;*
> *his words are more soothing than oil,*
> *   yet they are drawn swords.'*
>
> (Psalm 55:12–13, 20–21 NIV)

These words were penned out of David's heartbreak with Ahithophel, his most trusted adviser and confidante. Absalom, David's own son, had drawn him into a web of intrigue and betrayal. For four years they had conspired under the cover of friendship, oiled by smooth talk, before the trap was sprung (2 Samuel 15:7–12). The political spirit will bide its time – it has great patience as it plots and plans. During that time Absalom sat in the gate, a place of authority, seducing the hearts of the people. He would listen to their problems and complaints, subtly using them to undermine David. 'I understand – now, if I were king, it wouldn't be that way.' All Absalom needed was a listening ear and some feigned pastoral concern. And then through innuendo (no outright accusations) to sow seeds of doubt about David's integrity or capacity, very gently and patiently winning the hearts of the people to himself.

A spirit of compromise

Ahab-leaders are governed by expedience. They depend on

human ability to secure their interests. Consequently there is no fear of the Lord nor discernment. Personal survival and popularity become the guiding force in decision making.

The spirit of compromise promotes *peacekeepers* and discourages *peacemakers*. Before the Second World War Neville Chamberlain, Prime Minister of Great Britain, using a *policy of appeasement*, attempted to keep the peace by negotiating with the emerging Nazi menace. After signing the so-called Munich peace-pact with Hitler, he returned to Britain, foolishly heralding it as, 'Peace in our times'. Tragically it cost Czechoslovakia its freedom and accelerated the slide into full-scale war. Meanwhile, Churchill, the only man Hitler feared, had been strenuously warning of the dangers for over a decade. He boldly advocated complete resistance to Hitler. And it was to him that Great Britain and her allies eventually looked to break the Nazi tyranny and establish a lasting peace. Peace*keepers* compromise with evil for the sake of short-term political advantage. Peace*makers* confront evil, risking their popularity and reputation for truth and freedom.

Church leaders, under the influence of the spirit of compromise, sell out to *pastoral popularity* at the expense of *prophetic purity*. Sometimes the most pastoral thing is to be prophetic – to speak the truth in love so that the individual is brought back to the holiness of the Father's love – to a place of forgiveness and cleansing. By attempting to keep church members *happy* rather than making them *holy*, as peace*keepers*, Ahab-leaders neglect *character formation* as the primary goal of pastoral ministry. The true apostolic purpose of ministry, as declared by Paul, is then compromised:

> '*We proclaim him, admonishing and teaching everyone with all wisdom, so that we may present everyone perfect* [mature] *in Christ.'*   (Colossians 2:28 NIV)

How much of pastoral ministry is intentionally devoted to admonition and teaching in order to produce spiritually mature people? Overall pastors are not seen as spiritual directors or teachers whose role is to admonish and mould character, but as employees of the church to work as programme-managers and people-carers. The spirit of compromise reduces the ministry to a politically correct, people-pleasing peacekeeping corps.

A religious spirit

A deceitful religious spirit rode triumphantly into the kingdom on the back of Ahab's alliances. Jezebel became the patron of Baal's prophets (1 Kings 18:19–20) and Ahab the builder of his temple. Ahab also raised an Asherah pole (1 Kings 16:32–33), a phallic symbol, to celebrate the procreative powers of the earth. All this while maintaining the appearance of spirituality in the ritual worship of Yahweh.

An Ahab-leader pursues *appearance* over *purity*. Ahab, having a mind for image, named his children in the Lord's honour – Ahaziah ('Jehovah holds'), Jerhoram ('Jehovah is high') and Athaliah ('Jehovah is strong'). However, despite the religious facade he *'did more evil in the eyes of the LORD than any of those before him'* (1 Kings 16:30).

Lenin, the infidel revolutionary, was right when he said, 'Religion is the opiate of the people'. The spirit of religion *medicates the pain*, but it never *mentions the problem*. Living in denial, it slaps a gloss of religious sentiment over the rotting core of self, satisfied with its veneer of respectability.

When man's spirit takes control the Holy Spirit withdraws and *conservatism* replaces *conversion*. The supernatural knowledge of God is lost and the spirit of religion moves in. A culture of conformity takes over. *Social integration* replaces *spiritual intimacy* and Christianity becomes a folk-culture, offering soothing words of *'peace, peace'* (Jeremiah 6:14) to those who are already *'at ease in Zion'* (Amos 6:1). It endorses and promotes the predominate culture of the West – of *'personal peace and affluence'*, building contemporary cathedrals to the gods of productivity and power.

The spirit of religion maintains a *religious orthodoxy*, but not a *spiritual orthopraxy*. It defends correct belief, but deserts He who is the truth. Jesus said to the Jews,

> *'You search the Scriptures, because you think that in them you have eternal life; and it is these that bear witness of Me; and you are unwilling to come to Me, that you may have life.'*
>
> (John 5:39–40 NASB)

While championing the Scriptures, they refused to come to Him. In fact they sought to kill him (John 5:18). On the one hand the religious spirit will idolise the Scriptures, holding that they are the source of eternal life, but on the other it will seek to kill He who is the living Word! It will uphold the supremacy of Scripture but kill the visitation of God.

A territorial spirit

A *territorial spirit* manifests as idolatry and covetousness. This is seen in two ways – by the territorial nature of Baal worship and through Ahab's own greed and covetousness.

Firstly, a *territorial spirit* operates through an idol. Each town in ancient Israel was named after their adopted Baal (for example Baal Peor or Baal Hermon), thus Baal became the territorial spirit over that area. The frightening fact is that these towns were not in a pagan nation but in Israel – the old covenant church! In addition, the Baals were set up by the leadership – by Ahab and Jezebel! The Jezebel spirit takes territory through church leaders who have given themselves to the worship of Baal – the glorification of human power and productivity. They depend on church growth formulas and management techniques – on man's strength and ingenuity, unwittingly embracing an idolatry that opens them and their churches to alien spiritual forces. These strongholds then preside geographically and denominationally over the church. This manifests in the historic distrust between pastors. I recently had a mega-church pastor admit to me that the reason he refused to get involved with city-wide events was because research showed that large churches lose members through them!

Why are pastors so often afraid of the church over the road stealing their sheep? My experience of working with pastors cross-denominationally suggests that the territorial ownership of congregations goes far deeper than just being theological or even economic, as frightening as that is. Its underlying intensity displays the hallmarks of a demonic stronghold – an idol. Parishioners, in reality, are the idol's territorial possession and proof of its power. This is the spirit behind much of our traditional understanding of the 'local church'.

Secondly, a territorial spirit, operating through an Ahab-leader, covets and acquires the inheritance of others. It secures the kingdom through theft. Already established in a place of power, Ahab was ambitious to increase his holdings, further securing his position. He approached Naboth to acquire his vineyard saying, *'Let me have your vineyard ... since it is close to my palace ... '* (1 Kings 21:2).

Using his position for self-interest, Ahab heartlessly disregarded the welfare of others. Churches and leaders, when operating out of a human spirit, are forced to consolidate their position regardless of its effect on others. Because God is not sustaining that position they are plagued by insecurity. This whole dynamic lies behind the Western church's problem of *transfer growth* overtaking *conversion growth*.

Ahab's offer to purchase Naboth's vineyard was legitimately refused in Naboth's desire to honour the laws of inheritance (1 Kings 21:3; Numbers 36:7). Ahab returned home sullen and angry (1 Kings 21:4), which brings us to the next characteristic.

A spirit of anger and depression

While at a personality level, 'laid-back', Ahab at a character level was deeply stubborn. When his plans were frustrated it developed as internalised anger and consequent depression. The great international diplomat, sponsor of extensive capital works programmes and dexterous politician, *'lay on his bed sulking and refused to eat'* (1 Kings 21:4 NIV). Despite reigning as king, he could not rule his own emotions. I once watched a leader slide into a clinically diagnosed depression. Frustrated in his aspirations to secure a coveted position he was immobilised and unable to make leadership decisions until, like Ahab, he was suddenly stirred into action by the spirit of Jezebel:

> *'His wife Jezebel came in and asked him, "Why are you so sullen ... Is this how you act as king over Israel? Get up and eat ... I'll get you the vineyard of Naboth the Jezreelite."'*
>
> (1 Kings 21:5–7 NIV)

Stubbornness, anger and depression gave ground to Jezebel – to a spirit of witchcraft. This spirit will empower a leader, seemingly out of character, to use their position abusively to secure their own interests. By force Jezebel took control of events, resulting in Naboth's murder and the theft of his inheritance.

A spirit of witchcraft

The *spirit of witchcraft*, as represented by Jezebel, controls and manipulates others to satisfy a personal agenda (2 Kings 9:22). It begins as a work of the flesh (Galatians 5:20) but as a practised and habitual life-style it moves into the occult. What began with Ahab as a work of the flesh, in self-will and depression, ends with Jezebel in the demonic abuse of power. In this case, disguised as justice, she resorted to a violent exercise of naked power over Naboth to gain Ahab his enhanced position. The spirit of witch-craft inevitably abuses power for personal gain.

Let's now discover how Ahab and Jezebel partner to that end – to acquire Naboth's vineyard.

Jezebel and Ahab in partnership

Remembering that Ahab represents the leader who gives ground to the spirit of Jezebel let's see how they work together. First Kings 21 shows us.

Subverts the authority structure

Firstly, through the senior leader, *she subverts authority and the chain-of-command*:

> '... she wrote letters in Ahab's name ... to the elders and nobles in Naboth's city ...' (1 Kings 21:8)

A spirit of witchcraft seeks to operate under the aegis, the protection, of the senior authority ('wrote letters in Ahab's name'), subverting that authority to control the established authority structures ('the elders'). Rarely will an Ahab-leader dirty their own hands to implement their Jezebelic plans. Using either a *chain-of-command* or a *sphere-of-influence*, they prefer to set others up and operate from behind the scenes. The well-used cry from perpetrators of wartime atrocities, 'I was only obeying orders!' now makes sense.

Creates an appearance of spirituality

Secondly, she creates an appearance of spirituality – they were to proclaim a fast (1 Kings 21:9). This was the platform for launch-ing the attack on Naboth. Using smoke and mirrors the spirit of witchcraft creates an aura of spirituality while performing its diabolical deeds.

Creates an appearance of justice

Thirdly, she creates an appearance of justice by not only subverting the authority structure (the elders) but also the justice process (witnesses). She appointed two witnesses in accordance with the Mosaic law. But unfortunately for Naboth, they were *false* witnesses. To add insult to injury, the elders, compromised by Jezebel, packaged the false accusations in Scripture. They were directed by Jezebel to prime the false witnesses to, *'testify that he has cursed both God and the king'* (1 Kings 21:10). This was obviously in violation of the Law of Moses:

> *'Do not blaspheme God or curse the ruler of your people.'*
>
> (Exodus 22:28 NIV)

Naboth's refusal to sell his property to Ahab was purposely misconstrued as blasphemy against God. By implication therefore, the king had in effect become God; which is always the case under spiritually abusive leadership. Rather than faithfully representing God, the leader takes the place of God. And to touch the leader, is therefore to touch God. Naboth's righteous motivation to honour God in the law of inheritance was intentionally misconstrued by his accusers and used to justify his elimination. Controlling and abusive authority always recasts obedience to God as rebellion. But maligned motives and false accusations betray, beyond doubt, the satanic source of the attack, who himself is *'the father of lies'* (John 8:44) and *'the accuser of the brethren'* (Revelation 12:10).

The death of Christ was, likewise, achieved through a compromised authority structure. He was brought before the council consisting of Caiaphas and the elders, including false witnesses, who also accused him of blasphemy (Matthew 26:65). Throughout redemptive history, attacks inspired by the spirit of Jezebel, against true spiritual leaders, have always come through compromised leadership structures, therefore giving an appearance of legitimacy. Just as Jesus was falsely accused through the religious leaders of His day, so it is today.

> *'Therefore Jesus also, that He might sanctify the people through His own blood, suffered outside the gate. Hence, let us go out to Him outside the camp, bearing His reproach.'*
>
> (Hebrews 13:12–13 NASB)

Commits murder and robbery

Fourthly, she commits murder and robbery. By subverting the authority structures and their decision-making processes, Jezebel had Naboth murdered in the name of justice. She instructed them to *'take him out and stone him to death'* (1 Kings 21:10 NIV), which under the Law was the penalty applied to idolaters for their practical denial of God (Deuteronomy 13:6–11; 17:5). What a violation of justice! The real idolaters were the ones executing the judgment. To the naked eye Naboth's death was a judicial execution, but in reality was a case of murder for personal gain.

The death of Naboth was a work of Satan, who *'was a murderer from the beginning'* (John 8:44 NIV). The spirit of witchcraft has not changed. However, the threat is not so much from without but from within. Satan masquerades as an angel of light and his servants as servants of righteousness (2 Corinthians 11:14–15). He subverts leadership and uses it to fulfil his own designs – to destroy and kill. What is designed by God to be a channel of blessing and protection for His people is not only subverted, but also perverted. It becomes an avenue for wickedness and spiritual abuse.

Church conflicts invariably display these dynamics. Ambitious leaders, driven by the spirit of Jezebel, secure their positions by progressing from subtle device to naked power. When Naboth's vineyard cannot be obtained by negotiation the Jezebel spirit resorts to more desperate measures – to lies and murder. By using legitimate channels of authority her treacherous schemes are shrouded in an aura of respectability. But back stage, the spirit of control has already compromised the process and prejudiced the outcome.

Jesus prophesied that His followers would be put out of the synagogues and killed by those thinking they were serving God (John 16:2). However this required the formal process of excommunication.[3] Controlled by the spirit of Jezebel, the religious power structures would be used to legitimise the elimination of individuals who were a threat. By securing footholds in the lives of Ahab-leaders the spirit of Jezebel can subvert whole church boards and denominational structures to assassinate, by innuendo or false accusation, the reputations of truly prophetic or reforming leaders. Church history is replete with this process.

In the next chapter we will discover how the Jezebel spirit infiltrated the church through idolatrous authority structures from as early as the second century.

Chapter 9

Idolatry and Human Leadership

> *'They set up kings without my consent;*
> *they choose princes without my approval.*
> *With their silver and gold*
> *they make idols for themselves*
> *to their own destruction.'*
> (Hosea 8:4 NIV)

> *'A horrible and shocking thing*
> *has happened in the land:*
> *The prophets prophesy lies,*
> *the priests rule by their own authority,*
> *and my people love it this way.'*
> (Jeremiah 5:30–31 NIV)

I was sitting in a restaurant with several other pastors. Over lunch our conversation focused on the issue of revival as a particular perspective surfaced. One of them said that, 'We can't sit around praying for revival – we know what we have to do – all we have to do is – *do it*!' Explaining, this leader continued, 'Our job as pastors is to run our own churches and to reach our own neighbourhood.' Apart from a strong flavour of independence, it almost sounded right, and in our present system it is, no doubt, what most pastors are paid to do. But our continuing discussion revealed behind these statements a larger view. Revivals come and go – we have no influence over them – and so all we are meant to do is, to 'do church'.

Consequently, we shut our eyes to spiritual dynamics and hang onto the wheel driving the church like any other human organisation. We might even pray and ask God to bless our plans and programmes. But they are our plans and programmes, not His – they didn't come from His Spirit but from our own skill and training. We may even pay lip service to unity and revival, but in practice have lost any faith-expectation of the kingdom being advanced through sudden, powerful, or extensive outpourings of the Spirit. This is not to say that planning and programmes cannot play a subservient role in facilitating a measure of the grace of God, but they have become the head rather than the tail. We prefer to move ahead in our own strength than to wait for God.

The church's declaration of independence

How did this attitude enter the church? And what are its roots? To find the answer we must go back to the day when the Old Testament church cried out as a declaration of their independence from God.

'Give us a king!'

Samuel had grown old, his sons abused their privileges, the Ark of God's presence was gone, and the nation was ravaged by civil and moral anarchy.[1] Not only had the glory of God departed but they also faced a significant leadership crisis. Threatened by their enemies, the people lusted for a king like the other nations.

> *'So all the elders of Israel gathered together and came to Samuel ... They said to him, "You are old, and your sons do not walk in your ways; now appoint a king to lead us, such as all the other nations have."'*   (1 Samuel 8:4–5 NIV)

Human leadership

The single greatest change in the life of God's people was signalled. Profound and far reaching consequences were triggered from this event, determining the spiritual direction of Israel for generations. Their rejection of Samuel for a king was, in effect, the rejection of God as King. They were opting, instead, for human leadership. However, rather than giving them victory over their enemies, it opened the doors to an inrush of idolatry and demonic power, ending in their own defeat and captivity.

Foreshadowed by the Old Testament church

In this chapter we will uncover the significance for today's church of what was, in reality, Israel's declaration of independence. As a 'type'[2] it holds lessons for our day, which if heeded, will save God's people from further spiritual abuse on the one hand, while on the other accelerating his design for the transformation of the world through an end-time outpouring of the Spirit. It prophetically foreshadowed a miss-development in the church, dating from the second century, which quickly established religious strongholds and led the church into Babylonian captivity.

A prophetic generation

While the Reformation touched this miss-development it remains for a prophetic generation to lay the axe to the root. Like John the Baptist (Matthew 3:10) this prophetic generation will prepare the way of the Lord by uprooting and confronting the idolatries that led the church into captivity. Centuries-old bondages will be shattered as they receive the Father's heart and a zeal for His house. Through them the house of the Lord will be rebuilt as a house of prayer for all nations. They will deal with root causes – with the issues of the heart. Emerging from their wilderness preparations they will prophetically confront the historic idolatries of the church. Through brokenness and humility they will pull down the religious strongholds of pride that have held the church captive to the *elemental spirits of the universe* (Galatians 4:3, 9; Colossians 2:8, 20 RSV). They will call her back to intimacy with the Bridegroom and refuse to be motivated by their own need for significance – they will not pursue their own glory. They will see that the church has rejected Christ as King in favour of human control. And, like the prophet Hosea, they will confront the idolatry of human power structures. They too will declare in the white-hot holiness of God's anger,

> 'Where is your king, that he may save you?
>   Where are your rulers in all your towns,
> of whom you said,
>   "Give me a king and princes"?
> So in my anger I gave you a king,
>   and in my wrath I took him away.'

> (Hosea 13:10–11 NIV)

They will see that it was God who satisfied Israel's lust for a king, but also God who would take him away. But before we look at the consequences of Israel's new found independence we will consider its causes.

Leadership by expedience – a crisis of continuity and authority

They faced both a crisis of *continuity* and *authority*. Their request
for a king was pressured by expedience – by the tyranny of the
urgent – by crisis management. Prior to Samuel's leadership
Israel had been without a king with everyone doing what was
right in their own eyes (Judges 17:6; 18:1; 19:1; 21:25).[3] This
situation not only marked the whole period of the Judges,
preceding Samuel's call as a prophet, but the fear of its
reoccurrence ultimately precipitated his rejection, in preference
for a king. With Samuel's advancing age and imminent death,
Israel teetered again on the brink of anarchy – on *a crisis of
authority*.

This dilemma was compounded by a crisis of second generation leadership – *a crisis of continuity*. Samuel's sons *'did not walk
in his ways. They turned aside after dishonest gain and accepted
bribes and perverted justice'* (1 Samuel 8:3 NIV). Under these
pressures, to ensure continuity, Israel's elders demanded a
king.

The nation needed leadership and only a king would provide
it. In addition, invasion was imminent. With the Ammonites
moving against them they desperately needed military leadership. (1 Samuel 12:12). And who better than a strong and
authoritative king to provide it. But as the unfolding story
shows, decisions made by expedience are not usually wise.

Fulfilled in the New Testament church

This miss-development is directly paralleled in the life of the
new covenant church. By the turn of the second century the
first generation leaders – the apostles, the Samuels of their day
who led the church as men of the Spirit, had all passed from the
scene, hastening a *crisis of apostolic continuity and authority* – a
crisis of leadership. While the apostolic writings were in
circulation so were many others. Heresy and confusion pre-
vailed. The canonical Scriptures of the New Testament had not
yet fully formed and would not for another century or more.
Without the authority of both the Scriptures and the charismatic leadership of the first apostles, the second-century
church found itself facing the twin dilemma of escalating
heresy – a crisis of continuity and division – a crisis of authority.
What where they to do? Trust God to raise up a new generation
of 'Samuels' – anointed apostolic and prophetic leaders, or ask
for a king?

Apostles and prophets replaced by senior pastors!

Tragically, as Israel did, they opted for a king – for human government. As the church transitioned into the sub-apostolic era, the ascension-gift ministries of apostles and prophets were gradually replaced by the office of bishop.[4] It was believed that this office was the only legitimate continuity of apostolic authority and teaching (apostolic succession);[5] thereby addressing the two-horned dilemma of heresy – the crisis of continuity in apostolic teaching – and division – the crisis of apostolic authority.

Initially, the office of bishop was more akin to our present-day senior pastor, presiding over one local church. But as time progressed a bishop assumed superintendence over a number of congregations in a region. These became known as a diocese. As early as 110–117 AD, Ignatius, Bishop of Antioch, strongly advocated that one bishop (senior pastor) be in charge of each congregation.[6] According to Von Campenhausen, the former Chair of Ecclesiastical History at Heidelberg,

> 'In Ignatius a system of monarchical episcopacy (one bishop) has already been implemented, so that all important functions are in principle in the hands of the one bishop. The clergy itself no longer constitutes a single group of ... "leading" men ... but is sharply divided into grades. The "spiritual garland" of the presbyterate [elders] ... surrounds the one bishop [senior pastor] as his "council"; and below them both stand the ... the deacons.'[7]

What began as leadership through men of the Spirit (apostles, prophets and teachers – 1 Corinthians 12:28) serving as co-elders with the presbytery, had become by the second century a human structure governed by the office of bishop as the senior minister. He alone presided over the elders and the congregation. Referring to this hierarchy of clergy, Ignatius believed that, 'Without these there is nothing which can be called a church.'[8] Renwick explains,

> 'By the time of Ignatius ... one of the presbyters [elders] had been chosen to preside over the others. He had become a permanent pastor and president of the other presbyters or elders ... this president is the man whom Ignatius calls bishop because he is episcopos or "overseer".'[9]

This hierarchy of bishop or senior pastor, descending in order to the elders, deacons and congregation, was universal by the third century and went on to dominate the medieval Western church, determining leadership styles and structures to the present day.

Back to the future

Von Campenhausen points out that,

> ' . . . even the Reformation, which intended change and to a great extent achieved it, in this particular field of ecclesiastical office remained relatively conservative . . . Nevertheless it is here . . . that a real crisis in the early concept of office begins, and makes it increasingly impossible either to go back to earlier patterns or to persevere in traditional ways of thought.'[10]

I agree in the difficulty we face in persevering with our inherited and traditional leadership patterns. However, as the Holy Spirit renews and restores the church, as difficult as it is, we do have to go 'back to the future'. A crisis of spiritual authority and freedom was provoked by the Reformation, but not resolved. If God's purpose is the complete restoration of His church, eclipsing even the glory and power of the apostolic era, it is imperative that we recover the foundations of that era before we can move on. We must rediscover the foundations of true spiritual authority.

Some hard questions

If we are genuinely aspiring to spiritual breakthrough in the church, we cannot escape asking ourselves some hard questions. Is authority in the church organisational or spiritual? Are our present leadership structures really rooted in the apostolic revelation? Or, more to the point, is the concept of office, and specifically of senior pastor to be found in Scripture? And does it reflect a human control over the church? Like Israel, have we set up our own kings? We may or may not, as a denomination, have bishops and overseers presiding over multiple congregations of a region, but almost universally we do have a senior pastor holding a position with varying degrees of official authority. How true is this to the life of the apostolic church and, therefore, to the life of the Spirit?

The church thrived before the reign of the bishop. What we discover in the New Testament record is vastly different when compared to our present-day experience. It is also different from what had developed by the second and third centuries. Although as late as the *Didache*, a document probably dated towards the end of the first century, itinerant prophets and teachers were still functioning in perfect harmony with the local elders of the various congregations, but more of this in a moment.

The leadership model of the apostolic church

Gift or office?

So what was the leadership model of the apostolic church? Was it exercised through a charismatic gift or an organisational office – through *official power* or *spiritual authority*? Recognising that all life demands some structure to exist, how was the healthy tension between form and freedom resolved? Was the church led through the office of senior pastor or through apostles? Or was there another way altogether? Our answers will determine whether the body of Christ is presided over by the Spirit or by man.

God appoints first apostles, second prophets, and third teachers

Paul teaches that, *'God has appointed in the church, first apostles, second prophets, third teachers ... '* (1 Corinthians 12:28 NASB). Apostles, prophets and teachers were the lead-ministries of the apostolic church. Significantly they were not a hierarchy of *official positions*, but rather a sequence of *charismatic graces* – ministry anointings which, in their given order, *first* apostles, *second* prophets, *third* teachers, spearheaded the advance of the kingdom. In Ephesians Paul clearly shows that apostles, prophets and teachers are people, *gifted by the Spirit*, who in turn are given as a *gift to the body*:

> *'But to **each one** of us grace has been given as Christ apportioned it. This is why it says, "When he ascended on high, he ... **gave gifts to men** ... It was he who **gave some to be** apostles, some to be prophets, some to be evangelists, and some to be pastors and teachers.'*
> (Ephesians 4:7, 11 NIV)

People not positions

Apostles and prophets are *people* not *positions*. There are two steps in their calling and placement. First, the *person* receives a *ministry-gift* as an individual (*'to **each one** of us grace has been given'*). Secondly, that same *person* is then given to the body of Christ as a *gift-ministry* ('*When he ascended on high,* **he ... gave gifts to men** ... *he ... gave some to be apostles'* etc. [Ephesians 4:7, 11]). God, in His sovereignty, calls and anoints people, *not* positions.

New Testament apostleship – not an office but a gift!

Apostles, prophets and teachers are therefore men (or women)[11] of the Spirit. Their anointing is not the product of, or subject to any human organisation. Flowing from the ascension of Christ their gifts and callings are mediated directly by the Spirit:

> '*When he ascended on high,* **he** ... *gave gifts to men* ... '
>
> (Ephesians 4:7)

Their ministry anointing begins and ends with them in the sovereign calling of God. New Testament apostleship is therefore not an office to be succeeded to by future aspirants or to be granted by any church body. Rather it is a *spiritual gift* dispensed by sovereign means to an individual, who is in turn given as a gift to the body.

Confusion between spiritual authority and official power

Consequently, to promote the office of bishop, or in current terminology – senior pastor, as the continuance of apostolic or true spiritual authority is wrong. And yet this is what occurred in the second and third centuries and has been inherited by the present-day church as normative. The systemic disorder of Christ's body has, to a large degree, been caused by this continuing confusion between authentic *spiritual authority* and *official power*. This is reflected in the historic confusion between the *office* of senior pastor and the *gift* of apostle.

How did the apostles function?

So how did the apostles function, and who led the local congregation?

Christ anoints and appoints apostles but apostles appoint *elders* (Acts 14:23; Titus 1:5). While the former were mobile ministries, planting and caring for multiple congregations, functioning according to their relationships and the leading of the Spirit, elders were the local resident shepherds of one congregation, functioning as a team of general overseers. However, the latter, while free, never operated independently of their relationship with the apostles.[12]

How did the apostles relate to the churches?

So how did the apostles relate to the churches?

When the apostle wrote to the church in the city of Philippi he addressed them as *'the saints ... together with the overseers and deacons'* (Philippians 1:1 NIV).

Firstly, Paul primarily addressed himself to the *'saints'* – the believers. Why? Because they are the 'congregation of the Lord'[13] – the ones set apart as the royal priesthood (1 Peter 2:9; Revelation 1:6). As *king-priests* in the new covenant order, they are, themselves, a *priestly governing class* with direct access to God. Any mediation of a humanly derived *priestly-pastor class* between the congregation and Christ is antagonistic to the spirit of the gospel and true spiritual freedom. Neander, the great nineteenth-century professor of theology at the University of Berlin, held that the development of the monarchical bishop [senior pastor] '... was unfavourable to the life of the church; and ... promoted the formation of a priesthood foreign to the essence of that development of the kingdom of God which the New Testament sets forth ...' He believed that it stood, '... intimately connected with ... the formation of a sacerdotal [priestly] caste in the Christian church.'[14] From where God sits His congregation is free – they have not received a spirit of bondage but the *spirit of adoption* – they have become His children (Romans 8:15). Any clergy–laity distinction that elevates a priestly class, or an office, whether it is called bishop or senior pastor, over Christ's immediate rulership of His people is of the spirit of the anti-Christ. This is not to say that authority should not operate in the house of God. The question is – what kind of authority?

Secondly, Paul addressed himself not only to the *saints*, but also to the overseers or elders and deacons. Nowhere in the New Testament record does an apostle address himself to the bishop or senior pastor. And this is for one very simple reason – there were none! There is no evidence in the New Testament of one person presiding over the *elders* of a church, let alone the congregation.[15]

Diotrephes – the first senior pastor!

In fact the only possible allusion to a senior pastor is a negative one. The apostle John is confronted with a situation where a leader by the name of Diotrephes has not only obtained these rights but rejects John as an apostle – as a man of the Spirit (3 John 9). Von Campenhausen comments:

> 'The man of the Spirit, subject to no organisation and to no local authoritative body, clashes with the leader of the organised single congregation, who, it would seem, is already claiming monarchical rights for himself. He may therefore be described with confidence as a bishop, and as one that is fighting, just as Ignatius has required, for the solidarity of his congregation around himself ... Here then we come across an example of the exercise of that particular kind of episcopal authority which was to be of decisive importance in the wider development of spiritual office ...'[16]

In Diotrephes we have not only the first recorded *emergence of one leader* over the others, but also a *rejection of the trans-local ministry* of apostles and prophets in favour of a single senior local leader – the *senior minister*. Both are roundly condemned. Here we have the historic seeds of a very contemporary situation – the model of a senior minister presiding over the elders and operating independently of the ascension gift ministries of apostles, prophets and teachers.

In Diotrephes' case it was far more than a *structural* problem – it was a *spiritual* problem – an issue of the heart – of inner motivation.

The spirit of Diotrephes

Diotrephes 'loved to be *first* among them' (3 John 9). He was motivated by an inner need to be at the centre and in control. Every leader is tested on this in their own heart – in their need for recognition and significance. As far as we know, apart from personal ambition, there was no other issue. Diotrephes loved to have the *first place*. This is the same Greek word Paul used when speaking of Christ's place as head of the church:

> 'He is ... head of the body, the church ... so that He Himself might come to have first place in everything.'
>
> (Colossians 1:18 NASB)

His unresolved need for recognition caused him to unconsciously usurp the place of Christ in the life and affections of the congregation. How many times has this happened over two millennia of Christian history? In fact our inherited structures and values have only served to institutionalise and legitimise the spirit of Diotrephes.

Does Christ really have the *first place* in the leadership of the church? In sentiment, yes. But in reality, no – man does. We have usurped Christ's position as head of the church. Is it any wonder the body of Christ is crippled? Human control, exercised in the spirit of Diotrephes, has severed us from the central nervous system of the Spirit. The history of the Christian church is characterised by leaders who resort to less than worthy means to obtain a less than kingdom object – their own advancement.

This is not to say that every leader that has occupied church office is of the *spirit of Diotrephes*. Quite the opposite – multitudes of worthy men and women of God have served the Lord through traditional church positions. But whenever positions of *official power* exist, the fallen state of human nature, to whatever degree, will find it difficult to resist. Where there is a lack of anointing to fill the office, seduction and manipulation operate to both obtain and maintain a position. Spiritual gifting is self-evident and will make a way in the hearts of God's people. But where a leader without the anointing aspires to an office, self-promotion and manipulation are inevitable. And if the more subtle arts of flattery and innuendo do not work, the spirit of Diotrephes will resort to slander and the use of naked power. Diotrephes used *'wicked words'* (3 John 10 NASB), *'maliciously accusing'* (3 John 10 Goodspeed) John. Feeling that his position was threatened he maligned John's character (whether openly or covertly we don't know), seeking to undermine his credibility in the eyes of the congregation. When this didn't work he resorted to raw power:

> *'he refused to welcome the brothers* ... [and] *stopped those who wanted to do so and put them out of the church.'*
>
> (3 John 10b)

He refused to receive the apostolic team sent from John and exerted his senior ministerial power in putting those out of the church who wished to do so. The central nervous system of Christ's body, the men of the Spirit – apostles, prophets and teachers – was severed. With the rise of one leader over the others, not only was the congregation cut off from free association with the apostles, it was also cut off from the head of the body, Christ Himself.

Paul's prophetic warning

Calling the elders (remember, the office of senior pastor didn't exist) of the church in Ephesus together for a conference Paul prophetically warned them:

> *'I know that after I leave, savage wolves will come in among you and will not spare the flock. Even from your own number men will arise and distort the truth in order to draw away disciples after them. So be on your guard!'*   (Acts 20:29–31 NIV)

Jesus also warned about *pseudo-prophets* who would arise, looking like sheep and smelling like sheep, but who were inwardly ravenous wolves (Matthew 7:15). They would be predatory – hungry and looking to satisfy themselves. However, these 'wolves in sheep's clothing' are not wild-eyed off-the-map cult leaders. Jesus said they look like sheep – they look harmless. They wear business suits, speak in tongues and preach on Sundays. In fact, Paul said they would arise from among *themselves* – from among the preachers and the elders!

How would they be recognised? Firstly, by their inner *wolf-nature* – their ravenous *self-life* would feed on the flock for their own survival. Secondly they would *'arise'* from the team of elders. They will raise themselves above their peers, seeking pre-eminence. Thirdly, they would *'draw away disciples after them'* (Acts 20:30). Just as Ignatius advocated, the bishop or senior pastor becomes central to the unity of the congregation,[17] developing a cult of personal-loyalty. Lastly, they would *'distort the truth'* (Acts 20:30) to develop their personal following. This is not necessarily false doctrine. Their preaching and teaching may be doctrinally sound – remember they look and sound like sheep. But they twist and distort the truth in their personal dealings to gain the *first place* over other leaders and the congregation.

By the turn of the first century Paul's prophecy was fulfilled. The *plurality of elders* was overtaken by the *singularity of one senior minister* – the office of bishop. And through the advocacy of men such as Ignatius and Cyprian what can only be described as an aberration was mainstreamed into the life of the church.

Confusion of terms – elders, bishops and pastors

Consequently, the Western church's traditionally inherited structures have confused three important terms: *elders*, *bishops*, and *pastors*. Traditionally they have been seen as three distinct layers of church office: the *bishop* originally presiding over one congregation but in time over many, and therefore the *pastor* of each congregation, who in turn presided over the *elders*. It is important to note that Paul in his address to the Ephesian *elders* used *all three terms* inter-changeably, for *one category of person*. In Acts 20:17 he called the *presbuterous* or 'elders' of the church to meet with him. In Acts 20:28 he also referred to them as *episkopos* – as 'overseers' (NIV, NASB) or 'bishops' (NKJV, NRSV), reminding them that it was the Holy Spirit who placed them in this role. And in the same verse he exhorts them to *poimainein* (to feed and rule) or 'shepherd' (NASB, NRSV) the flock, which is the verb form of *poimen*, translated 'pastor' in Ephesians 4:11.

From this we see that firstly, Paul did not call for the bishop or senior pastor of the church, but the elders. They are the governing council of the church. The office of bishop or senior pastor did not exist. Secondly, we see the role of the Holy Spirit in appointing them – they have been gifted and positioned supernaturally by the Spirit as were the apostles, prophets, and teachers. Thirdly, the three terms apply to three aspects of the one person: elder refers to their *character*; overseer or bishop to their *sphere*; and shepherd or pastor to their *function*. In Paul's use of these terms there was no distinction between a bishop, elder, or pastor.[18] The *elders* are the pastors and the bishops of their congregation. All three terms are synonymous for the same person!

Protestant popes and priesthoods

If there were an office of leadership in the New Testament, it would be that of plural eldership.[19] However, the only reference to office in the New Testament is an invention of translators:

> *'If a man desire the office of a bishop, he desireth a good work.'*
> (1 Timothy 3:1 KJV; see also NKJV, NASB, NRSV)

In this case, the NIV is a more accurate rendering:

> *'If anyone sets his heart on being an overseer, he desires a noble task.'* (1 Timothy 3:1 NIV)

There is no corresponding word for 'office' in the Greek text.[20] The translators have literally pulled it out of the air, betraying the entrenchment of traditional structures and mindsets in the church! Rather than being treated as a living spiritual *organism*, the church has historically been managed as an *organisation*.

The only other potential reference to 'office' is in Hebrews, referring to the Old Testament priesthood (Hebrews 7:5 KJV). Nowhere in the Scripture record of the new covenant church, however, is there a term that refers to any kind of human priestly or leadership office. It is most definitely a concept imported from the Old Testament. In fact, it was borrowed from there by several of the early church fathers to legitimise the church's shift from *charismatic function* to *organisational position*. But imposing old covenant institutions on new covenant ministry only created a new priesthood. As Christ is the only mediator between God and man (1 Timothy 2:5), any usurpation of His priesthood can only be described as the spirit of anti-Christ. And yet that is exactly what happened as the concept of *official power* grew in the church. A priesthood developed, with abuses down through history that defy imagination.

While the Reformation addressed some of this, it did not resolve it. Because the concept of office and official power was perpetuated it has resulted in a plethora of abuses – of Protestant Popes and priesthoods. The usurping of *spiritual authority* by *official power* is at the root of the perennial problem of spiritual abuse and atrophy in the church. We will not see true apostles, prophets and teachers fully restored until the issue of office is resolved. The full restoration of true spiritual authority hinges on it.

So, what about senior pastors?

The only reference to the 'pastor' is in Ephesians 4:11. He (or she) is one of the ascension-gift ministries, who along with apostles, prophets, evangelists and teachers are *trans-local* in their sphere of ministry. In my view, the true Ephesians 4 *pastor* is exclusively trans-local, serving as a member of an apostolic team. They work with the apostle in shepherding the shepherds, the local elders.

The New Testament knows nothing of a local church position that looks anything like the current role of pastor or senior pastor. I suspect that many of those currently serving as senior pastors are either apostles or elders. But this will not be evident until some major shifts occur. One of these is the restoration of the city-church. This will cause major adjustments for those serving in leadership roles, including their understanding of the local church.

In apostolic times the local church was the church of the locality. It was the church of the city or the region,[21] and was defined *geographically* not *denominationally*. As God restores the apostolic unity of the church, denominational boundaries will become increasingly obsolete until only geographical ones remain. A church will no longer consist of those loyal to a particular denomination, leader or theological perspective, but of all those in a city who belong to the one Lord and the one faith (Ephesians 4:5).

As this occurs, every member of the body will discover their placement. This will emerge according to their gifts and anointing, not by academically or politically gaining a position. Some senior pastors will prove to be the apostles of the city. But they will need to come off the top of their congregations to function trans-locally in planting and overseeing multiple congregations. Even so, this kind of apostolic ministry will not be manifested in its full maturity unless it functions in the context of the emerging church of the city.

As servant-leaders these apostles will facilitate the phenomenon of the church simultaneously growing smaller and larger! As in apostolic times the church will increasingly live in the healthy tension between two polarities – the church in the home and the church in the city. House-churches will accelerate the harvest and facilitate shepherd care, while 'temple worship' will be revived in large city-wide celebrations, overflowing the largest public arenas. There will be many congregations but only one church. In fact many churches will merge regardless of denominational tags resurfacing as house-churches participating in regional or city-wide apostolic networks. Many church buildings will either be sold or become training centres for raising up labourers for the harvest. Otherwise the church will meet in the home or in large public arenas. Those 'senior pastors' who emerge as true apostles will be called to geography – to the city or to a larger region – not to a single congregation or denominational agenda. Other senior pastors will emerge as the true elders of the city, who will serve with the apostles, prophets and teachers in a collegiate style of leadership – as a joint-pastorate over the city.

What about elders?

But what about those who are currently serving as elders?

Biblically, the elders are the *shepherds* or *pastors* of the city church. And as such, they are spiritually mature people, anointed to teach and oversee the flock of that city (1 Timothy 3:2; Titus 1:7–9; Romans 12:7). They are not a business council or a traditional church board consisting of naturally accomplished men who surround the senior minister of what we currently understand to be the local church (i.e. one congregation). In fact some of those who are currently serving as elders, and even some senior pastors, will emerge as the *deacons* of the city church. Serving with the apostles and elders these deacons will function as strategy implementers and facilitators of city-wide unity, prayer and evangelism, while others will emerge as administrators of ministry to the poor and as stewards of church resources. And as already stated, some senior ministers will, with the emergence of the city church, surface as the true elders of the city. In a practical expression of unity in diversity they will display varied gifts and ministries (1 Corinthians 12:4–6) with a wide ranging impact, *overseeing* the flock together in plurality and humility of heart (1 Peter 5:1–5). This will occur in tandem with the trans-local ministries of apostles, prophets and teachers, some of whom will emerge from that city serving as co-elders with the city-wide presbytery. This is reflected in Peter's self-referencing as a *'fellow elder'* (1 Peter 5:1 NIV) while clearly functioning as an apostle.

The apostles and the elders

Just as the office of senior pastor did not govern the church, neither was it exclusively governed by the *gift* of an apostle. Its governance was clearly in the hands of the elders in its day-to-day life, who willingly co-laboured with those they received as apostolic (Acts 11:30; 14:23; 15:2, 4, 6; 16:4; Titus 1:5). Any authority that the apostles had with the elders was purely *spiritual* and *relational* – not organisational or official. They were apostles to one city but not to another. Epaphroditus was known as *'your messenger'* (Philippians 2:25) or literally 'your apostle', suggesting that while to the church in Philippi he was a relational overseer he was not such to others. No doubt Paul had this principle in mind when he said, *'Even though I may not be an apostle to others, surely I am to you!'* (1 Corinthians 9:2 NIV).

While *official power* functions *organisationally*, and is taken over another, *spiritual authority* serves *relationally* and is received by another. A true leader does not exercise power over another because of position. Rather they are given the authority by those who receive their leadership through relationship and trust. Recognition of spiritual authority is always voluntary and never coerced. A true elder will not *'lord it over the flock'*, but serve in humility and as an example (1 Peter 5:3).

Paul's apostolic bond with the churches, therefore, clearly reflects a relational and charismatic connection as opposed to a formalised office (1 Corinthians 4:14–21; 9:1–19; 2 Corinthians 6:11–13; 7:2–16; 11:5–20; 12:1–10, 11–13).

Each church was totally free to receive or reject apostolic personnel and policy according to their relationships. So the answer to our earlier question as to whether the New Testament model of leadership was based on office or gift is clear.

What is God's response to human government in the church?

As we have seen, just as Israel rejected God as king in their rejection of the prophet Samuel, the church rejected Christ as King when the office of bishop (the senior pastor) superseded the apostles and elders.

How did God view this miss-development? When Israel asked for a king to be like the other nations, Samuel was 'displeased' (1 Samuel 8:6). But the measure of the man was seen in his response. Rather than reacting to the people he responded to the Lord, who counselled him:

> **'Listen to all that the people are saying to you;** *it is not you they have rejected,* **but they have rejected me as their king.** *As they have done from the day I brought them up out of Egypt until this day,* **forsaking me and serving other gods** *... but warn them solemnly and* **let them know what the king who will reign over them will do.'**   (1 Samuel 8:7–9 NIV)

By refusing to react, Samuel received wisdom to know how to respond to Israel's defection. And God gave him important insights for today's church.

God shows mercy and provides for our weakness

First, Samuel was instructed to *'listen to all that the people were saying'* (1 Samuel 8:7 NIV). He was not to judge them but give them what they wanted. In fact, despite the heart condition of the people, he was to preside prophetically over his own replacement – over the establishment of the monarchy by anointing Saul as king.

God, in His mercy, had foreseen the weakness of His own people by allowing for a king in the law. Deuteronomy 17 prophetically foreshadowed, word-for-word, the people's request to Samuel:

> *'Let us set a king over us like all the nations around us.'*
> (Deuteronomy 17:14 NIV; compare 1 Samuel 8:5)

The Law then provided boundaries for the monarchy to protect both the people and their faith (Deuteronomy 17:15–20).

God knows our frailty and provides for it. Jesus highlighted this when He pointed out the law's provision for divorce:

> *'Moses permitted you to divorce your wives because your hearts were hard. But it was not this way from the beginning.'*
> (Matthew 19:8 NIV)

While divorce was not God's intent from the beginning, neither was the monarchy. Both, under the law, became His permissive will and were allowed because of the hardness of the people's hearts. God's original intent for Israel was that they be a *'kingdom of priests'* (Exodus 19:6) carrying His redemptive rule to all the nations of earth. But tragically they sold their birthright. Through their rejection of God as King, the congregation of the Lord traded its royal mandate for a human king. They had already relinquished their priesthood to Aaron, and now also their kingship to Saul.

Not until the new covenant would there be a people again called as 'kings and priests' (1 Peter 2:9; Revelation 1:6; 5:10). But tragically, the new covenant community fell into the same error. By rejecting the ascension-gift ministries of apostles and prophets they handed their *king-priest* role to a new *priestly ruling class* – the clergy, epitomised in the office of bishop – or senior pastor. However, as we learn from the Lord's direction to Samuel, even this is permissible and was not to be condemned. For it was through the monarchy that Messiah's seed was to be preserved, ultimately emerging as the son of David. In the mystery of His sovereignty He uses human frailty to bring redemption to the earth.

As we are not to condemn the monarchy, neither are we to

stand in judgment against the religious system. Like the monarchy it has preserved the seed of a coming visitation. Greater and more powerful seasons of revival and reformation are about to shake the institutional church. Just as Jesus came to His own as the son of David – a son of the monarchy – and Paul as a Hebrew of Hebrews (Philippians 3:5)[22] God will come again to the institutional church, providing it with a window of visitation. God is slow to anger and full of mercy (Psalm 145:8). Anger and judgmental attitudes towards the authority structures of the church are neither true to the heart of God nor worthy of Christ's bride. She will exude the mercy of God towards the visible church, interceding for her, and only speaking the truth in love (Ephesians 4:15). Even so, she will face a decision to receive or reject the coming visitation. And if she rejects it she will come under a greater discipline of God, being left spiritually desolate until she can turn and say, *'Blessed is he who comes in the name of the Lord'* (Matthew 23:39).

But God is grieved because we have rejected His messengers

Secondly, in rejecting Samuel, the one who came in the name of the Lord, the people were rejecting God:

> *'... it is not **you** [Samuel] they have rejected, **but they have rejected me as their king.**'*　　　　　　(1 Samuel 8:7 NIV)

This is one of the most sobering principles of God's economy. Jesus said,

> *'He who receives **you** receives **me**, and he who receives me receives the one who sent me. Anyone who receives a prophet because he is a **prophet** will receive a **prophet's** reward ... '*
> 　　　　　　　　　　　　　　　　(Matthew 10:40–41 NIV)

How we relate to men and women of the Spirit exposes how in reality we relate to the Spirit Himself.

We all know that 'if you don't like the message, you shoot the messenger'. Untold revelation and outpourings of the Spirit have been lost to the body of Christ because of our mishandling of the messenger. We have already seen how the Ephesians 4 ministries are given by the Holy Spirit, as *people*, to the body of Christ. The church's record of receiving and valuing those whom He sends as *apostles*, *prophets* and *teachers* is disastrous.

Jesus rebuked the religious system of His generation for this very reason. It was the product of generations of hypocrisy and violence towards the prophets:

> 'Woe to you, because you build tombs for the **prophets**, and it was your forefathers who killed them. So you testify that you approve of what your forefathers did; they killed the **prophets**, and you build their tombs.'   (Matthew 23:29–32)

How easy it is to miss the visitation of God. Feel the grieving heart of God as Jesus cries out to the church of His generation:

> 'He saw the city and wept over it, saying, "If you had known in this day, even you, the things which make for peace! But now they have been hidden from your eyes. For the days shall come upon you when your enemies ... will level you to the ground ... and they will not leave in you one stone upon another, **because you did not recognize the time of your visitation.**"'
> (Luke 19:41–44 NASB)

What is the lesson? *Divine visitation is incarnational.* God comes in the form of *people* – He gifts them by the Spirit and gives them to the church. But the religious system usually refuses to recognise them because they either lack the pedigree or the position to warrant attention. The resumes of Jesus and the disciples were not too impressive. The carpenter's boy from Nazareth and a rag-tag team of ignorant fishermen didn't rate on the Richter scale of religious power – but they were sent from God. And to the degree their generation received *them*, to that degree they received *God*.

Spiritual breakthrough in the Western church is contingent on one thing – receiving those sent by the Spirit. God has a habit, though, of coming to mangers, carpenters, and fishermen – He reveals himself to babes, to the uneducated and the unrecognised. He uses *'the things that are not – to nullify the things that are'* (1 Corinthians 1:28).

As in Hosea's day, human control has become so mainstream that, *'the prophet is considered a fool, and the man of the spirit insane'* (Hosea 9:7).

The question, therefore, is whether we are willing to turn our inherited leadership values and structures on their head.

So, when the second- and third-century church replaced the

men of the Spirit with the bishop – with official power – they were not rejecting men, but God.

God views a human king as idolatry

Thirdly, Samuel was shown that by rejecting him as prophet, Israel was not only rejecting God but, in fact, pursuing other gods:

> '... *but they have rejected me as their king. As they have done from the day I brought them up out of Egypt until this day,* **forsaking me and serving other gods.**'   (1 Samuel 8:7–8 NIV)

The kingship was the product of the nation's idolatry, and was proven to be so by its unfolding history as the kings, by-and-large, led the people further away from the Lord in their pursuit of false gods.

As a prophet Hosea recognised the connection between idolatry and human government:

> 'They set up kings without my consent;
>   they choose princes without my approval.
> With their silver and gold
>   they make idols for themselves
> to their own destruction.'
>
> (Hosea 8:4 NIV)

Israel lusted after a king so they could be *'like the other nations'*. He became their worldly guarantee of success, their *'arm of flesh'* (2 Chronicles 32:8). The Western church's rapid decline in a post-modern world demands answers. In a panicked state of cultural-cringe, instead of seeking the Lord we have turned to worldly means and, more tragically, to worldly values in order to win the world's respect. Certainly it is crucial that we communicate and administrate with excellence and creativity. But this is not the same as adopting the world's values – its gods of success and power.

It is one thing to have inherited the power structures of the church dating from the second and third centuries; it is another to renew, in our generation our allegiance to them – to the *king* – to a system of human control. Consequently, contemporary ministry success is achieved more through proficient programme management, slick communication and entertainment than through the power of a life lived close to God. Success is not so much measured by Christ-likeness as by numerical increase. We figure that to have relevance in our culture we must create an image of power and success, little realising our folly is open to the world's gaze.

We have tragically succumbed to another spirit and lost our savour. This has surfaced dramatically through recent survey results from George Barna, showing that only 32% of born-again adults and 9% of born-again teenagers in the USA believe in moral absolutes![23] Christ has been deposed by human control and worldly values – by a false god.

God warned them about the abuse of authority

Fourthly, Samuel was to warn the people of the abuse they would suffer through the kingship:

> *'... warn them solemnly and **let them know what the king who will reign over them will do**.'*   (1 Samuel 8:7–9)

Firstly, Samuel warned them that their sons and daughters would be enslaved by the king (1 Samuel 8:10–13). How many generations of young people have been spiritually bankrupted by a religious system that is geared only to preserve the status quo? And how many young pastors started out with the fire of God in their bones only to be shipwrecked on a system that exists to make people *happy* but never *holy*. How many have been rudely awakened to discover that they have been hired to merely 'hatch, match and dispatch' – to preside over the rights of passage, providing some religious solace along the way. Rather than ruling as princes with God themselves, the next generation has been enslaved to human power and institutional agendas.

Secondly, Samuel warned them that a human king would consume their productivity in maintaining his system (1 Samuel 8:14–17). How many dollars have been lost to the kingdom of God – to gospel expansion and to the discipling of the nations – consumed instead on an infrastructure unrelated to kingdom growth and world transformation.

It is significant that the human king of the Old Testament church required ten percent of everything they owned (1 Samuel 8:14–18). This and other factors suggest it is time to review how tithing is taught and practised in much of the Evangelical and Pentecostal church. The fact that tithing was legislated by law in the 6th century as the church went into spiritual decline; that it is not *explicitly* taught in the New Testament, nor mentioned in the *Didache* (the earliest known document of church practice and polity); and that the new covenant is a better covenant calling us to a more exacting righteousness than the old, all suggest that it is time to review this issue.

This is not to dismiss Jesus' and Paul's teaching on finance, but rather bring it to the fore and rediscover the joy of totally abandoned giving. This was the experience of the first generation of believers when

> *'No-one claimed that any of his possessions was his own . . . For from time to time those who owned lands or houses sold them, brought the money from the sales and put it at the apostles' feet.'*
> (Acts 4:32, 34–35 NIV)

Obviously a higher law was in operation here than the old covenant law of tithing. In fact it was the law of the spirit of life in Christ Jesus (Romans 8:2) where not ten percent, but one hundred percent belonged to God.[24]

So in conclusion, the foundations of the church were flawed from the second century. From that time onwards, true *spiritual authority* was superseded by *official power*.

The prophetic response to human government

Prophets are *seers*, and as such, will see into the root cause of the church's defection. But how do they handle what they see? Samuel modelled the mature prophetic response.

He confronted and comforted

After installing Saul as king he showed them, through a miraculous sign, the gravity of their rejection of God as their King:

> *'Now then, stand still and see this great thing the LORD is about to do before your eyes! Is it not wheat harvest now? I will call upon the LORD to send thunder and rain. And you will realise what an evil thing you did in the eyes of the LORD when you asked for a king.'*
> (1 Samuel 12:16–17 NIV)

At the word of Samuel the Lord sent rain and thunder, in the dry season, to prophetically highlight the people's rebellion. They were smitten, and in awe they pleaded for mercy.

Samuel not only *confronted* but he also *comforted*. He exhorted them not to be afraid and not to turn away from the Lord after idols, because *'the Lord will not reject his people'* (1 Samuel 12:22). He assured them of their place in the heart of God:

> *'... because the Lord was pleased to make you his own.'*
>   (1 Samuel 12:22)

He continued to intercede and teach

He then declared his own response:

> *'As for me, far be it from me that I should sin against the Lord by failing to pray for you. And I will teach you the way that is good and right.'*   (1 Samuel 12:23 NIV)

Here is the strategy for the man of the Spirit – *intercessory prayer* and *teaching*. Despite the pain of Israel's defection (1 Samuel 8:6) and his personal rejection, Samuel recommitted to his prophetic call.

What a lesson to seers! He did not allow his spirit to be affected – no bitterness, no anger – only mercy and grace. And out of this grace he proactively engaged the heart of God in prophetic intercession and teaching until his assignment was completed.

SECTION 3

Back to the Future – the Breakthrough

Restoring the Glory of God

Chapter 10

Uprooting and Pulling Down

'See, today I appoint you over nations and kingdoms to uproot and tear down, to destroy and overthrow, to build and to plant.'
(Jeremiah 1:10 NIV)

'To every thing there is a season,
and a time to every purpose under the heaven ... a time to plant,
and a time to pluck up that which is planted ...'
(Ecclesiastes 3:1–2 KJV)

In Section 2 I sought to show what, in my view, is the major hindrance to revival. We saw it historically typified in Israel, the old covenant church, as idolatry – described by the prophets as spiritual adultery. Moving from the type to the anti-type, from Israel to the church, it is likewise the primary issue for the contemporary Western church. Driving the manifest presence of God from her, idolatry lies at the heart of the church's malaise.

But God doesn't leave us in our mess. He has promised, as we will discover in chapter 11, to bring deliverance and restoration. However, to do so He takes us 'back to the future' – back to beginnings. He first uproots everything He has not planted, clearing the ground of our 'stuff' before He starts to rebuild. The future of the church is, therefore, in her foundations – in her beginnings.

The next four chapters (Chapters 10–13) will show how the church might move into her destiny as she returns to the beginnings of bridal intimacy and covenant-love – in fact to the One who is from the *'beginning'* (Isaiah 41:4; Proverbs 8:23; Revelation 1:17).

Revelation is foundational to the church (Matthew 16:18). But the revelation of what – the latest 'end-time' teaching or church growth formula? Absolutely not! Peter, in a flash of understanding, declared to Jesus, *'You are the Christ, the Son of the living God!'*

(Matthew 16:16). Jesus immediately responded, *'Upon **this** rock I will build my church'* (Matthew 16:18).

But what was the rock – was it Peter, as many claim, or something more? That it was Peter is partially true in that the church is built on the foundation of the apostles and prophets (Ephesians 2:20). But it was something far more – it was the rock of *revelation* – and more particularly, the revelation of God in Christ. As Paul declared, there is no other foundation, which can be laid (1 Corinthians 3:11). Consequently the work of reformation and revival will consistently call each generation back to the beginnings, to the apostolic foundation of intimacy with God in Christ.

The spirit of prophecy is the testimony of Jesus (Revelation 19:10). Moving in this spirit, John called the church to return to her *'first love'* (Revelation 2:4), and Jeremiah called Israel to *'the devotion of her youth'* (Jeremiah 2:2). The judgment of captivity fell on Israel for one reason – they had forsaken bridal intimacy:

> *'I will pronounce my judgments on my people*
> > ***because of their wickedness in forsaking me**,*
> *in burning incense to other gods*
> > *and in worshipping what their hands have made.'*
> > > (Jeremiah 1:16 NIV)

By turning to the works of their own hands they had forsaken the Lord – the *'fountain of living water'* and *'dug their own cisterns'* (Jeremiah 2:13).

Jeremiah was therefore commissioned to call them back to the *fountain* and *foundation* of intimacy with God. But first their idolatrous strongholds needed to be dismantled – to be uprooted and torn down. If the church is to be rebuilt and restored on the foundation of intimacy with God, the rubble of human pride and protocol will be removed first. Idolatrous strongholds will be brought down before the process of rebuilding can begin. And before Christ's high-priestly prayer of John 17 – the dream of one flock with one Shepherd – can be realised, the territorial Baals of *productivity* and *power* will be demolished. God Himself turns His face in judgment against the idols of power – they are in fact, as Hosea prophesied, *'idols for destruction'* (Hosea 8:4). And as we shall see in this chapter, the prophetic role is not only to serve as a *proclaimer* of imminent judgment against idolatry, but as an *interpreter* of those judgments when they fall. To fulfil this, Jeremiah's commission contained *four negatives* but only *two positives*. Before the positive activity of *'building and planting'* could go forward the false gods needed to be uprooted, torn down, destroyed, and overthrown (Jeremiah 1:10 NIV).

As God pours out His Spirit in revival, the work of the prophet often appears to be more negative than positive. Because among other things the prophet serves as the *proclaimer* and *interpreter* of God's judgments, they invariably confront heart attitudes and human systems that have violated the holiness of God. They 'stand before the Lord' and represent His holiness to men, calling them back into the arms of covenant-love. Their sometimes adversarial role is often misunderstood. It emanates from their vision of God – of His majesty and holiness – and of the imminence of the coming kingdom. Consequently their whole call and passion, rooted in the revelation of God, moves them as voices crying in the wilderness to prepare the way of the Lord.

While the prophet is imbued with a vision of the invisible – of what *is to come*, natural men can only see what *has been* or what *is* – the status quo. Any suggestion of 'uprooting', 'tearing down', or 'destroying' is deeply disturbing. The natural or carnal person is either rooted in the security of the past (tradition) or the present (success and power). They therefore look to *institutional* continuity – walking by sight, trusting in the work of human hands, in created things – in position, possessions, or power. Whereas the man or woman of the Spirit, seeing Him who is invisible, looks to *spiritual* continuity – to the prophetic unfolding of God's kingdom purpose. Knowing that man doesn't live by bread alone (Matthew 4:4) they look to the *now* word proceeding from the mouth of God (Revelation 2:7). They are looking for the city whose builder and maker is God (Hebrews 11:10). They therefore exult in the prophetic proclamation that *'Babylon the Great is fallen!'* (Revelation 18:2).

Babylon the Great is fallen

Babylon – the church seduced by a spirit of pride

The prophets all declare the ultimate fall of Babylon – her uprooting and complete destruction (Isaiah 21:9; Jeremiah 51:8; Revelation 14:8; 18:2, 10). But what is Babylon? Is it Islam, the Roman Catholic Church or perhaps the global financial system? Or could it be America, as some are currently claiming? However, we have already seen in Chapter 7 that the Babylon of Revelation can actually symbolise the *church*! (Revelation 11:8; 16:19; 17:18).

Seduced by religion and the spirit of pride the city of God can, in reality, become the city of man – Babylon itself! We are unwise, though, in attempting to identify her with a particular denomination, organisation or group. Babylon is a *spirit* before it is a *system*. While it can be variously described as a religious spirit or a political spirit, and even a worldly or commercial spirit, it is behind all these things a spirit of *pride*. Isaiah exposed this when he prophesied Babylon's fall:

> 'You said, "I will continue forever –
>   the eternal queen!"
> But you did not consider these things
>   or reflect on what might happen.
>
> 'Now then, listen, you wanton creature,
>   lounging in your security
> and saying to yourself,
>   "I am, and there is none besides me.
> I will never be a widow
>   or suffer the loss of children."
> Both of these will overtake you
>   in a moment, on a single day:
>   loss of children and widowhood.
> They will come upon you in full measure,
>   in spite of your many sorceries
>   and all your potent spells.
> You have trusted in your wickedness
>   and have said, "No-one sees me."
> Your wisdom and knowledge mislead you
>   when you say to yourself,
>   "I am, and there is none besides me."
> Disaster will come upon you,
>   and you will not know how to conjure it away.
> A calamity will fall upon you
>   that you cannot ward off with a ransom;
> a catastrophe you cannot foresee
>   will suddenly come upon you.'
>   (Isaiah 47:7–11 NIV; see also Revelation 18:7–8)

We mistakenly look for Babylon *out there* when all the while it is *in here* – in us. We have fallen prey to spiritual pride, boasting in our pedigree as Pentecostals, Evangelicals, or Conservatives. We say, '*I am, and there is none besides me*' (Isaiah 47:8).

We feel smugly secure, trusting in our doctrinal orthodoxy and in our Protestant cathedrals of success and power: *'You said, 'I will continue forever – the eternal queen!''* (Isaiah 47:7). Whether we are Evangelical, Pentecostal, or Conservative we have fallen prey to the spirit of pride, unwittingly committing adultery with the gods of this age.

Babylon – a home for spiritual powers

Babylon, through her pride, becomes *'a home for demons and a haunt for every evil spirit'* (Revelation 18:2 NIV; see also Ephesians 6:12).

Principalities and powers are given a base of operation within the church itself (Ephesians 4:27). Like the religious establishment of Jesus' and Paul's day it gives the appearance of godliness, but even religious 'flesh' provides ground for demonic activity. Uncrucified *self*, in leaders and people alike, provides legal access for Satan to rule over entire religious structures and organisations. By operating out of *self*-will, *self*-promotion or *self*-justification we can build and maintain churches and ministries independently of God. Rooted in pride they can become strongholds that ultimately resist the knowledge of God. What begins in the *Spirit* can be maintained by the *flesh* (Galatians 3:3) and end in *demonic* control (Galatians 5:20). The church of God, led astray by carnal pseudo-apostles and pastors (1 Corinthians 3:1; 2 Corinthians 11:13) can, while maintaining an appearance of Evangelical or Pentecostal orthodoxy, become the very 'synagogue of Satan' (Revelation 2:9; 3:9).

What better strategy than to set up a base of operations in the enemy's camp! A church, while maintaining religious respectability, can become a home for spirits of witchcraft, sensuality, and control.

Pride and the work of our own hands

Babylon – the *spirit of pride*, is described as a 'great whore' (Revelation 17:1). And with the mystery name – *'Mother of All Prostitutes and of Idol Worship Everywhere around the World'* (Revelation 17:5) – she is the source of *spiritual adultery*. A condition any individual, group, or movement can experience where the *spirit of pride*, to whatever degree, has been given permission to operate. Pride opens the door to other gods – to the work of our own hands – to human effort, productivity and power. This is not to deny a biblical work ethic. Sure we labour, but it is the Lord who builds the house, or gives the increase (Psalm 127:1; 1 Corinthians 3:6). Rather than trusting in the Lord we therefore turn to our own devices – to human programming and promotion. It is the same anti-Christ spirit which operates in the world religions, the world system and as we have seen, adulterously within the church. As a *whore* it is seductive and insidious. And as the *'Mother of . . . Idol Worship Everywhere around the World'*, it generates a pervasive and universal religious spirit to which all believers, churches and denominations are susceptible.

Idolatry and the Western church

And so the Western church, which should have been *salt* and *light* to the world (Matthew 5:13–14) has instead become its source of darkness. As the church goes – so goes the world. She has been designed and mandated by God to lead the world. But her true prophetic calling has been subverted through her own idolatry. And she has become, instead, a false-prophet, leading the world into darkness. Self-deceived, we foolishly point the finger at the world's darkness, not realising our own 'lampstand' has been taken out (Revelation 2:5 NIV). In our proud boasting we say, *'I am rich; I have acquired wealth and do not need a thing'* (Revelation 3:17 NIV).

Instead of living as a kingdom *counter-culture* we have become another Western *sub-culture*, trapped in our Evangelical and Pentecostal ghettos of cultural irrelevance. And in a pathetic parody of our prophetic witness we pronounce judgment on the world, forgetting that it begins in the house of God (1 Peter 4:17).

The Western church can be likened to the man that Jesus delivered from an evil spirit. After searching for a place to rest the demon finally decided to return. Finding the house swept clean and unoccupied it capitalised on the opportunity by gathering seven friends more wicked and moved back in. And so the final condition of the man was worse than the first (Matthew 12:45).

The outpouring of the Holy Spirit in the first several centuries swept the house clean. But instead of continuing to be filled with the Spirit it remained 'unoccupied', attempting to appear 'clean' and in 'order', *'having a form of godliness . . . '* (2 Timothy 3:5 NIV). Despite this first-century cleansing of God's house, the emptiness of human power structures by the third, fourth, and fifth centuries began to create a spiritual vacuum, inviting the re-entry of a stronger demonic power. It returned seven-fold. The demons of idolatry, pride, sensuality, greed and witchcraft, which had ruled over previously God-less societies, returned as a 'baptised paganism'. Peter's prophecy of the coming apostasy was fulfilled:

> *'If they have escaped the corruption of the world by knowing our Lord and Saviour Jesus Christ and are again entangled in it and overcome, they are worse off at the end than they were at the beginning ... Of them the proverbs are true: "A dog returns to its vomit," and, "A sow that is washed goes back to her wallowing in the mud."'*   (2 Peter 2:20, 22 NIV)

The spirit of Babylon repossessed the church so that its final condition, and therefore the final condition of Western culture, became worse than the first.

Attack on America

As I write, the world is coping with the immediate aftermath of the Islamic terrorist attack on New York and Washington of 11 September 2001. A day when the world as we have known it changed. In fact this is a watershed, a marking off of a new era for the Western world. But what is the nature of this era and what is God doing through it?

First let me say that I see in a glass darkly, and what I see I only see in part (1 Corinthians 13:12). I know there are various perspectives on this and that not all the truth is ever revealed to any one person. We only receive in part. But as each of us puts that part forward we discover the whole counsel of God.

Before I comment any further we need to consider the prayer of Habakkuk:

> *'Lord, I have heard of your fame;*
> *   I stand in awe of your deeds, O Lord.*
> *Renew them in our day,*
> *   in our time make them known;*
> **in wrath remember mercy**.'   (Habakkuk 3:2 NIV)

The prophet, in the midst of turmoil and judgment, cried out to the Lord for His intervention – for His vindication and deliverance in the face of injustice and the onslaught of evil. Above all else our God is a God of compassion who remembers His covenant-mercy and delights to pour out His tender loving-kindness – in wrath He will always remember mercy. In fact as James teaches, *'Mercy triumphs over judgment!'* (James 2:13).

11 September 2001, despite the deep human tragedy, displays the hand of a merciful God. The average hijacked plane was less than a third full. It has been estimated that there could have been more than 90,000 lives lost in the towers as opposed to less than 3,000. Many Christians who would normally have been at their offices were for various reasons prevented from being there. Numerous stories of amazing, if not miraculous, escape were heard after the attack. And the plane downed by the heroic action of several passengers who just happened to be committed Christians, was most probably targeting either the White House or the Capitol. In fact it seems probable that the plane that crashed into the Pentagon was actually assigned to one of these far softer targets, but failed to make it. In the wake of the attack the outpouring of prayer across America and around the world has been enormous. And this is only adding to the already historic move of the '2 Chronicles 7:14' prayer and repentance which has been sweeping across the USA and the world over the last 6–8 years. In wrath God remembers mercy.

But how do we understand the wrath? We do not seem to have too many problems with the mercy, but it is hard for us to come to terms with God's wrath and judgment.

Distinguishing between two kinds of judgment

At this point it is important to clarify something. There is a misunderstanding in the minds of many about the judgment of God. We must distinguish between what I would call *eschatological* judgment[1] and *remedial* judgment. The former includes the cataclysmic judgments surrounding the Second Coming and the final judgment itself. These are eternal judgments and they are permanent. *Remedial* judgment relates to the chastisements of God upon His children, which are temporary and are designed to be redemptive. Their purpose is to restore and bring them back to Him. In warning of imminent captivity Jeremiah pronounced these kind of judgments:

> *'I will pronounce my judgments on my people because of their wickedness in forsaking me, in burning incense to other gods and in worshipping what their hands have made.'*
>
> (Jeremiah 1:16 NIV)

Israel's judgments through their many military defeats and various captivities were of this kind. Even their continued partial blindness to the gospel is a temporary and *remedial* judgment – a chastisement.

In my view the terrorist attack on America is exactly that – a *remedial* judgment. But is it a judgment on the nation or on the church? Paul said of Christ in Ephesians:

> *'And God placed all things under his feet and appointed him to be head over everything **for the church**.'*
>
> (Ephesians 1:22 NIV)

There is no question that God judges nations (Matthew 25:32–33; Jeremiah 18:5–10). But the whole movement of history exists for one purpose – His church. Jesus laid His life down for her, and as the apple of His eye the ascended Christ jealously controls 'all things' for His Bride. Kings and presidents, nations and civilisations, religions and ideologies – all rise and fall according to His design for a glorious Bride – a mature and perfected church. There is no demonic ruler that doesn't first come under the authority of Christ. He has been given *all* authority in heaven and on earth (Matthew 28:18; Ephesians 1:22–23). Angelic prince powers currently governing whole populations, civilisations and religions, including Islam, only do so with the permission of He who is the King of kings, awaiting the appointed time when He will present their possessions to His Bride as her inheritance.

11 September (911) – an emergency call to the church!

In the meantime God will use these powers to perfect His people. It is significant that Islam only emerged during the 7th century – in my view as a rod of divine discipline on some of the greatest darkness of the church. By this time she was not only divided between east and west but also embroiled in bitter doctrinal disputes and mired in a prevailing worldliness. The events of 11 September (9/11 or 911) are primarily an *emergency call* – a prophetic warning to the church.

Instead of the rod of the Assyrian and Babylonian Empires, as in biblical times, God is disciplining His church through the false religious empire of Islam. Sobering precedents have already occurred in history and there is nothing to say that we are exempt from their reoccurrence. Egypt was a Christian nation boasting a rich and ancient heritage in the gospel, but by 651 AD it had fallen to Islamic invasion. So also modern-day Turkey (ancient Asia Minor), the field of Paul's amazingly fruitful endeavours – today it is ruled by Islam.[2] In fact within decades of Mohammed's visions, three of the greatest centres of early Christianity had fallen – Jerusalem, Antioch, and Alexandria. Not to mention the whole Iberian Peninsula (Spain and Portugal), though this was later won back. With the fall of the Roman Empire it is estimated that one-half of Christendom fell under the power of Islam. By 1453 they had won the jewel in the crown, with the fall of the eastern citadel of Christianity – Constantinople (today's Istanbul).[3] The historic Church of St. Sophia became a mosque, and the city became the ruling centre for Islam. The Ottoman Turks swept through Greece, Bulgaria, the Balkans and Hungary, finally knocking on the backdoor of Western Europe in the siege of Vienna in 1529 and again in 1683.

This proved to be one of the major turning points of history. In the final siege of 1683 up to 200,000 Moslem troops surrounded Vienna in a 60-day siege. By the final day the walls of the city had been breached and the city, in a weakened state, was about to fall. But through the last minute intervention of Jan Sobieski, the warrior-king of Poland, Vienna was providentially delivered, preserving Christianity and more particularly Reformation Christianity, as the dominant faith of Western Europe. One contemporary report of the siege acknowledged that, 'Heaven favourably heard the Prayers and Tears of a Cast-down and Mournful People, and retorted the Terror on a powerful Enemy, and drove him from the Walls of Vienna'.[4]

It is not insignificant, nor a coincidence, that the last day of the siege when the Moslem army was most dominant and Vienna about to fall was – 11 September. This date is etched into the memory of the Islamic world, and 11 September 2001 is a loud and clear message that radical Islam is back to complete the unfinished business of 1683 – the total victory of Allah over the Christian West.

The history of the Christian movement vividly illustrates the truth of Jesus' warning that if salt loses its flavour it will be thrown out and trodden under the feet of men (Matthew 5:13). Let us have ears to hear not only the warnings of history, but also of current events.

Paul's warning to the church

Paul also warned the church,

> *'Do not be haughty, but fear. For if God did not spare the natural branches, He may not spare you either. Therefore consider the **goodness** and **severity** of God: on those who fell, severity; but toward you, goodness, if you continue in His goodness. Otherwise you also will be cut off.'* (Romans 11:20–22 NKJV)

He is referring to the discipline of God on Israel – *'the natural branches'* – and the cutting off of Israel from faith. If the church arrogantly presumes, through its disobedience, on the *goodness* of God they too run the risk of experiencing His *severity* – of being cut off. In fact the word 'severity' literally means 'to cut off'. According to Vine[5] the 'severity' of God refers to His 'temporary retributive dealings', and was used as a term in the ancient papyri for 'the exacting to the full the provisions of a statute'.

What is Paul saying? He is warning that God will carry out the covenant sanctions – the *remedial judgments* of Deuteronomy 28 and Leviticus 26. These passages not only include the *blessings*, which America and the Christian West have so abundantly enjoyed, but also the *curses*, which can include sudden ruin, and military or economic reverses to the point of invasion and captivity (Leviticus 26:14–33).

Because Israel broke covenant through idolatry and unbelief, she not only experienced the incremental judgments of God (disease and natural disasters, war, invasion and finally captivity) but was also cut off from the land and, more significantly, was cut off from the presence of God. According to Paul this too can happen to the new covenant church.

The message of God's severity – strange to Western ears

Western Christianity is an expert on the *goodness* of God. We sing and write about it. We preach it from our pulpits, broadcast it over the airwaves and multiply it through every electronic means – as we should. But because we don't balance it by teaching the whole counsel of God – His goodness *and* severity, it becomes *self*-serving and breeds a *self*-indulgent religion governed by personal convenience and affluence. To talk about the *severity* of God is strange to our Western ears. And yet it was the message preached by the prophets. Couched in the language of love they warned of God's severity to those who worshipped other gods, foreshadowing their imminent captivity if they refused to turn back. They would be *'trodden under foot of men'* (Matthew 5:13). With neither fear nor favour, these prophets faithfully presented the severity of God to their generation.

Even so, the people of God felt they were immune from disaster:

> *'... they said, "He will do nothing!*
> *No harm will come to us;*
> *we will never see sword or famine.'*　　(Jeremiah 5:12 NIV)

Apart from Jeremiah and several other true prophets, the religious leaders of the day only confirmed the people in their feelings of invincibility and the sense that 'it will never happen to us'. For them it was business as usual:

> *'They dress the wound of my people*
> *as though it were not serious.*
> *"Peace, peace," they say,*
> *when there is no peace.'*　　(Jeremiah 6:14 NIV)

And yet the Lord warned them against these kinds of leaders:

> **'Do not listen to what the prophets are prophesying to**
> **you;**
> **they fill you with false hopes.**
> **They speak visions from their own minds,**
> *not from the mouth of the LORD ...*
> *they say, "No harm will come to you."*
> *But which of them has stood in the council of the LORD*
> *to see or hear his word?*
> *Who has listened and heard his word ...*
> *I did not send these prophets,*
> *yet they have run with their message ...*
> **But if they had stood in my council,**
> **they would have proclaimed my words to my people**
> *and would have turned them from their evil ways*
> *and from their evil deeds.'*
>
> 　　(Jeremiah 23:16–18, 21–22 NIV)

If the popular prophets of Jeremiah's day had *'stood in the council of the LORD'* they would have warned of imminent judgment.

And in doing so, they would have turned the hearts of the people back to God.

The message and ministry of the prophet

The true prophet is a 'covenant-mediator'. This is seen in the word of the Lord through Jeremiah:

> *'Listen to the terms of this covenant and follow them . . . I warned them again and again, saying, "Obey me." But they did not listen or pay attention; instead, they followed the stubbornness of their evil hearts. So I brought on them all the curses of the covenant I had commanded them to follow but that they did not keep . . . They have followed other gods to serve them. Both the house of Israel and the house of Judah have broken the covenant . . . Therefore "I will bring on them a disaster they cannot escape."'*
> (Jeremiah 11:6–11 NIV)

The prophetic spirit goes out in both old and new covenants to draw the hearts of the people back to covenant love – back to holiness and intimacy with God. When Jesus was asked which was the greatest commandment in the Law He answered from the *'shema'* of Deuteronomy 6,

> *'"Love the Lord your God with all your heart and with all your soul and with all your mind." This is the first and greatest commandment. And the second is like it: "Love your neighbour as yourself."* **All the Law and the Prophets** *hang on these two commandments.'*
> (Matthew 22:37–40 NIV)

Both, the covenant (the law) and the prophetic ministry (the prophets) are fulfilled when the people of God return to the Lord with all their hearts. Contrary to what many may think, Jesus did not come to abolish the Law and the Prophets, but to actually fulfil them (Matthew 5:17). The new covenant puts within us such a heart for God that the covenant, summed up in the greatest commandment, is finally fulfilled.

Consequently the function of a prophet in today's church has not substantially changed from that of his or her old covenant counterpart – to call the people of God back to covenant obedience and love. While their method of delivery may be original, their message is not. They give witness to the covenant, and more importantly, to the unchangeable character and nature of the covenant God. By restating in the power of the Spirit the terms of that covenant, including its sanctions (remedial judgments and blessings), they call the hearts of the people back to the embrace of God's holy love. John, a New Testament prophet, fearlessly fulfilled this ministry when he confronted the spiritual love-life of the Ephesian Church, calling them back from where they had fallen:

> *'You have forsaken your first love. Remember the height from which you have fallen! Repent and do the things you did at first.'*
> (Revelation 2:4–5 NIV)

In calling them back to covenant-love – to the *goodness* of God, John also sanctioned it with a remedial judgment – the *severity* of God:

> *'If you do not repent, I will come to you and remove your lampstand . . .'*
> (Revelation 2:5b)

Violating the covenant has consequences, even in the New Testament.

This prophetic call to return to covenant love is embedded in the covenant sanctions (remedial judgments) of Leviticus 26. After twenty-five verses of sanctions they culminate in the invitation to return to the Lord (see Leviticus 26:40–45 NIV). The sanctions are designed to be remedial – to bring us back to the Lord. Therefore the function of the prophet is not only to sound warnings of imminent judgment, but also to discern the hand of God in the judgments as they happen, interpreting accurately, in the light of the covenant, what God is doing and why. The love-covenant, with its *stipulations* (commandments) and *sanctions* (blessings and curses), is the grid through which we interpret and come to understand the circumstances of God's people. It is a prophetic touchstone, the reference point for God's dealings with His people. Either blessing or cursing flow from this covenant of love, depending on whether God's holy nature has been honoured or violated.

In the church today we have caricatured the prophet as a prognosticator, looking to them for personal words of direction or comfort. And in some cases for warnings of natural disasters. In doing so we have missed the point, minimising and domesticating the prophetic ministry. There is no question that personal prophecy and prediction are elements of the prophetic gifting. But the real weight of the prophet's calling is concentrated in the covenant. Through this touchstone they articulate God's ways with His people.

As God draws history to a conclusion, bringing all things together in Christ (Ephesians 1:10) He will restore the prophetic ministry to truly biblical proportions where they will again stand in the council of the Lord (Jeremiah 23:22). In a spirit of meekness, but with great power, they will rebuke not only the church, but also strong nations – their governments, kings and presidents, calling them back to the ways of the Lord – back to covenant love. They will prophesy over the church and over cities and nations, changing their spiritual atmosphere, preparing the way of the Lord. Never before have we so desperately needed to hear from heaven. In these epochal days as God sets the stage for the greatest display of His glory in history, give us again men and women who are moved by a different spirit. Those who are more than conference celebrities and 'anointed' entertainers, more than professional pastors and programme promoters. Those who, coming out of the presence of God, are *seers* and *truth-tellers*, prophesying as 'covenant-mediators and interpreters', drawing the church and the nations back to the heart of God.

The Western church – under the discipline of God

Babylon is in the church – and it is falling! God is bringing it down – He is removing everything that can be shaken (Hebrews 12:27). The Son of Man is sending out His angels to weed out of the kingdom everything that causes offence (Matthew 25:41). Jesus, referring to the Pharisaic religious system, declared,

> *'Every plant that my heavenly Father has not planted will be pulled up by the roots.'*   (Matthew 15:13 NIV)

The *spirit of pride and religion* that has been secure in the bosom of the church for centuries is in the process of being exposed and rooted out.

God's *remedial judgments* are always incremental. The Lord is slow to anger and full of compassion. In His great mercy He sends His messengers, again-and-again, to call His people back to Himself before He sends His judgments – military defeats, economic recession, destructive weather patterns, disease or plagues. Israel was cut off as the final remedial judgment, only after years of prophetic pleading and escalating chastisements. But how far are we in this process? I submit that the West is much further down the path of remedial judgment than we want to admit.

The last one hundred years have already seen the Western nations experience the agonies of two World Wars and a major depression. According to Gil Elliot in his book, *The Twentieth Century Book of the Dead*, more people were killed globally in the 20th century by war and ideological or ethnic purging than have lived and died throughout the whole of history! 170 million were killed in government sponsored genocide apart from actual war![6]

The hour is far later than we have imagined. Our so-called enlightened age has been one of the darkest, and yet one of great renewal and reformation in the church. The Lord has not only been coming to us in seasons of judgment but also in mercy. Even so, if we miss the window of 11 September by refusing to discern the dealings of God and humble ourselves then we will be subjected to increasingly heavier chastisements.

We are still in a season of grace – God in His wrath remembers mercy. Now is the time to turn from our proud ways – from the works of our own hands – to humble our hearts and seek the Lord. Humility, repentance and reconciliation are the only weapons that will roll back the judgments that are most certainly coming. Our deepening heart-response to the call of covenant-love will bring down, once-and-for-all, the Babylonian principalities of pride and religion that have, for centuries, held the church in captivity.

Now for building and planting – in the next chapter we will consider the biblical promise of restoration.

Chapter 11

Building and Planting

'See, today I appoint you over nations and kingdoms ...
to build and to plant.'
(Jeremiah 1:10 NIV)

'My eyes will watch over them for their good,
and I will bring them back to this land. I will build them up and
not tear them down; I will plant them and not uproot them.
I will give them a heart to know me, that I am the LORD ...
for they will return to me with all their heart.'
(Jeremiah 24:6–7 NIV)

By the fourth century the church had universally succumbed to
the spirit of Babylon – she had gone into spiritual captivity. As
with ancient Israel, the glory had departed and was replaced by
human control – the *'arm of flesh'* (2 Chronicles 32:8). But the
good news is that God never leaves His people in captivity. In
fact after seventy years in Babylon He pulled off the ultimate
jailbreak! He came to 'turn their captivity' (Psalm 126:4) – to set
them free and restore their former glory. Jeremiah as a prophet of
the captivity declared that God would,

*' ... **restore** the fortunes of Jacob's tents*
and have compassion on his dwellings;
*the city will be **rebuilt** on her ruins ...*
From them will come songs of thanksgiving
and the sound of rejoicing.'   (Jeremiah 30:18–19)

The restoration

Refreshing and restoration
God is about restoration. Peter preaching on the day of Pentecost
understood the outpouring of the Spirit not only in terms of
refreshing but also in terms of *restoration*. He promised that times

of *refreshing* would come from the presence of the Lord before He returns and that He would remain in heaven *'until the times of* **restoration** *of all things, which God has spoken by the mouth of all His holy prophets . . . '* (Acts 3:21 NKJV).

Consequently God pours out His Spirit not only to refresh or to revive, but also to restore. But what is God restoring? It is *'all things, which God has spoken by the mouth of all His holy prophets'* (Acts 3:21 NKJV).

Restoration foreshadowed by the prophets

From the beginning the prophets have foreshadowed a great restoration. The whole book of Joel centres on this theme. Israel, through her backsliding, had come under a divine judgment, but restoration was promised not only by Joel (2:25–26), but by Isaiah (49:6), Jeremiah (30:3, 17–18), Amos (9:11–15), and particularly by Ezekiel who describes the glory of God departing (Ezekiel 10) and then its restoration (Ezekiel 33–48). Ezekiel's vision of the valley of dry bones, Magog, the temple, and the river are all prophetic of the end-time restoration and victory of the church.

But what is God restoring?

Jesus had been raised from the dead. But before He ascended to the Father He stopped-over to be with His disciples. It was on their frail shoulders that the entire destiny of the human race and God's redemptive purpose now rested. You would think this was the opportunity for Jesus to guarantee success. That He would give them the necessary clues on how to 'do church' – how to build powerful programmes, attract the crowds, structure for growth and preach hot sermons. But no – all He did was give them a forty-day crash course on the *kingdom of God!* (Acts 1:3)

From this we can conclude two things: that an understanding of the *kingdom* must be pivotal to the future of Christ's cause; and secondly that we must be on the wrong track!

Surely, the fact that Jesus referred to the *kingdom* fifty-six times in the Gospel of Matthew, but only three times to the *church* should tell us something. Space does not permit us to explore this further, but briefly – the church is not the kingdom. Rather, the church, in God's economy, is only part of the kingdom. Even so, we have minimised the kingdom and centred on the church, making it one of our greatest idolatries. Satan's tactic has always been to replace the *rule of God* with the *rule of the church* – and therefore with institutional religion.

The disciples were no different. Being good Jews they immediately asked, *'Lord, is this the time when you will restore the kingdom to Israel?'* (Acts 1:6 NRSV). Coming out of their Hebrew prophetic tradition they possessed an expectation of a restored messianic kingdom – a golden age of God's righteousness and peace. But they misunderstood its nature, viewing it along *institutional* and *national-elitist* lines, looking for a Jewish Messiah who would deliver them from Roman tyranny. However, it was not until Paul's revelation of the gospel that Christ's kingdom was understood to be the reverse – in fact to be *spiritual* and *universal*.

Even so, the disciple's expectation of the imminent restoration of the kingdom was valid. Ezekiel, during the Babylonian captivity, prophesied of a future new covenant restoration of the kingdom as the return of Eden's paradise:

> *'Thus says the Lord GOD, "On the day that I cleanse you from all your iniquities, I will cause the cities to be inhabited, and the waste places will be rebuilt ... And they will say, 'This desolate land has become like the garden of Eden; and the waste, desolate, and ruined cities are fortified and inhabited.' Then the nations that are left round about you will know that I, the LORD, have rebuilt the ruined places and planted that which was desolate; I, the LORD, have spoken and will do it."'*   (Ezekiel 36:33–36 NASB)

The restoration of the kingdom will return humanity to the open communion enjoyed by our first parents. In the book of Revelation a restored Eden is symbolised by the *'tree of life'* and the *'river of the water of life'* flowing from under *'the throne'*. The Spirit of God will flow like a river to the nations, healing them from the effects and ravages of sin, reshaping the world into a kingdom paradise (Revelation 22:1–3).

Weymouth, translating Ephesians 1:10, picks up this Messianic promise of the kingdom, explaining that God's purpose is, 'for the government of the world when the times are ripe for it – the purpose which He has cherished in His own mind of *restoring the whole creation* to find its one Head in Christ'.

Fulfilled in the church

However, before we can fully understand the *restoration* promises of the Old Testament we need to discuss briefly the interpretation of Old Testament prophecy.[1] Prophecy can have a double application – first to the immediate circumstances of Israel and second to the larger eschatological (end-time) reality of Christ and His church. We must understand that the restoration prophecies were never fully satisfied in the post-exilic history of Israel. The promised glory of the latter house, for example, being greater than the former (Haggai 2:9)[2] was never literally fulfilled in their return from Babylon. The temple, rebuilt under the leadership of Ezra and Nehemiah, and later under the Herods, never equalled the former glory of Solomon's temple. While the prophecies of a kingdom restoration have received a measure of fulfilment in the deliverance of Israel from Babylon and the post-exilic restoration of the temple, they are not fully satisfied until Messianic times in Christ and His church.

Peter, speaking to the New Testament church explained that

> '... *the prophets, who spoke of the grace that was to come to you*, searched intently and with the greatest care, trying to find out the time and circumstances to which the Spirit of Christ in them was pointing when he **predicted the sufferings of Christ and the glories that would follow**. It was revealed to them that **they were not serving themselves but you**, when they spoke of the things that have now been told you by those who have preached the gospel to you by the Holy Spirit sent from heaven.'
>
> (1 Peter 1:10–12 NIV)

The prophets did not fully understand *'the time and circumstances to which the Spirit of Christ in them was pointing'*. In addition to speaking to their own time, they were speaking through the entire Old Testament economy, not only as prophecy but also as a type (Colossians 2:27; Hebrews 8:5; 10:1)[3] of the *'sufferings of Christ and the glories that would follow'*. The prophecies of restoration, therefore, reach their climax in *'the sufferings of Christ'*. And more particularly in what Peter describes as, *'the glories that would follow'* – the outpouring of the Spirit in the church, and her last-day deliverance from spiritual Babylon. Therefore as the prophet declared, *'the glory of the latter house'* – the new covenant church – would be *'greater than the former'* – the old covenant church (Haggai 2:9).

Israel and the church – first the natural, then the spiritual
One of the principles of God's economy is that of 'first the natural then the spiritual' (1 Corinthians 15:46). The *natural* prefigures the *spiritual*. In this sense, *natural* Israel serves as a type

and shadow – the anti-type and substance being found in the *spiritual* Israel – the church of the new covenant, in which there is neither Jew nor Gentile (Galatians 3:28; Ephesians 2:11; 3:6). Paul alludes to this when he refers to the 'new creation' as the 'Israel of God' in which natural circumcision is of no account (Galatians 6:16).[4] 'The circumcision', by his reckoning, are those *'who worship by the Spirit of God, who glory in Christ Jesus, and who put no confidence in the flesh'* (Philippians 3:3 NIV).

Circumcision is no longer *outward* and *natural* – but *inward* and *spiritual*:

> *'A man is not a Jew if he is only one outwardly, nor is circumcision merely outward and physical. No, a man is a Jew if he is one inwardly; and circumcision is circumcision of the heart, by the Spirit, not by the written code.'*   (Romans 2:28–29 NIV)

So who is a true Jew? According to Paul he is not one born *naturally by the flesh*, but *inwardly by the Spirit*. The natural precedes and prefigures the spiritual. Therefore, as Paul says, *'For not all who are descended from Israel are Israel'* (Romans 9:6 NIV). One is *natural* – the other, *spiritual*.

'First the natural' – an interpretative principle

There is much confusion surrounding the relationship of Israel and the church. This principle of 'first the natural then the spiritual' is integral to our understanding of it. It shows that the relationship is primarily typological as Israel foreshadowed the future reality of the church.

'First the natural then the spiritual' is an important *interpretative principle*, and is used by the writer to the Hebrews. Addressed to the first generation of Hebrew believers it is an exhortation to fully transition from the old to the new covenant. In comparing and contrasting the new economy with the old, the writer juxtaposes *natural* and *spiritual* Israel:

> *'But you have come to Mount Zion, to the **heavenly Jerusalem**, the city of the living God. You have come to thousands upon thousands of angels in joyful assembly, to the **church** ... '*
> (Hebrews 12:22–23 NIV)

Natural (earthly) Jerusalem, or Zion, serves as a type, prefiguring the *spiritual* (heavenly) Jerusalem – the church. Therefore the prophetic promises given to *natural* Israel find their fulfilment in the *spiritual* Israel as the seed of Abraham (Galatians 3:29).

There is, therefore, both continuity and discontinuity between Israel and the church. Continuity in the *natural* finding its fulfilment in the *spiritual*. Discontinuity in the *spiritual* crowning and completing all that the *natural* prefigured. All the kingdom promises of God are now climaxed through His church in which there is neither Jew nor Greek:

> *'His intent was that **now, through the church**, the manifold wisdom of God should be made known to the rulers and authorities in the heavenly realms, according to his eternal purpose which he accomplished in Christ Jesus our Lord.'*
>
> (Ephesians 3:10–11 NIV)

Israel destined for revival – a blessing to the nations

Paul predicts, however, that *natural* Israel has a glorious future as they come to their 'fullness' in the *spiritual*. Israel is destined to experience a massive end-time revival and in-gathering as part of the *'one new man'* – the body of Christ, in which the *'dividing wall of hostility'* between Jew and Gentile is destroyed (Ephesians 2:14–17 NIV). Paul explains,

> *' . . . if their* [i.e. Israel's] *transgression means riches for the world, and their loss means riches for the Gentiles, how much greater riches will their **fulness** bring!'*
>
> (Romans 11:11–12 NIV)

Not only does Paul promise that *'all Israel will be saved'* (Romans 11:26), but that their revival and restoration will release even greater blessing to the Gentiles. Because of Israel's unbelief salvation has come to the Gentiles. So if their *'rejection is the reconciliation of the world'* (Romans 11:15a), Paul asks, what can their restoration be but *'life from the dead'*? (Romans 11:15b) – the source of even greater blessing. Their *'fulness'* – their turning to the Lord in repentance and faith – will trigger an unparalleled era of signs and wonders across the nations – a season of the most intensive and extensive outpouring of God's power ever experienced. At this point, with the in-gathering of Israel, the church will be complete, attaining to the fullness of the stature of Christ, experiencing the full manifestation of His resurrection life.

When will Israel experience revival?

The in-gathering of the Jews will climax an extraordinary wave
of global revival. Israel, as a people, will turn to the Lord *after* the
full in-gathering of the Gentiles. Paul explains

> *'that a partial hardening has happened to Israel **until** the fulness*
> *of the Gentiles has come in; and thus all Israel will be saved ...'*
> (Romans 11:25–26 NASB)

The timing of Israel's revival is clear: it is not *'**until** the fulness of
the Gentiles'*. A sweeping revival in Israel and the Jewish diaspora
will climax the in-gathering of the nations. Moved to *'envy'*
(Romans 11:11, 14 NIV) by the powerful transformation of one
city and nation after another they will turn to the Lord. Being
grafted back in through the gospel (Romans 11:23; 2 Corinthians
3:14–16) they will enjoy all the promises of restoration, along
with the Gentiles, as the Israel of God in which there is neither
Jew nor Greek (Galatians 3:28; Ephesians 3:6; Colossians 3:11).
Their inclusion again in the household of faith, swept in by a
wave of world revival, will introduce the most glorious period of
history – when *'the glory of the LORD will cover the earth as the waters
cover the sea'* (Habakkuk 2:14).

Having explained the relationship between Israel and the
church as type and antitype,[5] or as prophecy and fulfilment, we
can now turn to some specific Old Testament prophecies. Rather
than taking them as referring exclusively to natural Israel, using
the interpretative principle of 'first the natural', we will look at
them as speaking through Israel to the church as the climax of
God's redemptive purpose. We will view the revived and restored
body of Christ, including the final in-gathering of the Jews, as
the crowning act of His redemptive purpose and the fulfilment
of the Old Testament restoration promises.

Ezekiel's prophecy of the last day church

Idolatry and the glory of God

Ezekiel was a prophet of the Babylonian captivity. He showed
how idolatry caused the glory of God to lift from the old
covenant church (Ezekiel 8 – 10; 12 – 22). And he foreshadowed
the coming restoration and the return of the glory under the new
covenant (Ezekiel 36; 37) to a new and greater temple, the body

of Christ (Ezekiel 40 – 43), from which the river of God would flow to the healing of the nations (Ezekiel 47; Revelation 22).

His prophecies speak to the glorious restoration of the church in this generation. Like ancient Israel, having lost the glory of God within several generations of its birth the church was in need of revival and reformation. Languishing in its Babylonian captivity, God intervened with what we now call the Reformation. The period of the *'restoration of all things'* was ushered in (Acts 3:21 NASB) – a *kairos*[6] time in which the temple of God, the church, will be restored and filled with the glory of God. In these times of refreshing and restoration the Holy Spirit will increasingly flow like a river to the healing of the nations, bringing the presence of Christ and His justice and peace to the earth (Isaiah 25:7–8).

The veil will be taken from the understanding of this generation. They will see that idolatry has driven the glory of God from His sanctuary and that only repentance will restore it. A new breed of apostles and prophets will arise as powerfully anointed preachers and teachers, calling this generation back to covenant faithfulness – to radical holiness. Filled with the spirit of the fear of the Lord they will, under the authority of the Word of God, declare the prophetic purposes of God over peoples and nations, pronouncing His covenant blessings and judgments with a power unequalled by previous generations.

Idolatry and the new covenant

Living in the light of God's holy love, this new breed of apostles and prophets will expose idolatry as the cause of the church's Babylonian captivity. And as ministers of the new covenant they will bring restoration through the power of the Spirit:

> *' . . . when the people of Israel were living in their own land, they defiled it . . . So I poured out my wrath on them because they . . . had defiled it with their idols. I dispersed them among the nations . . . I will gather you from all the countries and bring you back . . . I will sprinkle clean water on you, and you will be clean; I will cleanse you from all your impurities and from all your idols. I will give you a new heart and put a new spirit in you; I will remove from you your heart of stone and give you a heart of flesh. And I will put my Spirit in you and move you to follow my decrees . . . '*
>
> (Ezekiel 36:17–19, 24–27 NIV)

Consequently a new breed of Christian will arise. Delivered from a *spirit of pride* and cleansed from their idols they will live under an open heaven, enjoying unhindered communion with God and the full manifestation of His power.

Living under this open heaven,

> *'No longer will a man teach his neighbour,*
> *or a man his brother saying, "Know the* LORD,*"*
> *because* **they will all know me**,
> *from the least of them to the greatest.'*
>
> (Jeremiah 31:34; Hebrews 8:11 NIV)

Every human system that dared to usurp Christ's pre-eminence will be removed and the people of God will be free.

The valley of dry bones – personal renewal to corporate reformation

Renewal prepares the way for *reformation*. Immediately after the promise of a new heart and a new spirit of Ezekiel 36 the prophet received the revelation (Ezekiel 37) of the coming together of the body of Christ, the church, according to Ephesians 4.

And so *personal renewal* becomes *corporate reformation*. Ezekiel 37 foreshadows a massive restoration across the world-wide body of Christ as it is raised to life again. With *'bone coming to bone'* (Ezekiel 37:7) there will be a commotion, *'a rattling sound'* (Ezekiel 37:7 NIV), a *'shaking'* (KJV) as the *'noise'* (KJV) of revival and reformation is heard across the earth. True revival is always noisy and chaotic as the power of God shakes the status quo. The familiar contours of church life – of our religious graveyards – will be disturbed. Those who experience personal revival will be uprooted and repositioned as they are drawn into new relationships by the *'ligaments'* (Ephesians 4:16 NIV) of a *'kindred spirit'* (Philippians 2:20 NASB). They will discover the brother or sister they never had, those who have been given a new heart and spirit, who are moved by the heart of God and are 'current' in the *'new thing'* (Isaiah 43:19) He is doing. Old ways and old allegiances will be broken. And as we yield to God in this, moving us from the familiar ruts of the dry valley floor, we will experience divine connections which will lift us to new levels of anointing and effectiveness. These connections are not the old and familiar political alliances motivated by personal advantage, but supernatural connections, orchestrated by sovereign means. The body of Christ will be

> *'. . . joined and held together by every supporting ligament,* [the whole body] *growing and building itself up in love, as each part does its work.'*
> (Ephesians 4:16)

Just when the church looks as though it is spiritually dead – lying where it fell in defeat, dislocated and divided – an awesome display of divine power will raise it to its glorious destiny:

> *'So I prophesied as He commanded me, and the breath came into them, and they came to life, and stood on their feet, an exceedingly great army.'*
> (Ezekiel 37:10 NASB)

Revived and restored to apostolic unity and power the true church will arise as the army of God, triumphing over the enemies of Christ in the power of the Spirit.

No man or movement can organise this – it is the work of God. Many have tried and failed. Just as the Shepherding Movement attempted during the 1970s and 80s, false or carnal apostolic movements will arise presuming to *'steady the ark'* (2 Samuel 6:6). In the name of unity, they will attempt to bring 'order' to the work of God through human control. But no one will be able to lay claim to what only God can do. As Ezekiel prophesied it was the breath of God that came into them, raising them up as a mighty army (Ezekiel 37:10). The end-time restoration of the church is a sovereign work of the Spirit. Be warned, there is no method, model, man, or movement that can produce it. No apostolic or city-reaching strategy will be able to lay claim to what only God can do. Jesus' prayer of John 17 for unity is totally impossible. That is why Jesus prayed it! He knew that man could not do it. And therefore it will only be answered through an extraordinary outpouring of the Spirit, for it is

> *'"Not by might, nor by power, but by my Spirit," says the* L*ORD Almighty.'*
> (Zechariah 4:6 NIV)

Just as the Lord promised, the revival and restoration of the body of Christ – its deliverance from Babylon, and restoration of apostolic unity – will be an act of God.

'... *I am going to open your graves ... I will bring you back ... I*
will put my Spirit in you and you will live ... Then you will know
*that **I the** L*ORD **have spoken, and I have done it** ...'
(Ezekiel 37:12–14 NIV)

The restoration of David's tabernacle

Every outpouring of the Spirit signals a transition from an old
order to the new. And it usually creates conflict.

In obedience to a vision, Peter's groundbreaking visit to
Cornelius (Acts 10) shook the status quo, taking the gospel and
the outpouring of the Spirit beyond its original Jewish confines.
But some Jews demanded that the new Gentile believers submit
to circumcision, and therefore to a ritual law for salvation. In
effect they were saying, *'The old way of doing it is God's way!'* How
was this *'new thing'* (Isaiah 43:19) to be understood? It was totally
outside their frame of reference, it flew in the face of religious
protocol – in fact from where they sat you could not come to
God outside of their revelation. To put it colloquially, it was
either their way or the highway!

To resolve the issue the apostles and elders gathered in
Jerusalem. After hearing Peter's testimony of the outpouring of
the Spirit on the Gentiles, and after much heated debate, James
stood up and resolved the problem by reading from the prophet
Amos:

'The words of the prophets are in agreement with this [i.e. with
Peter's experience of the Gentile outpouring], *as it is written,*

*"After this **I will return***
    *and rebuild David's fallen tent.***
*Its ruins I will rebuild,***
    *and I will restore it,***
    that the remnant of men may seek the Lord,
    and all the Gentiles who bear my name ..."'
(Acts 15:15–17 NIV)

James interpreted the 'new thing' that God was doing (the
outpouring of the Spirit on the Gentiles) as the *restoration of*
David's tabernacle.

But what does the *restoration of David's tabernacle* actually
mean?

Transition to a new order – a time for change!

David's tabernacle signifies a *transition to a new order*. The Ark of God's presence, which had been lost, was not restored to Moses' but to David's tabernacle. The restoration of God's presence represents a new order of things. The old order of Moses' tabernacle had forfeited the Ark under the spiritually delinquent leadership of Eli (1 Samuel 2). And so when the time for its restoration arrived, the Ark did not return to the old structure but to a new one – to David's tabernacle. New wine requires new wineskins. The Holy Spirit inevitably breaks out despite our best attempts to domesticate Him through personal or denominational agendas. He cannot be contained or tamed by our religious cultures – He is the omnipotent God and the creative power behind the universe! Renewal always creates revolution, moving us on from old ways and old structures.

Despite this, the old structure of Moses' tabernacle stood for another thirty-five to forty years until the building of Solomon's Temple. There was an overlap between the old and the new – a period of transition. In fact David appointed priests and worship leaders from the new order of his tabernacle to minister in the old (1 Chronicles 16:37–43; 21:28–30; 2 Chronicles 1:1–6). God always provides a *window of transition* as the old decreases and the new increases (John 3:30) – a lead-time before the old is superseded by the new. Moses' tabernacle, whose worship was previously silent, enjoyed the renewal of its worship under David's new priesthood. God has been visiting the old order of the institutional church for the last thirty-five to forty years through the Charismatic Renewal, the 'Third Wave', and the 'Toronto Blessing', bringing renewal and giving lead-time.

But now is the time for change. There is a shifting in the heavenlies. The lead-time is rapidly expiring as the church steps into an acceleration of God's purposes. Within every *window of transition* there is a *kairos* moment – a moment of intersection as the new order eclipses the old – a point of no return. We cannot stay with the old order forever. Although it has enjoyed the benefits of renewed worship the Ark has moved on. While we need to learn from what God did in the past, like the scribe of the kingdom who brings out things both old and new (Matthew 13:52) we must commit to following the Ark of God's presence, no matter where it leads. David did not become the curator of a religious museum – of Moses' tabernacle. The only thing that transferred from Moses' to David's tabernacle was the Ark of the

Covenant, nothing else. All the familiar patterns were gone – all the old securities and structures were finished with. But the one thing that did not change was the *Ark of God's presence* and His *covenant character*. He is the one who declared, *'I am the* LORD *and I change not'* (Malachi 3:6 KJV).

All else is shifting sand. Everything that can be shaken will be shaken – everything temporal – even structures that were raised up under the design of God for a previous generation. We have no choice but to leave the security of the past and pursue the Ark of His manifest presence.

While the old order has been enjoying a season of renewal, God has been preparing the new order – an *underground church*. Hidden from the eye of the old institutions, those with a *heart of David*, have been trained in their *caves of Adullam*, (1 Samuel 22:1; 2 Samuel 23:13)[7] – in places of anonymity and suffering, ready for a day of promotion in the Spirit. God holds them under wraps until a chosen moment in history. They are those who are in distress and in debt – those who have been marginalised by the old order of human power – those viewed as dissenters and discontents but who in the timing of God emerge as David's mighty men – as the leaders of the new kingdom order:

> *'But God chose the foolish things of the world to shame the wise; God chose the weak things of the world to shame the strong. He chose the lowly things of this world and the despised things – and the things that are not – to nullify the things that are, so that no-one may boast before him.'*   (1 Corinthians 1:27–29 NIV)

In the next five to ten years we will see *alternative forms of church and worship*, after the heart of David, filled with an *uncontrolled spiritual passion* that will be used of God to reach a new generation. It won't be new methods of church growth but a new spirit of radical holiness, of worship – with a passion for the presence of God. As a kingdom counter-culture, house churches, underground youth churches and alternative forms of ministry will restore true spirituality. Like a vine growing over a wall they will transcend every man-made boundary, extending into previously unreached people groups – to the poor and the disenfranchised of this world. They will break the patterns and protocols of the religious system to touch God and reach their generation.

Restoration of God's manifest presence – the defeat of the programme idol!

David's tabernacle signifies the *restoration of God's manifest presence*. As mentioned previously, the Ark of God's presence had been lost under Eli's priesthood, captured in battle by the Philistines. The news killed Eli. His daughter-in-law immediately gave birth, naming her son *Ichabod*, meaning, 'the glory has departed'. From then on, throughout Samuel's ministry and Saul's kingship, Israel was without the Ark – without the manifest presence of God. It was not until David's reign that the Ark was restored.

Tragically, David's first attempt to bring back the Ark failed. Loading it onto the back of a new cart, he presumed to restore the presence of God in his own strength and with his own methods. The oxen stumbled and Uzza, who was assisting, instinctively reached out to steady it. In a flash he was struck down! Confused, David fled, leaving the Ark in the care of Obed-Edom; he did not return for another three months. During that time he sought the Lord, coming to the realisation that,

> *'We did not enquire of him about **how to do it** in the prescribed way.'*
> (1 Chronicles 15:13 NIV)

Evidently God is very particular about *how* we do His work. God's *work* is to be done God's *way* – not ours. Our good intentions and good ideas are not good enough. We feel that if we are sincere or creative God will be happy but unfortunately we can be *sincerely* and *creatively* wrong. We build our 'new carts' – our new programmes and strategies – and think all we need to do is get the wheels turning – get the programmes going and the wheels of religious activity moving, and God will be pleased. But no – He was angered (1 Chronicles 13:10). Why? Because we are trusting in the machinery of ministry – in our own plans and programmes rather than in Him.

So how was the Ark to be restored? On the shoulders of the *priests* (1 Chronicles 15:11–15). God uses *men* (and women) not *methods*. He puts His treasure in earthen vessels – in people. But only in a particular kind of person – the *Levites* and the *priests* – those who have been separated by the anointing to minister to Him. The only way the Ark of His presence will be restored is on the shoulders of those who stand before Him in their priestly ministry, offering the spiritual sacrifices of a consecrated life –

and of intercessory prayer and worship (1 Peter 2:5). They are those who with a heart of worship, separate themselves to spend time alone with Him, refusing to be distracted by the madding crowd of pressing things – not content until they are soaking in His presence and even then still hungry for more. They are those who with a pure heart and clean hands wait on Him for who He *is*, not for what He *does*. They will achieve things in the spirit realm, and therefore on earth, that those using human methods never can.

Restoration of true spiritual authority – the defeat of the ministry idol!

David's tabernacle typifies the restoration of *true spiritual authority*. Jesus, as the son of David, is the fulfilment of that type.

Jesus' authority did not come from the religious system, but from the incarnation of truth:

> *'And the Word ... became flesh (human, incarnate) and **tabernacled** (fixed His tent of flesh, lived a while) among us; and we [actually] saw His glory (His honor, His majesty), such glory as an only begotten son receives from his father, full of grace ... and truth.'*　　　　　　　　　　　(John 1:14 Amplified)

It was living out of the brokenness of a heart-relationship with the Father that gave Jesus His authority (see John 5:19, 30; 8:42). It was therefore a *spiritual* authority, not dependent on the structures or systems of men. It was an *incarnational* authority, rather than *positional*.

Likewise David's authority emanated from his heart-communion with God. He spoke out of that passion when, as newly anointed king, he announced to the people,

> *'Let us bring the ark of our God back to us, for we did not enquire of it during the reign of Saul.'*　　　(1 Chronicles 13:3 NIV)

But Saul, by contrast, when he had the opportunity as king, neglected to promote the presence of God altogether. The reason? It was not a consideration in his personal life. As a leader, *private passion* usually determines *public policy*. His soul was not towards the Lord which became evident as his reign unfolded. On the other hand, David's first concern as king was to prepare a place for the presence of God. Because he had already developed a *heart of worship* in private, it was the most natural thing to promote the presence of God in public. What I would describe as *the trembling heart of worship* became the exclusive source of his authority with God and with his people.

Saul's authority was fixed in human strength. He typifies the *human government* of the old order. He was *'an impressive young man without equal'* (1 Samuel 9:2a NIV) and *'from his shoulders and up he was taller than any of the people'* (1 Samuel 9:2b NASB). The religious system is impressed by appearances – by worldly values – by human stature and strength. Saul was a *head* and *shoulders* man who used his natural reasoning (head) and natural strength (shoulders) to do the work of God.

Space doesn't permit a full study of Saul's life and leadership. However, the root cause for his loss of the kingdom was an *unbroken self-life*. Even when Saul was 'eyeballed' by the prophet Samuel for his blatant disobedience in sacrificing the best of the flock, he persistently defended himself, deflecting the truth by blame-shifting. Samuel responded with a frightening pronouncement:

> *'Does the* LORD *delight in burnt offerings and sacrifices as much in obeying the voice of the* LORD*? To obey is better than sacrifice, and to heed is better than the fat of rams. For rebellion is like the sin of divination, and arrogance like the evil of idolatry. Because you have rejected the word of the* LORD*, he has rejected you as king.'*
> (1 Samuel 15:22–23 NIV)

Saul offered a sacrifice to God from *self*-will. This seemingly spiritual act was done in *'stubbornness'* or *'rebellion'* (NKJV), which Samuel explained, in fact, as *'idolatry'* and *'witchcraft'*. What is Samuel saying? He is saying that *ministry* (our service to God) *can become idolatry and witchcraft! Self*-will is a satanic principle, whether it is exercised in gross sin or in the service of God:

> *'Not everyone who says to Me, "Lord, Lord," will enter the kingdom of heaven; but he who does the will of My Father who is in heaven. Many will say to Me on that day, "Lord, Lord, did we not prophesy in Your name, and in Your name cast out demons, and in Your name perform many miracles?" And then I will declare to them, "I never knew you;* DEPART FROM ME, YOU WHO PRACTICE LAWLESSNESS.*" '* (Matthew 7:21–23 NASB)

It is possible to prophesy, cast out demons and move in the miraculous in disobedience to the Father – it is possible to *'practice lawlessness'* in the things of the Spirit and to be without restraint in the work of God! To habitually do ministry out of self-will and rebellion!

How can this be? The gifts of God are irrevocable (Romans 11:29). They are not given or retained because of our good works or behaviour. They are a grace gift – a *charisma*, freely bestowed on the same grounds as salvation: independently of character, by grace, through faith (Ephesians 2:8). Consequently the work of God can be led by those who lead out of *charisma* at the expense of *character* – those who may pay lip service to the lordship of Christ but do their own thing – who in fact operate in a spirit of rebellion and witchcraft.

Witchcraft and idolatry are, according to Paul, both *'works of the flesh'* (Galatians 5:20). However, exercising leadership in the flesh, in human strength – as in the case of Saul – eventually gives ground to demonic oppression and ultimately to kingdom dispossession. Saul was overtaken by an evil spirit and the kingdom passed to David (1 Samuel 16:14–16, 23; 18:10). Eventually the government of God lifts from Saul's leadership and rests on another. It is eclipsed by a new order.

However, before David's new order leadership could emerge, he served the old order (1 Samuel 16:21) honouring Saul (1 Samuel 24:5–6) but trusting in the Lord for promotion (2 Samuel 5:12; 1 Chronicles 14:2). Even so, the anointing transferred to David, despite Saul's continuing but temporary position as king (1 Samuel 16:13–14). This time of transition between the old and the new tested David's walk with God. The anointing lifted from Saul's life, an evil spirit tormented him, and he was moved to jealousy and fear at David's evident favour with God (1 Samuel 18:10–14). Now, demonically driven, it was not long before he attempted to take David's life (1 Samuel 19:9–10), leading to David's fugitive existence and wilderness years. His patron and mentor who possessed the power to lift him to the throne, driven by a murderous jealousy, was now his enemy. Despite the lie of his current circumstances, David, as a seventeen-year-old youth, had been anointed for the kingship. Now he had to trust the Lord to bring it to pass.

True spiritual authority does not come from a *position* – it comes from God's *presence* through times of *pressure* – from the crucible of wilderness testing. Jesus, the son of David, having learned obedience, emerged from the wilderness in the power of the Spirit – with true spiritual authority (Luke 4:14). The prince of this world, Satan, could find nothing in Him (John 14:30). There was nothing in Jesus that answered to the spirit of the world. So too with David. God used the isolation and injustice of his straitened circumstances to purify his inner life – to humble him and draw him further into Himself. In contrast to Saul's unbroken self-life David embraced the dealings of God that caused him to inherit the kingdom – the dealings that produced the one sacrifice that God will not despise – the sacrifice of *'a broken and contrite heart'* (Psalm 51:17 NIV). Brokenness is the only ground of true spiritual authority. The kingdom belongs to the poor in spirit (Matthew 5:3).

Restoration of true worship – the defeat of the worship idol!

David's tabernacle typifies the restoration of *true worship*. God is stirring the heart of this generation to pursue a passion for Him after the spirit and structure of David's tabernacle. All over the world we are beginning to see a resurgence of 24/7 intercessory worship. From a 6th-century Bangor, Ireland monastery to the 18th-century Herrnhut ('the Lord's Watch') in Saxony with the Moravians and now to this generation, God has raised up the sound of 24/7 worship. David set apart musicians and singers who ministered to the Lord around the clock (1 Chronicles 9:33; 15:16–22; 25:1–31; Psalm 134:1).

But it is one thing to restore the *structure*, it is another to restore the *spirit* of David's tabernacle. Amos prophesied its restoration during a time marked by prosperity and spiritual decline. While on the one hand, the people's military and economic strength increased, on the other their spiritual life decreased. Seduced by the surrounding idolatry they worshipped both God and Baal, superficially maintaining their ritual worship but secretly having deeply defected. Prosperity had lulled them into a false sense of security until they were rudely awakened by the word of the Lord:

> *'I hate, I despise your religious feasts;*
> *I cannot stand your assemblies.*
> *Even though you bring me burnt offerings and grain offerings,*
> *I will not accept them.*
> *Though you bring choice fellowship offerings,*
> *I will have no regard for them.*

> *Away with the noise of your songs!*
>   *I will not listen to the music of your harps.*
> *But let justice roll on like a river,*
>   *righteousness like a never-failing stream!'*
>
> (Amos 5:21–24 NIV)

Our services, seminars, concerts and conferences, the noise of our chorus singing and music can all offend the heart of God. We are mistaken to think that worship consists of our creativity and professionalism, our presentation of music or preaching. Worship has little to do with *public performance* and everything to do with *private purity*. It emanates from the *private pain* of surrender – it is the fragrance of a life abandoned to God. A life lived for His pleasure. It is what the Father is searching for, and the only thing that will satisfy Him (John 4:21–24). It has nothing to do with our musical expertise, album sales or artistic success and everything to do with the *private pleasure* of being abandoned to the Father's love.

I recently visited the website of a major Christian publisher. They were conducting a survey of churches with the question emblazoned across the top of the page: *'Are the seats in your church comfortable?'* I was taken-aback. 'Honestly!' I thought, 'Who cares!' But obviously someone does – why else would they be asking? Anaesthetised by our post-war affluence and the afterglow of a bygone Christian era we are unaware of how far we have fallen. Apart from God giving us a revelation of His own holy nature, we have no yardstick by which to measure the church, or the culture. Fortunately, though, this is exactly what is happening. God is bringing back the plumbline of worship *'as it used to be'* (Amos 9:11; Acts 15:16). Worship not according to our traditional patterns or even our contemporary culture, but according to the tabernacle of David.

So what does this mean? To have worship restored as it was under David's tabernacle for Amos's generation and for ours, means to be cleansed of idolatry – to have our hearts fixed on the Lord (Psalm 57:7 KJV) – to worship only Him. As David so poignantly asked –

> *'Who may ascend the hill of the* LORD*?*
>   *Who may stand in his holy place?*
> *He who has clean hands and a pure heart,*
>   *who does not lift up his soul to an idol*
>   *or swear by what is false.'*   (Psalm 24:3–4 NIV)

Every false allegiance and affection – every false god – was thrown to the ground in David's passion and pursuit of the true and living God. It means laying down every priority, agenda and value system that is contrary to the heart and character of God.

As the *'anointed ... sweet psalmist of Israel'* (2 Samuel 23:1), David, was above all else a true worshipper. Expressed in worship he possessed a thirst for the living God. He learned in his youth to commune with God in the solitariness of his father's sheep fields. Before moving the hearts of men as the great warrior-king his heart was first moved by God in the secret place. He desired only one thing – to be in His presence, near to the heart of God. He knew how to 'waste' time with the Lord – to seek His face and to gaze on His beauty. It became the secret of David's power. And he learned, therefore, to trust in the Lord, who through life's troubles proved Himself to be a secure stronghold. The Lord, through experience, became David's refuge and strength. Even in his youth David had become so attuned to God's heart as a worshipper that the Lord could say of him, *'I have found David ... a man after my own heart'* (Acts 13:22 NIV).

But David was not only a worshipper – he was a *warrior-king*. To have worship restored like it was under David suggests there are heights of praise and worship – that there is a way of being near to the heart of God that will be a weapon of warfare to cast down demonic powers over whole cities and nations (Psalm 149). True worship after the heart of David, I believe, will release the presence of God into the nations, displacing every demonic power until history finally declares, *'The kingdoms of this world have become the kingdom of our Lord and of his Christ ... '* (Revelation 11:15). In other words – until the completion of the great commission.

Completion of the great commission – winning back planet earth!
Lastly, the restoration of David's tabernacle signals the *completion of the great commission*:

> *'I will ...*
>   *rebuild David's fallen tent ...*
>   *and I will restore it,*
> *that the remnant of men may seek the Lord,*
>   *and all the Gentiles who bear my name.'*

(Acts 15:16–17 NIV)

Through the restoration of David's tabernacle, God's redemptive purpose for the earth will be accomplished. David prophesied that,

> '***All the ends of the earth***
> ***will remember and turn to the*** Lord,
> *and all the families of the nations*
> *will bow down before him,*
> *for dominion belongs to the* Lord
> *and he rules over the nations.'*   (Psalm 22:27–28 NIV)

As a prophet David saw down through the ages to the time when Jesus, as the son of David, would harvest the nations in the power of the Spirit. There is no room in David's prophetic reach for the defeat of the gospel or the defeat of Christ's body on earth (Psalm 110; Acts 2:34–35; Hebrews 10:13; 1 Corinthians 15:25).

Charles Haddon Spurgeon, the great 19th-century London preacher, was of the same mind:

> 'David was not a believer in the theory that the world will grow worse and worse, and that the dispensation will wind up with general darkness, and idolatry. Earth's sun is to go down amid tenfold night if some of our prophetic brethren are to be believed. Not so do we expect, but we look for a day when the dwellers in all lands shall learn righteousness, shall trust in the saviour, shall worship thee alone ... The modern notion has greatly damped the zeal of the church ... and the sooner it is to be shown unscriptural the better for the cause of God. It neither consorts with prophecy, honours God, nor inspires the church with ardour. Far hence be it driven.'[8]

Any prophetic scheme that robs the church of her revival destiny, the gospel of its power, or Christ of His victory in this present age must be seen for what it is – a delusion of demonic design, sent to disrupt the advance of the kingdom of God on earth.

Again quoting Spurgeon, referring to the power and destiny of the gospel in transforming the planet, he said,

> '... many in the Church are giving up the idea of it except on the occasion of the advent of Christ, which as it chimes

in with our own idleness, is likely to be a popular doctrine. I myself believe that King Jesus will reign, and the idols be utterly abolished; but I expect the same power which turned the world upside down once will still continue to do it. The Holy Ghost would never suffer the imputation to rest upon His holy name that He was not able to convert the world.'[9]

We have conveniently put off the final victory of Christ until the Second Coming, and forgotten that it was His first coming that conquered death and hell – that broke the power of sin and purchased men for God. We have forgotten that it was not the Second Coming, but His first that signalled the beginning of His reign, releasing the mighty rivers of His Spirit into the first-century world and bringing heaven to earth. And we have especially forgotten that the victory of His first coming mandates us to disciple whole nations (Matthew 18:18–20). Jesus has already destroyed the works of the evil one (1 John 3:8; Hebrews 2:14). We have already been given authority over the devil (Matthew 10:1) and commanded to occupy until He comes (Luke 19:13 KJV). We are not looking to the Second Coming for what the first coming has already achieved. Rather we look to the Second Coming as the awesome climax of what God in Christ has done through the cross, and is doing progressively through powerful outpourings of His Spirit. Let us be clear: Christ's kingdom *has come definitively*, through His ascension to the Father; *is coming progressively*, through increased outpourings of the Spirit; and *will come consummately*, at the glorious climax of history – at the Second Coming of Christ.

He will return for a worshipping Bride – a perfect and mature church, moving in the restoration of David's tabernacle, and experiencing the full realisation of all He purchased at the cross (Ephesians 4:13; 5:27). At this glorious climax she will offer to Him a world renewed in the power of the kingdom (Matthew 13:33; 1 Corinthians 15:24–25).

Let's now discover the key to winning back planet earth.

Chapter 12

Redeeming the Planet

'Then I saw in the right hand of him who sat on the throne
a scroll with ... seven seals ...'
(Revelation 5:1)

John, the writer of Revelation, saw into heaven – into the throne room. And in the hand of the One sitting on the throne was a scroll sealed with seven seals. The question echoed throughout heaven and earth,

'Who is worthy to break the seals and open the scroll?'
(Revelation 5:2 NIV)

But there was no one. John, broken, wept until finally the only one worthy was found. He was *'the Lion of the tribe of Judah, the Root of David ...'* (Revelation 5:5). And immediately John saw a Lamb standing in the centre of the throne. The Lamb took the scroll from the hand of Him who sat on the throne at which the four living creatures and the twenty-four elders fell down and worshipped (Revelation 5:6–8).

The atmosphere of heaven was filled with portent. The only one worthy to open the scroll had been found. Ceremoniously presented with the sacred document the whole of heaven and earth paused, awaiting its opening. But what was it – what did it mean – what was the significance of this momentous event?

The new covenant – title-deed to the planet

The scroll – the *biblion*, is nothing less than *the title deed to a redeemed planet*.[1] The fact that it was a *biblion* and closed with seven seals told John's Asiatic audience that it was a testament – a

covenant.[2] In their day, when the testator died it was ceremoniously and publicly unsealed, read aloud, and then executed.
The seven seals signify that the document is the promise of a
future inheritance – a coming kingdom. Its intent, signed and
sealed in ages past, is now to be carried out. Its presentation in
heaven declares that Christ is now receiving His inheritance as
redeemer and ruler of the earth (Psalms 2; 110). He is the Lion of
Judah, the Root of David – both regal titles – He is the King
of kings, and the Lamb of God.

This covenant-document was written *'on both sides'* (Revelation 5:1 NIV). The tables of the Law were also inscribed in
duplicate, front and back (Exodus 32:15), and then placed in
the Ark of the Covenant – in the presence of God's glory (Exodus
25:16, 21; 40:20; Deuteronomy 10:2). This was in accordance
with ancient eastern custom when a victorious king would
impose a treaty-covenant on the vanquished. Two copies of the
treaty, one for each party, would be drawn up as a legal
document and presented in the house of their god as a witness.
The relationship between the two, the victorious king and the
vassal, was then governed by the terms of that covenant.

The great commandment – key to relationship with God

The implications of this are staggering. Back in Chapter 10, we
saw how God relates to His people through covenant. Christ has
not revoked the Law and the Prophets – rather He has fulfilled
them and summed them up in the *shema* of Deuteronomy 6
from which He proclaimed the great commandment:

> ' "*Love the Lord your God with all your heart and with all your
> soul and with all your mind.*" *This is the first and greatest
> commandment. And the second is like it: "Love your neighbour as
> yourself." All the Law and the Prophets hang on these two
> commandments.*'　　　　(Matthew 22:37–40 NIV)

The covenant summed up in the great commandment is a
romance, first with God and secondly with one another. In
Christ, God has made a covenant with the earth – with individuals, churches, cities and nations. And just as the treaty-
covenant of ancient kings gave a foundation for their dealings
together so the *new covenant*, encapsulated in the great commandment, has become the *touchstone* for how God relates to us.

God also dealt with Israel, the old covenant church, based on the
same commandment – the *shema*. It was their marriage covenant
with Yahweh. God's nature did not change with the transition
from the old to the new covenant. He is still a holy God who
reaches out with His redeeming love-covenant to His creation.
But if we forsake Him and give our affections to other gods – to
other lovers – then there are covenant consequences. Remedial
dealings are sent from God into our lives as individuals, families,
churches and nations. These are brought by the Father of
compassion and mercy as a discipline (Hebrews 12:1–12), not
to destroy us but to bring us back to Him – to restore us to the
intimacy and purity of covenant-love:

> ' *"I am with you and will save you,"*
>   declares the LORD.
> *"Though I completely destroy all the nations*
>   *among which I scatter you,*
>   **I will not completely destroy you.**
> **I will discipline you but only with justice;**
>   *I will not let you go entirely unpunished.'*
>
> (Jeremiah 30:11 NIV)

The great commandment – key to the glory of God

The Ark of the Covenant and the glory of God

The Ark of the Covenant was so named because it contained the
covenant. A box-shaped receptacle approximately 4 feet long
and 2 feet deep, it carried the two tables of the Law – the
covenant stipulations – and was covered with a blood-sprinkled
mercy seat over which the *shekinah* glory hovered under the
watchful gaze and outstretched wings of two golden cherubim.

What a beautiful picture of how God manifests His presence.
The love-covenant, the great commandment, was broken by our
unfaithfulness, bringing us under the sanctions of God's holy
law. But through the shedding of blood, mercy not only covers
the violated covenant but also renews it. And now, like the eyes
of the cherubim, the gaze of heaven is fixed not on the broken
covenant and its curses, but on the sprinkled blood of the mercy
seat. The blood of Christ covers our sins, we receive the Father's
mercy, and the love-covenant is renewed. God's holiness is
satisfied, our love relationship is restored, and the Father's glory
is manifest.

Glory and government

God not only *reveals* Himself but *rules* from between the wings of the cherubim – from the Ark of the Covenant – He is the one who '*sits* **enthroned** *between the cherubim*' (Psalm 80:1).

God *governs* His creation by covenant – blessing or cursing according to whether or not the love-covenant, the great commandment, is obeyed. John's vision of the Lion of Judah, the Root of David standing in the throne and opening the seals of the covenant speaks of *God's government*. The Lion, David, and the throne are all symbols of rulership. Through obedience to the covenant Israel would possess the land and rule – through disobedience they would be dispossessed and enslaved. We either rule in life through Christ, or are defeated, depending on whether we keep the terms of the covenant. We are either given territory to rule over or denied territory, according to our love-relationship with Jesus.

The covenant document presented to the Lamb of Revelation 5 was none other than the *new covenant*. It is nothing less than the title-deed to the planet. But it has conditions. And they are two-fold: *to love the Lord with all that is within us; and love our neighbour as ourselves*. Our obedience to these will unseal the church's title deed to a redeemed earth. If she responds to the romancing of her heavenly Bridegroom, and out of a heart ravished by Him loves her neighbour as herself then she will receive the blessing of the covenant – *glory* and *government* – nothing less than the glory of God and the government of the world.

When the seals of the *new covenant* were opened, and the inheritance received, the elders and the living creatures fell down before the Lamb – the King, and worshipped, singing a new song,

> 'You are worthy to take the scroll
>   and to open its seals,
> because you were slain,
>   and with your blood you purchased men for God
>   from every tribe and language and people and nation.
> You have made them to be **a kingdom and priests**
>   to serve our God,
>   **and they will reign on the earth**.'
>
> (Revelation 5:9–10 NIV)

The worshipping Bride, harvested from every tribe, language, people and nation will rule on the earth as king-priests. As *priests*, loving the Lord through worship and intercession, they will enter the blessings of the covenant and rule as *kings*.

The glory departs and returns because of the covenant

John was not the only one shown the scroll – the covenant document. Ezekiel also saw a scroll, written on both sides with *'words of lament and mourning and woe'* (Ezekiel 2:10), which he was then commanded to eat. This was the covenant with its *sanctions* – its remedial judgments (lament, mourning and woe) for Israel's unfaithfulness. Only after eating and digesting it was he able to go and speak to the house of Israel. The love-covenant is the heart of the prophetic oracle. Without experiencing the impassioned heart of the divine lover the prophet is not qualified to speak. He was to show Israel that their idolatries were wounds to the heart of an aggrieved lover, and that their unfaithfulness to the Lord and His covenant caused the glory of God to depart. It was the cause of their defeat and their captivity. According to Deuteronomy 28 and Leviticus 26, these 'woes' were merely the consequence of violating their love-relationship with Yahweh.

However, God always relates to us in a redemptive way. After proclaiming God's holiness in the face of Israel's idolatry, and interpreting their misfortunes through the covenant, Ezekiel received a vision of the glory of God returning to a greater temple, far larger and superior to anything they had ever seen (Ezekiel 40–43). Some have said this temple (Ezekiel's temple) will be a literal one built by Israel during the millennium. But will the God who has gone on record as saying He does not dwell in temples made by human hands (Acts 7:48) be satisfied with a house of bricks and mortar? Neither is He likely to be impressed with a reversion to an old covenant that has been fulfilled by one that is declared a better covenant with better promises (Hebrews 8:6; see also Isaiah 1:10–12; 66:3). In Chapter 10 we explored in detail why Ezekiel's prophecies speak of the last-day glory of the church. Ezekiel's temple described in chapters 40 – 43 is a picture of none other than the restored church – the mature body of Christ grown to the fullness of Christ's own stature. But the glory returns to Ezekiel's end-time temple on the grounds of the covenant. The church, disciplined by her Babylonian captivity, will return to her first love – to her love-covenant with Jesus, her heavenly Bridegroom. Ezekiel, after the grief of seeing Israel's idolatry, finally saw the glory of God descend and return to this new and better temple. As he saw the glory of this end-time temple he heard a voice say,

> *'Son of man, this is the place of my throne and the place for the soles of my feet. This is where I will live among the Israelites for ever. The house of Israel will never again defile my holy name – neither they nor their kings – by their prostitution and the lifeless idols of their kings at their high places. When they placed their threshold next to my threshold and their doorposts beside my doorposts, with only a wall between me and them, they defiled my holy name by their detestable practices. So I destroyed them in my anger. Now let them put away from me their prostitution and the lifeless idols of their kings, and I will live among them for ever.'*
>
> (Ezekiel 43:7–9 NIV)

In other words if the church – the Israel of God – will expel her idols and live in obedience to the great commandment, the glory will return!

The great commandment – key to revival and reformation

Josiah, the reformer and revivalist king, also discovered the power of the covenant. In fact the rediscovery of the 'book of the law' (most probably Deuteronomy or possibly the whole Pentateuch) in the temple proved to be the catalyst for Josiah's revival. On reading it Josiah's heart broke and he cried out,

> *'Great is the LORD's anger that burns against us because our fathers have not obeyed the words of this book; they have not acted in accordance with all that is written there concerning us.'*
>
> (2 Kings 22:13 NIV)

Josiah looked at their circumstances and saw the covenant curses in operation. He immediately turned to Hilkiah, the prophetess, to get a word from the Lord. True to the prophetic touchstone of the covenant she prophesied,

> *'I am going to bring disaster on this place and its people, according to everything written in the book ... Because they have forsaken me and burned incense to other gods and provoked me to anger by all the idols their hands have made ...'*
>
> (2 Kings 22:16–17)

But to Josiah she said,

> '**Because your heart was responsive and you humbled yourself** *before the* LORD *when you heard what I have spoken against this place and its people, that they would become accursed and laid waste,* **and because you tore your robes and wept in my presence,** *I have heard you* ... **Your eyes will not see all the disaster** *I am going to bring on this place.'*

(2 Kings 22:19–20)

Through humility and brokenness Josiah averted the judgment of God. He renewed the covenant and removed the worship of Baal from the temple, embarking on a holy rampage, destroying, pulling down and desecrating the altars and high places. He then revived the true worship of Yahweh (2 Kings 23).

Falling on our faces

Worship and intercession

As well as the covenant-document, John, Ezekiel, Josiah and the elders had something else in common – they all *fell on their faces* when they saw the glory of God. When the elders saw the Lamb with the scroll, they fell down before Him, each one holding a *harp* and a *bowl* (Revelation 5:8), representing *worship* and *intercession* respectively. Worship and intercession are the two wings that will carry the Bride into the presence of God and the fullness of His kingdom.

When we experience true worship God begins to share His heart and mind. We begin to intercede out of His will and out of what touches Him (Romans 8:26–27).

Some of the most powerful times of intercession I have seen were born out of worship. In the early 1970s our church played a significant role in hosting and spreading the renewal in Australia, particularly in the city of Sydney. When Paul and Bunty Collins arrived in Sydney they planned to hold healing meetings having come directly out of a powerful signs and wonders move in New Zealand. But God had other ideas. At the first meeting, despite their plans, spontaneous worship broke out and that's all they could do. Coming to the next meeting there were twice as many people and they thought, 'OK, that was last week – we'll move out in healing this week'. But again God had His way. Worship with spontaneous singing in the Spirit broke out and again filled the whole service. Catching the drift, Paul and Bunty learned to host the Holy Spirit so that praise and worship became the key that unlocked the door to renewal for Sydney. In a city where many had failed previously, people were being saved, healed and baptised in the Spirit. The meetings grew exponentially and became a powerful centre of the renewal whereby many thousands were introduced to the things of the Spirit.

The highlight of the week became our Monday night 'world-wide prayer meeting'. We never knew what God was going to do. There was no agenda for these meetings. Apart from worship and responding to the heart of God there was no plan. After only one or two worship choruses, the congregation of up to several hundred people would be powerfully lifted into the heavenlies by the song of the Lord and spontaneous singing in the Spirit. I recall one particular night when this happened and a spirit of intercession fell on several so that they began to weep and travail in prayer. As it fell, the remainder of the congregation continued in worship and were lifted several notches in their intensity and, as the intercessory travail continued, into aggressive warfare and then high praise. At this point there was an explosion of applause, exuberant shouting and singing in the Spirit – there was an overwhelming sense of breakthrough and victory. The burden of intercession lifted and a powerful spirit of rejoicing was released. What had happened? At the height of that awesome worship God had simultaneously laid the nation of the Philippines on the hearts of several intercessors. From the travail and breakthrough in prayer of that night the work had been done, and very quickly the Lord put together a team of about 12 people including Paul and Bunty with their young family. They were sent out to Manila where a highly influential centre of renewal was established which is still operating to this day. But it had first been born in the Spirit, on the wings of worship and intercession, back in our Sydney prayer meeting.[3]

No wonder the elders fell before the throne with a *harp* and a *bowl* – in worship and intercession!

The four horsemen of the apocalypse released – revival, war, recession, disease

Out of this atmosphere of worship and intercession, the seals of the new covenant are fully opened (Revelation 5) and the four horsemen of the apocalypse are released (Revelation 6). The power and the glory of the kingdom – God's end-time purposes – His mercy and His judgments, are only released in their fullness through the worshipping Bride – through the church returning to her love-covenant with Jesus – to the great commandment. Overflowing from the heights of passionate and pure worship into an intercessory identification with the heart of God, the seals of covenant blessings and curses are broken and released into the earth.

First a *white horse* went forth, whose rider held a *bow* and was given a *crown*. Commentators differ, but in my view this is the white horse of *revival* – the white horse of the gospel going out in the power of the Spirit, 'conquering and to conquer' (Revelation 6:2). It signifies the victorious advance of the kingdom in the nations until the fullness of the Gentiles has come in – until, *'The kingdom of the world has become the kingdom of our Lord and of his Christ'* (Revelation 11:15 NIV)

Second a *red horse* was released, *'taking peace from the earth'*, signifying war (Revelation 6:4). At the same time as the covenant blessing of revival, the remedial judgment of war is released. For example the 1859 prayer revival, starting in America, preceded the Civil War by only several years. And the First World War followed hard on the heels of the great Welsh Revival of 1904 and the Azusa Street Revival of 1906. God, in His wrath, remembers mercy by often pouring out His Spirit before He pours out His judgments. The second half of the 20th century has been marked by unusual seasons of refreshing through the Charismatic Renewal, Third Wave Movements and the 'Toronto Blessing'. However, we are now entering a period of increasing judgment as the purposes of God accelerate across the earth. The pace of revival, reformation, and war will increase.

Third a *black horse* went forth whose rider held a pair of *scales*, symbolising *economic recession* (Revelation 6:5–6). The Western economies were rocked by the 1929 Depression, triggering enormous unemployment and suffering. We are again facing grave economic uncertainties as we enter the 21st century with various crashes and recessions over the last fifteen years.

Fourth a *pale horse* appeared whose rider, named *Death*, was given power to kill not only through war and recession but also by disease (Revelation 6:8). We are not only facing the Grim

Reaper in HIV AIDS but now also in the terrorist threat of bio-warfare. Anthrax has already been released in the USA and it appears that some rogue states and terrorist organisations have the capacity to use more sophisticated bio-weapons such as smallpox.

Hinge-times in history

Now some may say, 'Come on, these things have happened all through history, in one form or another!' I agree, they have. Even so, in my view, they are released with increased ferocity during what I would call *hinge-times* of history – periods of transition on which new epochs and eras swing. For example Reformation Europe was marked by these four phenomena from before 1500 to approximately 1648 with the end of the Thirty Years War. The prevailing atmosphere was presaged with apocalyptic storm clouds, with expectations of divine judgment and the imminent return of Christ. The Pope was seen as the anti-Christ and Luther as the prophet Elijah sent to prepare the way of the Lord. They saw the *white horse* of revival in the Reformation; the *red horse* of war in the numerous peasant uprisings, the Islamic insurgence and the Thirty Years War; the *black horse* in endemic peasant poverty; and the *pale horse* in the plague which decimated approximately one-third of Europe. With the four horsemen trampling European soil with such incredible ferocity they felt the end of the world was near. But by the mid-17th century these four phenomena began to subside. Europe had been radically reshaped politically and spiritually and was now settling into a new era. The kingdom of God had made a quantum leap forward.

Likewise the period of 1950 to 2025 is a *hinge-time* in history. A hinge on which swings an era of global transformation – of culmination when massive spiritual awakenings and harvest will finally bring heaven to earth. As a time of transition it will prepare the way for a final world-wide transformation when

> 'the mountain of the LORD's temple will be established
>   as chief among the mountains;
> it will be raised above the hills,
>   and all nations will stream to it.'
>
> (Isaiah 2:2 NIV)

It will be an era of powerful spiritual awakenings. Whole communities, cities and nations, one after another, will be so transformed that justice and peace will prevail throughout the earth. God will fulfil His promise that,

> *'Many peoples will come and say,*
>
> *"Come, let us go up to the mountain of the* Lord *...*
> *He will teach us his ways ..."*
> *The law will go out from Zion ...*
> *He will judge between the nations*
>   *and will settle disputes for many peoples.*
> *They will beat their swords into ploughshares*
>   *and their spears into pruning hooks.*
> *Nation will not take up sword against nation,*
>   *nor will they train for war anymore.'*
>
> (Isaiah 2:3–4 NIV)

In the meantime the four horsemen will continue to ride. This transitional period will continue to be marked by accelerating revival, war, recession and disease – in wrath God will remember mercy as the covenant blessings and judgments go forth, renewing and disciplining first the church and then the nations until they return to the Lord and the kingdom fully comes.

Chapter 13

The Prescription – Brokenness on Earth, Openness in Heaven

Restoring the Glory of God

'... the land was radiant with his glory ... I fell face down ... and the glory of the Lord filled the temple.'
(Ezekiel 43:2–5)

'... and the elders fell down and worshipped.'
(Revelation 5:14)

In summary, I have so far attempted two things in this book. First, to provide a prophetic forecast of the church's future, and second, a diagnosis of the hindrances to that future – to full-scale revival and world-wide community transformation. It is one thing, though, to diagnose and prognosticate, it is another to prescribe – to provide answers. Even so, I cannot overemphasise that the right prescription can only be found in a true and accurate diagnosis. In fact, our refusal to face the diagnosis has caused us to pursue all manner of superficial solutions and panaceas which focus on relieving symptoms but never healing the disease. The yielding to truth, though, in itself is a healing. But to return to my point, once the diagnosis is clear a doctor who doesn't know what treatment to prescribe is not all that useful. This is the challenge of our closing chapter.

We all hunger for the Spirit of God to touch down in our cities and nations. But our latest church growth programmes and our new apostolic paradigms, nor even our city-reaching strategies, are not doing it. Why is this? Because the final answer is not *structural*, it is *spiritual*. Our Western psyche is geared to be in control. And so we unwittingly prefer our *programmes* to His *presence*. While God is never capricious, He is unpredictable. If this is true, it demands that we, in response, pursue *spirit* over *structure*. But for us to make the switch, something has to change in us. God is after something we have not been willing to give – a transaction through which we lose not only control, but also ourselves. He wants *us*. He wants our surrender – and He is looking for it now.

'Come out from among them!' – a call to holiness and intimacy

Causing confusion among commentators Paul, seemingly out of context, in his second letter to the Corinthians, issues a clarion call to holiness and intimacy with God – *a call to come out of Babylon*:

> *'Do not be bound together with unbelievers; for what partnership have righteousness and lawlessness, or what fellowship has light with darkness? Or what harmony has Christ with Belial ... Or what agreement has the temple of God with idols? For we are the temple of the living God; just as God said,*
>
> *"I will dwell in them and walk among them;*
> *And I will be their God, and they shall be My people.*
> *Therefore, come out from their midst and be separate,"*
>   *says the Lord.*
> *"And do not touch what is unclean;*
> *And I will welcome you.*
> *And I will be a father to you,*
> *And you shall be sons and daughters to Me,"*
> *Says the Lord Almighty.*
>
> *Therefore ... let us cleanse ourselves from all defilement of flesh and spirit, perfecting holiness in the fear of God.'*
>
> (2 Corinthians 6:14 – 7:1 NASB)

But what was the context of this call? Why did Paul issue it? The answer is found in the reason for Paul's whole Corinthian correspondence. It was centred in one thing – the underlying opposition of the so-called *super-apostles*.[1] Sandwiched in the middle of an energetic defence of his apostleship Paul issued this call to holiness and intimacy. But why here? Because a false apostolic movement had imbided the spirit of the age, being driven by values contrary to the Spirit of Christ. It was in effect, pagan and demonic (2 Corinthians 6:14–16). While the *pop-apostles* of Corinth *'masqueraded as servants of righteousness'* (2 Corinthians 11:15) they were, under the masks of their spirituality and success, sons of Belial (2 Corinthians 11:15).

Therefore, in a prophetic spirit, Paul called the church to come out from Babylon (2 Corinthians 6:17. See also Isaiah 48:20; 52:11; Jeremiah 50:8; 51:6, 9, 45; Revelation 18:4). But this is only one half of the equation – the uprooting and tearing down of Jeremiah's prophetic commission. The other half is the call to intimacy:

> *'And I will be a father to you,*
> *And you shall be sons and daughters to Me.'*
>
> (2 Corinthians 6:18 NASB)

This is the building and planting of the Jeremiah call. God always calls us 'out of' to take us 'into' – *out of* Babylon and *into* the holiness of God.

The parallel with our generation is obvious. A false apostolic movement is in the process of emerging along with the authentic. Initially, like the Corinthian *super-apostles*, it will be very popular and appear to be highly successful. But in time as abuses become more obvious it will muddy the waters for the genuine. Because of this, it will so compromise the term *apostolic* that its use, rather than becoming easier, will actually become more difficult. It will be evident that many have appropriated an *apostolic charisma* without paying an *apostolic cost* – that they have merely implemented *apostolic paradigms* without living in *apostolic purity*. That they have created *new wineskins* only to fill them with the *old wine* of Babylon – the spirit of competition, self-seeking and pride.

But at the same time, the Spirit of God is calling out a true apostolic movement to Himself – to come out from the deceit and pride of Babylon and return to holiness and intimacy.

The sins of the spirit

So how do we come out of the bondage and deception of Babylon? And how can we be sure we are part of the true end-time restoration of apostolic Christianity? As Paul explained it is by '*cleans*[ing] *ourselves from all defilement of* **flesh** *and* **spirit**, *perfecting holiness in the fear of God*' (2 Corinthians 7:1 NASB).

We are not only defiled by the sins of the *flesh* but also by the sins of the *spirit*. The former are obvious. But the latter – the sins of the spirit – are hidden. They are the sins of motive, attitude, and affection – the things that make us do what we do. This is where the *pride of life* lives – where we worship the work of our own hands, taking pride in our own accomplishments and success. It's where we give allegiance to the false gods of success and power – the gods of ministry, position and prestige – the false images of self. It is where we live and feel – and where we are most vulnerable. It is, therefore, where we are the most defensive – where we have established fortified strongholds for our own survival.

The stronghold of self

As I have sought to highlight, the stronghold of *self* is our greatest single roadblock to spiritual breakthrough. When we allow God into this hidden realm – into the deepest parts of our spirit by surrendering *self*-will and *self*-justification, all heaven will break loose. When God has a people with whom He can entrust Himself, through whom He can live and act, supernatural things will occur – heaven will come to earth. He is waiting for a people who will not use Him – who will not use the gifts and the power of God for *self*-aggrandisement. As leaders reconsecrate themselves, laying down *self*-promotion and *self*-effort, God will have room to move again, to be who He is, not only in their own lives but also in the church. False gods will fall to the ground. The product of our own hands – our images, our ministries, our plans and strategies – and our egos – will be consumed as wood, hay, and stubble in the flames of God's presence. Pastors and leaders will not only surrender their positions and their possessions but even their paycheques to obey God and move into their destiny in the *emerging church*.

Those who are not influential or powerful by human standards will arise from obscurity to lead what God is doing. Man will get out of the way. Christ will rule in the church. And the prince of this world will be cast down. There will be an *open heaven* over entire cities and nations. And what once took years of difficult labour will happen in days and weeks as new believers, children and teenagers are used by God to bring about supernatural healing and deliverance. God will break all the rules as underground youth churches and alternative forms of worship move under the power of God to harvest a new generation. Young apostles and prophets will emerge from this underground church and provide prophetic leadership for the work of God into the next era.

But how will all this happen – how does heaven come to earth?

The divine prescription

As we have just seen, Paul prescribes the antidote to Babylon by exhorting us to *'cleanse ourselves from all defilement of flesh and spirit, perfecting holiness **in the fear of God'*** (2 Corinthians 7:1 NASB).

The fear of the Lord is the hatred of evil (Proverbs 8:13; 19:9; Psalm 34:11–14). It is the spring from which holiness flows (Isaiah 11:2–3; Proverbs 14:27) and it provides the inner motivation to cleanse ourselves from the sins of the flesh and of the spirit.

In that sense, therefore, the fear of the Lord is the beginning of wisdom (Proverbs 9:10). And we know that

> *'the wisdom from above is first pure, then peaceable, gentle, willing to yield, full of mercy and good fruits, without a trace of partiality or hypocrisy.'*   (James 3:17 NRSV)

So, *'the wisdom **from above'*** in a very real sense brings heaven to earth. As heaven's wisdom, the fear of the Lord will teach us His ways, causing renewal of heart, restoration of relationships, and the rebuilding of the house of prayer.

Renewal of heart

The forerunner-ministry of John the Baptist was designed to *'prepare the way of the Lord'* (Luke 3:4–6). Before every historic visitation of God the Holy Spirit has prepared the way by significant dealings with the human heart. Every human attempt to rebuild Eden (religious and political) lacks the one ingredient that only God can give – a renewed heart. A renewed heart comes only through the regenerating and sanctifying power of the Spirit.

Therefore every true visitation of God, in some measure, is preceded by the call to a deeper identification with the cross and to a fuller experience of the Spirit[2] – and through these to closer conformity to the image of Christ.

This usually comes through 'the dealings of God' (Hebrews 12:4–11). God allows things in His wisdom which He could stop by His power:

> *'And we know that in all things God works for the good of those who love him, who have been called according to his purpose.'*
> (Romans 8:28 NIV)

As Forrest Gump observed, 'Life is like a box of chocolates – you never know what you're going to get'. God works in *'all things'*, including pain. But why? The very next verse tells us – that we might be *'conformed to the likeness of his Son'* (Romans 8:29 NIV). The vicissitudes of life – its unpredictable and often painful experiences, are allowed by God for one purpose: to press us into a deeper identification with the cross of Christ and the life of the Spirit, through which we are more closely conformed to His image and glory.

A few verses earlier Paul clearly shows that sharing in Christ's suffering qualifies us to share in his glory:

> *'Now if we are children, then we are heirs – heirs of God and co-heirs with Christ, if indeed we share in his sufferings in order that we may also share in his glory.'*   (Romans 8:17)

In fact, our experience of suffering works into us a glory *'beyond all measure'* (2 Corinthians 4:17 NRSV). Paul connects our present *'light'* and *'momentary'* suffering with the *'eternal weight of glory'*. The good news, though, is that the measure of glory always outweighs the measure of suffering. But the fact remains – no suffering, no glory.

And so the *weight* of the coming visitation will be measured by our suffering. But how does this work? If we co-operate with Him then in times of suffering the Holy Spirit will create within us three conditions of heart: *purity*, *brokenness*, and *humility*.

Purity of heart

> *'Blessed are the pure in heart,*
> *for they will see God.'*

> (Matthew 5:8 NIV)

'Who may ascend the hill of the LORD*?*
Who may stand in his holy place?
He who has clean hands and a pure heart ...

Lift up your heads, O you gates;
be lifted up you ancient doors,
that the King of glory may come in.
Who is this King of glory?
The LORD *strong and mighty,*
the LORD *mighty in battle.'*   (Psalm 24:3–4, 7–8 NIV)

When confronted by the enemy in 2 Chronicles 16, Asa faced the choice of relying on human strength – on the army of the king of Aram – or on the Lord. Despite previously leading the people in revival, in the moment of crisis he tragically chose human ability – to trust in the king of Aram. The window of victory over the enemy closed. And because he did not look to the Lord the prophet declared,

> *'For the eyes of the* LORD *flash back and forth over the whole earth to display His strength on behalf of those **whose heart is full of integrity toward Him**.'*   (2 Chronicles 16:9 Berkeley)

Asa's heart was not pure, causing him to walk by sight and trust in human contrivance rather than in the Lord.

The Western church likewise faces overwhelming odds. But what will we do? Are our hearts pure toward the Lord? Will we proudly continue to bow to the gods of rationalism and intellectualism, doubting and refusing to believe? Will we continue to turn to what we know and trust – to the Baals of *productivity* and *power*, to the work of our own hands – to better techniques and methods? Or will we turn to the Lord?

Brokenness of heart

'The sacrifices of God are a broken spirit;
a broken and a contrite heart,
O God, you will not despise.'   (Psalm 51:17 NIV)

'For this is what the high and lofty One says –
he who lives for ever, whose name is holy:
"I live in a high and holy place,
but also with him who is contrite and lowly in spirit,

> *to revive the spirit of the lowly*
> >   *and to revive the heart of the contrite.'*   (Isaiah 57:15 NIV)

> *'Blessed are the poor in spirit,*
> >   *for theirs is the kingdom of heaven.'*   (Matthew 5:3 NIV)

Our hearts, in their natural state, are proud. Apart from the renewing work of the Spirit we are unbroken and resistant to the searching light of truth. Before David's prophetic confrontation with Nathan, he had concealed the reality of his true condition – of his sin with Bathsheba and the murder of Uriah – for twelve months. When confronted, though, he didn't blame-shift – there was no self-justification. He didn't rationalise but broke, receiving truth against himself.[3]

It is not possible to experience true revival without brokenness. *Brokenness on earth* will always create *openness in heaven*.

Humility of heart

> *'God opposes the proud but gives grace to the humble.'*
> >   (James 4:6 NIV)

> *'He has showed you, O man, what is good.*
> >   *And what does the* LORD *require of you?*
> *To act justly and to love mercy*
> >   *and to walk humbly with your God.'*   (Micah 6:8 NIV)

This kind of humility is to occur

> *'not only when their eye is on you and to win their favour, but with sincerity of heart and reverence for the Lord.'*
> >   (Colossians 3:22 NIV)

We are learning how to play to an audience of one. Even so humility is not only *devotional* but also *relational*. It is done in the fear of God but is expressed toward men. Do I unconsciously feel better about myself by finding fault in others? Do I humorously or otherwise put others down? Do I find it difficult to admit I was wrong, or ask somebody for their forgiveness? Do I justify myself and rationalise my behaviour? Do I compete for position or recognition? Do I suffer from feelings of envy or jealousy and find it difficult to praise another person? Do I experience an inner resistance when being counselled, corrected, or instructed?

Do I have difficulty in receiving from others? Just a few of the symptoms of pride.

I recall vividly the inner struggle I experienced when starting out in ministry as my closest friend was promoted and favoured over me. Every Sunday when he led the worship or preached, was for me an exercise of holiness and of humbling my heart as I struggled with feelings of jealousy until I was free.

The spirit of pride is the root cause of spiritual decline:

> *'Pride goes before destruction,*
> *And a haughty spirit before stumbling.'*
>
> (Proverbs 16:18 NASB)

It was historically the cause of the church's fall – causing it to stumble from the ways of God into politics and power. Therefore the church's recovery will be in the opposite spirit – in the spirit of humility:

> *'A man's pride will bring him low,*
> *But a humble spirit will obtain honor.'*   (Proverbs 29:23 NASB)

The wisdom-writer understood the source of all life's problems – our heart. He exhorts us to

> *'Watch over* [our] *heart(s) with all diligence,*
> *For from it flow the springs of life.'*   (Proverbs 4:23 NASB)

Church, let us learn the lesson and bow our hearts before *'the Father of spirits'*, who through His moulding touch disciplines us so that we might share His holiness (Hebrews 12:5–12). Our dealings with the Father are to one end – that He might so mould our spirits – our motives, attitudes, and affections – that we might commune with His heart and nature. Father come, breathe upon us and break our hearts.

John Bunyan said that, 'When we pray it is better to let our heart be without words, than for our words to be without heart.' And so let's camp here a moment. Let this be a *selah*[4] time as we dwell on these words penned by John Donne five centuries ago. Let us feel the *pathos* of this cry as we pray,

> 'Batter my heart, three-person'd God; for, you
> As yet but knock, breath, shine, and seek to mend;

That I may rise, and stand, o'erthrow me, and bend
Your force, to break, blow, burn and make me new.
I, like an usurp'd town, to another due,
Labour to admit you, but Oh, to no end,
Reason your viceroy in me, me should defend,
But is captiv'd, and proves weak or untrue.
Yet dearly I love you, and would be loved fain,
But am betroth'd unto your enemy:
Divorce me, untie, or break that knot again,
Take me to you, imprison me, for I
Except you enthral me, never shall be free,
Nor ever chaste, except you ravish me.'

Restoration of relationship

*'See, I will send you the prophet Elijah before that great and
dreadful day of the LORD comes. He will turn the hearts of the
fathers to their children, and the hearts of the children to their
fathers; or else I will come and strike the land with a curse.'*
(Malachi 4:5–6 NIV)

*' "To be sure, Elijah comes and will restore all things" . . . he was
talking to them about John the Baptist.'*
(Matthew 17:11, 13 NIV)

The prophetic forerunner spirit prepares the way for visitation by
bringing restoration to relationships.

In times of revival hearts begin to bow again before the majesty
of His felt presence. God begins to require purity, brokenness and
humility in all of our relationships. If we come to the altar
knowing our brother has something against us, we are commanded to go and first be reconciled (Matthew 5:21–26). Is it
possible that our worship and our sacrifices, our singing and our
praying, are actually grieving the heart of God? (Isaiah 1:13–20).
Absolutely!

No amount of praying or religious exercise will move God
when unresolved relationships and offences break our fellowship
with Him and with one another.

*'If any one says, "I love God," yet hates his brother, he is a liar.
For any one who does not love his brother, whom he has seen,*

cannot love God, whom he has not seen. And he has given us this command: Whoever loves God must also love his brother.'

(1 John 4:19–21 NIV)

If we are serious in our pursuit of God then we cannot escape the light of God searching our hearts on these issues. He will not permit us to move on until our hearts break in repentance and restitution. In fact, He will resist us. No amount of good intention, human planning or effort will move us forward if we have unresolved attitudes of bitterness and resentment.

If you need to write a letter, make a telephone call or see somebody, whatever the cost – do it. Weighty matters are at stake. We are in travail for the visitation of God to the earth – for an outpouring of the Spirit to awaken and transform our world.

One of the specific areas the Holy Spirit is speaking about is the relationship of the fathers to the sons. While it is fitting for sons to honour their fathers, both natural and spiritual, the order of Malachi's prophecy is very significant. The hearts of the fathers are first turned to their sons before the hearts of the sons are turned to the fathers (Malachi 4:5–6). The initiative is with the fathers. David, the man after the heart of God, prayed,

> *'Even when I am old and grey,*
> *do not forsake me, O God,*
> *till I declare your power to the **next generation**,*
> *your might to all who are to come.'*   (Psalm 71:18 NIV)

The whole DNA of fatherhood is geared to raising up sons – to releasing a new generation. Pastors and ministry leaders please hear me – this means a change of heart and ultimately letting go. Let's stop making excuses and pass on the baton!

Rebuilding the house of prayer

> *'See, I will send my messenger* [John the Baptist], *who will prepare the way before me. Then suddenly the* Lord *you are seeking will come to his temple ... But who can endure the day of his coming? Who can stand when he appears? For he will be like a refiner's fire or a launderer's soap. He will sit as a refiner and purifier of silver; he will purify the Levites and refine them like gold and silver.'*
> (Malachi 3:1–3 NIV)

> *'It is written ... "My house will be called a house of prayer, but you are making it a 'den of robbers'."'*   (Matthew 21:13 NIV)

> *'And I will pour out on the house of David ... a spirit of grace and supplication.'*   (Zechariah 12:10 NIV)

The prophetic forerunner spirit prepares the way for Christ to come and cleanse His temple. His first advent set the pattern for every future visitation. Here lies the core diagnosis as outlined in this book. When Jesus came, the temple of God was filled with worldly transactions and those making gain for themselves. *Self-*seeking and worldly values, as explained, predominate in the Western church. Too often ministerial success and status are determined by worldly measures – in dollars and numbers. While these can certainly multiply under the blessing of God they are not our motive, nor our goal. Neither are they the measure of our obedience to the will of God.

The seduction, though, of trading our ministry gift for personal gain is powerful. Even so, ministers and leaders do not, overall, trade for financial advantage. The enemy of our soul is more subtle. We sell ourselves for the acceptance of our people or peers – for popularity, prestige, or position. Our personal security, our reputation, our recognition and our ministerial success are maintained by this mercurial spirit. By selling ourselves for personal advantage the house of God has thrown out the welcome mat to opportunism and commercialism – in fact to what the prophets called a *'spirit of prostitution'* (Hosea 5:4).

Western Christianity has become almost totally narcissistic as we worship our own image in God's house. But the prophets declare that when Jesus comes to His house all idolatry will be purged and His glory will fill the temple. But He will not share it with another. It is *His* house and *His* glory. How much of our ministry comes from our need to seek our own glory – for personal significance and a sense of identity? (John 7:18) To the degree that we seek *our* glory, the glory of *God* cannot return to the temple. Are we willing, as John the Baptist was, to decrease in order that He should increase?

The snake in my backyard
This is the rub. The theme of our discussion has been 'snakes in the temple'. But what is at the heart of the serpent's seduction, of his work of deception and idolatry in the church? It is the

promise that *we* shall becomes as gods – that *we* can be in control. His entry point is *self* – self-interest and self-seeking. This is the root of deception and control. And therefore it is also the test of what is *true* and *false*. It's not so much what's in your theology, important though that is – it's what's in your heart.

> *'He who speaks from himself seeks his own glory; but He who is seeking the glory of the one who sent Him is a man of truth, there is nothing false in Him.'*   (John 7:18)

I would have been about 5 or 6 years old when my Dad cornered and killed a large snake in our backyard. He moved onto another project, leaving my older brother and me alone with two things: the dead snake and the sharp end of a shovel. Well, boys being boys the two inevitably met. So what had previously been one really long snake was suddenly a lot of little short ones! Although it was already dead, I can still remember the exultant feeling with which we performed our grisly task – of having power over that carcass.

Likewise that old serpent, the devil, was cornered and killed by our heavenly Father 2,000 years ago. And we are now triumphing over his remains. With every response of faith and obedience – with every denial of *self* to follow Jesus – the cross (the 'sharp end of the shovel') dismembers that already dead body of sin.

Christ, as the seed of the woman, has already fatally crushed the head of the serpent (Genesis 3:15). When the seventy returned exulting in their new-found victory over demons Jesus reminded them that this was because He had seen *'Satan fall like lightning from heaven'* (Luke 10:18). He therefore continues,

> *'**I have given you authority to trample on snakes** and scorpions and to overcome all the power of the enemy.'*   (Luke 10:19 NIV)

Satan, sin and self were once-and-for-all destroyed at the cross (Colossians 2:15; Romans 6:6). They were put under the feet of Christ (Ephesians 1:22). But now by our daily obedience, as Paul says, every act of disobedience is being punished (2 Corinthians 10:6) until finally *'The God of peace will . . . crush Satan under [**our**] feet'* (Romans 16:20).

In other words, the carcass of Satan, sin and self will be so completely dismembered that the victory is not only *potentially*, but *experientially* our own.

We must understand that immediately after experiencing their victory over demons Jesus counselled the seventy to rather *'rejoice that their names are written in heaven'* (Luke 10:20).

He pointed out that the Father has *'hidden these things from the wise and learned, and revealed them to little children'* (Luke 10:21 NIV).

What is Jesus saying? Ultimate victory over Satan, sin, and self – or more particularly, over the demons of deception, pride, and idolatry, is given to those who are known in heaven. The Son has shown us the Father and on the basis of this intimate relationship victory is not given to the mighty and the worldly powerful, nor to the wise and the learned, but to babes. To those who have forsaken the worldly weapons of warfare – the weapons of prestige, power and position; and who have instead cast themselves upon God, wielding the weapons of humility and meekness, boasting not of their own accomplishments but of the cross of Christ that the glory might be God's. This is the only way we will crush, in final victory, the head of the serpent, destroying forever the powers of witchcraft, deception and pride that have ruled in the church. The meek will inherit the earth (Matthew 5:5). God will pour out His Spirit in the harvest of the nations. But only when we forsake the weapons of the *flesh* and embrace, once and for all, the weakness of the cross.

So the divine antidote to the house of God being a place of commerce is the *cross*. But how does this work? Only as it is restored as a house of prayer. True worshippers cannot worship in spirit and truth with *self* still on the throne. The more we gaze upon the awesome majesty of our God the smaller we are in our own sight. When we 'lose ourselves' in worship we are, effectively, activating the full power of the *'law of the spirit of life in Christ Jesus'* – we are set free from the *'law of sin and death'* (Romans 8:2) – from Satan and from *self*. Only as we obey the great commandment in loving God with all our heart, soul, mind, and strength, and our neighbour as ourselves (Mark 12:29–31) is the central nervous system of *self* finally severed.

In conclusion therefore, *'let us cleanse ourselves from all defilement of ... spirit, perfecting holiness in the fear of God'* (2 Corinthians 7:1 NASB). Can I say yes to the *'refiner's fire'* – to the searching, probing, and cleansing light of His Spirit? Can I pray as David did:

> '*Search me, O God, and know my heart;*
>   *test me and know my anxious thoughts.*
> *See if there is any offensive way in me,*
>   *and lead me in the way everlasting.*'

(Psalm 139:23–24 NIV)

Pastors, leaders and people – what is your motive for ministry? Are you seeking great things for yourself? Why do you 'do church' – why are you 'doing' small groups, counselling and pastoral care? Why do you 'do' music and worship? Are you looking to gain a sense of *personal significance* or to give a sense of *paternal satisfaction* – to bring pleasure to the Father's heart?

It is time to find a new *starting point* – to return to the heart of the Father for from *Him* and through *Him* and to *Him* are all things – and to return to His purpose for a family conformed to His own image. To return to the apostolic foundation of intimacy with God in Christ.

Come Holy Spirit, renew our hearts, restore our relationships and rebuild the Father's house of prayer. People, pray for yourselves – it is time to return to the Lord – to finish 'playing church' and living for self. Pray for your leaders – pray that their hearts will be touched by the love of the Father and by His eternal purpose – that they will return to what truly matters. Support and love them, esteem them highly for their work – for they bear a greater judgment (James 3:1).

Above all – in brokenness may we fall on our faces in the light of the glory of His presence. May our lives truly be a house of prayer for all nations. Even so, come Lord Jesus.

Notes

Introduction

1. *Polemic/polemical* – a controversial discussion involving dispute.

Chapter 1

1. A new paradigm of church which is non-institutional – without the traditional structures and constraints which buildings can represent. See *Church Without Walls: Moving Beyond Traditional Boundaries*, by Jim Peterson, published by NavPress, Colorado Springs, 1992.
2. For further discussion of the city-church and its government refer to Chapter 9, 'Idolatry and Human Leadership', p. 123ff.
3. For further information on Melbourne's city-wide pastors and intercessors prayer movement, go to their website at www.transformingmelbourne.org or www.pastornet.net.au/mpn/ or write to Melbourne Pastors Network, PO Box 2536, Cheltenham VIC 3192, Australia.
4. *Linguistic Key to the Greek NT*, p. 531.
5. *Britannica World Language Dictionary*, p. 208.
6. Jonathan Edwards, Vol. 1, p. 605ff.
7. *Joel-News-International-367*, 18 June 2001, www.joelnews.org
8. From Patrick Johnson's book, *Operation World*, quoted by *Joel-News-International-395*, 13 February 2002.

Chapter 2

1. Tony Campolo in a public address at Waverley Christian Fellowship, Melbourne, Australia, 18th March 1999. See Acts 7:48 and 17:24.
2. Acts 8:4, 12, 35; 9:20; 10:42; 11:20; 13:5, 38, 44, 49; 14:3, 7, 15, 21; 15:35; 16:10, 32; 17:2–3, 11; 18:5, 25, 28; 19:8–10, 20; 20:20–21, 25; 22:14–15; 26:16–20; 28:23, 31.
3. See W.E. Vine, *Expository Dictionary of Old and New Testament Words*, p. 343.
4. Quoted by Iain Murray, *Revival and Revivalism*, p. 387.
5. Lead Story: 'Hundreds Leave Their Pastorate Each Month', *Charisma News Service*, February 26, 2001, Vol. 2 No. 249; www.charismanews.com
6. *Ibid.*
7. J.B. Lightfoot, *Epistle to the Philippians*, p. 150; for the meaning of *ginosko* (know) see also B.F. Westcott, *The Gospel According to St John*, p. 239.
8. DeVern Fromke, *The Ultimate Intention*, p. 10.
9. Basic US educational test.
10. *Pointers*, Bulletin of the Christian Research Association, March 2000, Vol. 10, Issue 1.

Chapter 3

1. Francis Schaeffer, *The Church at the End of the Twentieth Century*, p. 156.
2. For a helpful overview of these and other revivals going back to the 1700s refer to Geoff Waugh's book, *Flashpoints of Revival*. Also Richard Riss' two titles are very helpful – *Latter Rain – the Latter Rain Movement of 1948 and the Mid-Twentieth Century Evangelical Awakening*, and *A Survey of 20th Century Revival Movements in North America*.

Chapter 4

1. *Britannica World Language Dictionary*, p.653.
2. *Ibid*, p. 1060.
3. 'Group of 12 (G12)' – a popular church growth strategy used in South and Central America, beginning to be used in the West also. The whole structure of the church flows from a founding group of 12 who each lead another group of 12 and so on, as the church grows through multiplication.
4. Doug Small, *Alive Ministries*. Quoted, with permission, from personal correspondence with the author, 2nd May 2001. It is now in print as *Transformation Themes: Recovering Pieces of Truth that Liberate* (Alive Ministries: Kannapolis, NC; 2001), Alive Ministries: Project Pray; P.O. Box 1245; Kannapolis, NC 28082. www.aliveministries.org
5. *Britannica World Language Dictionary*, p. 1383.

Chapter 5

1. *Theological Wordbook of the Old Testament*, Vol. 2 p. 850ff.
2. ISBE pp. 268, 2514; 2 Kings 17:17; 21:6; 21:9; Schulz p. 92. The images reflect their embrace of heathen nature-worship. Ezekiel has already encountered the *'idol of jealousy'* (Ezekiel 8:3, 5) in the north gate of the temple which is most probably a representation of Baal or Asherah. Manasseh had previously set up an Asherah pole, a phallic symbol, in the temple (2 Kings 21:7). As a fertility cult with its pedigree in Ishtar, the Babylonian/Assyrian Queen of Heaven (Jeremiah 7:18; 44:17–25; ISBE pp. 268, 2514), the worship of Asherah and Baal took Israel to depths that exceeded even the surrounding nations (2 Kings 21:9), engaging in orgiastic worship, child sacrifice, snake worship, and the occult (2 Kings 17:17; 21:6; Schulz p. 92).
3. Tim Dowley (ed.), *The History of Christianity*, p. 62.
4. John Stott, *Tyndale NT Commentaries, The Letters of John*, p. 105.

Chapter 6

1. Samuel J. Schultz, *The Old Testament Speaks*, p. 92; ISBE, Vol. , pp. 345ff., 542ff.
2. R.K. Harrison, *Introduction to the Old Testament*, p. 365.
3. J.I. Packer, *A Passion for Faithfulness*, pp. 205, 206.
4. Richard Rohr, *Simplicity*, p. 56.
5. *Ibid*, p. 57.
6. See Emile Durkheim, *The Elementary Forms of Religious Life*.

Chapter 7

1. By 'institutional church' (or 'religious system') I refer to the entrenched attitudes of ownership and control that, in time, occupy human organisational structures. The wind of the Spirit blows where it wills – we do not know where it comes from nor where it is going (John 3:8). Only humility and highly fluid structures are able to quickly respond when God moves. But once a leader or a 'movement' refuses to move on with God it establishes its own autonomy – its own control. It becomes 'institutionalized', depending on human power structures for survival. From my observation, even the more recent emergence of many so-called 'apostolic models' of church are as prone, if not more so, to the pitfalls of control as traditional denominational structures. Often the paradigm difference is only semantic rather than substantive. Human nature is the same regardless of paradigms or structures. Chapter 9, 'Idolatry and Human Leadership', deals with these issues.

2. Compare Revelation 18:10; 16:19; 17:18 and 11:8. See David Chilton, *Days of Vengeance*, pp. 362ff., 421ff. While one may not fully agree with his complete theological position or all the details of his exegesis, in my opinion Chilton's commentary on Revelation, after twenty-five years of pursuing an interest in this subject, provides one of the most hermeneutically sound and plausible interpretations I have seen. I commend it to your attention.

3. See also Luke 10:18 for Jesus' application of this Isaiah passage to Satan.

4. Revelation 17 and Chilton, *ibid*, pp. 421ff.

5. Chilton, *ibid*, p. 129. He also states, 'In the Greek Old Testament (the version used by the early church), it is a common prophetic expression for rebellious, idolatrous Israel about to be destroyed and driven from the Land (Jeremiah 1:14; 10:18; Ezekiel 7:7; 36:17; Hosea 4:1, 3; Joel 1:2, 14; 2:1; Zephaniah 1:18), based on its original usage in the historical books of the Bible for rebellious, idolatrous pagans about to be destroyed and driven from the Land (Numbers 32:17; 33:52, 55; Josh 7:9; 9:24; Judges 1:32; 2 Sam 5:6; 1 Chronicles 11:4; 22:18; Nehemiah 9:24); Israel has become a nation of pagans, and is about to be destroyed, exiled, and supplanted by a new nation, the Church.'

6. *Enhanced Strong's Lexicon*, Oak Harbor, WA: Logos Research Systems, Inc., 1995.

Chapter 8

1. For the interested student, refer to the scholarly work on this subject by Clinton Arnold, *Ephesians: Power and Magic – The Concept of Power in Ephesians in Light of Its Historical Setting*.

2. For an explanation of pragmatism refer to Chapter 4.

3. Leon Morris, *The Gospel According to John*, NICNT, p. 692.

Chapter 9

1. See Judges 18 – 21 and 1 Samuel 4 – 8. The books of 1 and 2 Samuel flow chronologically from the time of the Judges, Samuel being the last of the judges and the first of the prophets. The theme of Samuel is the rejection

of the 'theocracy' (the rule of God) and establishment of the 'monarchy' (the rule of man). The theme of 1 and 2 Kings is its failure.

2. See 1 Corinthians 10:6, 11 – the history of the old covenant (OC) church, Israel, occurred as 'examples' (NIV) or as 'types' (Gr. *tupos*) for our warning in the new covenant (NC) church. The word *tupos* denotes an impression or mark made by a stamp or die. The OC church, in essence, is a 'type' – an impression or mark made by the die or stamp of the future NC church, which is called the 'antitype'. As such a 'type' is a prefiguring – a prophetic foreshadowing of a future reality. The epistle to the Hebrews shows that OC institutions are a 'shadow' of future spiritual realities (Hebrews 8:5; 10:1). Just as a shadow has no substance of itself and points to the actual object causing it, the OC order pointed to the reality of the NC – Christ and His church. Therefore significant events, people, and institutions of the OC prophetically foreshadow spiritual realities and warnings for the NC church.

3. The moral and spiritual anarchy of the period of the judges overlaps the story of Samuel and the establishment of the monarchy.

4. David Wright, *The History of Christianity*, pp. 118–120; Henry Chadwick, *The Early Church*, pp. 41–53.

5. Apostolic succession was not fully developed until the third century owing to the advocacy of Cyprian, Bishop of Carthage (248–258). However, it was present in the climate of the second century with the emphasis on apostolic *tradition* and *teaching*. But by the third it had grown to the succession of apostolic *office*, tracing from the first apostles a line of succession through the bishops. (see R.E. Higginson, *Evangelical Dictionary of Theology*, p. 73).

6. Michael A. Smith, *The History of Christianity*, p. 83.

7. Von Campenhausen, *Ecclesiastical Authority and Spiritual Power in the Church of the First Three Centuries*, p. 97.

8. Quoted by Von Campenhausen, *ibid*, p. 99.

9. A.M. Renwick, *The Story of the Church*, p. 27.

10. Von Campenhausen, p. 294.

11. Refer to David Cannistraci, *The Gift of Apostle*, pp. 86–90 for a discussion on women apostles.

12. See Watchman Nee, *The Church and the Work*, Vols. 1, 2, 3, for a biblical and practical explanation of the apostle and his relationship with the churches; also Robert Banks, *Paul's Idea of Community*, pp. 159ff.

13. The old covenant church, in assembly, is designated, 'the congregation of the Lord' (see Deuteronomy 23:2ff.), or in Hebrew the *qahal*; which is rendered about 100 times in the LXX (Septuagint) by the Greek word *ecclesia*, from which we derive our English word 'church'. The *qahal* refers to the whole congregation assembled either for war, worship, or government.

14. Neander, *Church History*, Vol. 1, pp. 268–269.

15. Some view James, in Jerusalem, as a senior pastor. However, the question needs to be asked whether the Jerusalem church or the Antioch church is the normative model of the Gentile church. In any case, there is no explicit internal evidence that shows James occupying the position of senior pastor (bishop). As the Lord's brother, a witness of the resurrection, and an apostle of the parent Jerusalem church he understandably carried

significant weight. He was recognised by Paul, along with Peter and John as a 'pillar' of the church (Galatians 2:9).

16. Von Campenhausen, pp. 122–123.

17. Von Campenhausen p. 101.

18. Renwick p. 20.

19. See Alexander Strauch's, *Biblical Eldership*, for a useful exegetical and practical guide to the functioning of eldership teams.

20. The same applies to Acts 1:20 (NASB) in referring to Judas. The translators have arbitrarily replaced the Greek term *episkope*, otherwise rendered 'bishop' or 'overseer', with the English word 'office', again betraying the entrenched concept of *official power* in the church.

21. **The city churches:**
    The church of Antioch (of Syria) (Acts 11:25–26)
    The church of Caesarea (Acts 18:22)
    The church of Cenchrea (Romans 16:1)
    The church of Corinth (1 Corinthians 1:2)
    The church of Ephesus (Revelation 2:1)
    The church of Jerusalem (Acts 8:1)
    The church of Laodicea (Colossians 4:16)
    The church of Pergamum (Revelation 2:12)
    The church of Philadelphia (Revelation 3:7)
    The church of Sardis (Revelation 3:1)
    The church of Smyrna (Revelation 2:8)
    The church of Thessalonica (1 Thessalonians 1:1)
    The church of Thyatira (Revelation 2:18)
    The churches of the region:
    The churches of Asia (1 Corinthians 16:19)
    The churches of Cilicia (Acts 15:41)
    The churches of the Gentiles (Romans 16:4)
    The churches of Galatia (Galatians 1:2)

22. Paul's strategy was to go to the Jew first as the synagogues often provided the seed of gospel expansion. See also Romans 1:16; Acts 3:26; 9:20; 13:5, 14, 46.

23. News Release, 12 February 2002. www.barna.org

24. For a brief history of tithing see the *Evangelical Dictionary of Theology*, p. 1097; Latourette, Vol. 1 p. 356; and for an excellent discussion on the theological/biblical issues surrounding tithing see the useful article by Gerald Hawthorne of Wheaton College, *The New International Dictionary of New Testament Theology*, Vol. 3, pp. 851–855.

Chapter 10

1. From the Greek, *eschaton*, meaning 'last' or 'final'; see 1 Peter 1:5, 20; Revelation 1:11–17.

2. Latourette, Vol. 1, pp. 273, 288.

3. *Ibid*, p. 602.

4. http://www.hillsdale.edu/dept/History/Documents/War/LouisXIV/ 1683-Vienna-Siege.htm

5. Vine, W.E., *Vine's Expository Dictionary of Old and New Testament Words*, Riverside, Iowa, 1981.

6. R.J. Rummel, www.hawaii.edu

Chapter 11

1. This area causes unnecessary confusion and conflict in the body of Christ. Most of us have, often unconsciously, imbibed the perspective of a particular millennial school, or method of interpretation, equating it with Evangelical or Pentecostal orthodoxy, when in fact no school can stake this claim. Refer to Bernard Ramm's, *Protestant Biblical Interpretation* for a balanced and very useful handling of the very difficult issue of interpreting prophecy; pp. 241–247.
2. The biblical principle of restoration stipulates that more is restored than was lost (see Exodus 22:1–9; Leviticus 6:1–5; Deuteronomy 22:1–3; Proverbs 6:31; Job 42:10–12).
3. Refer Ramm p. 258.
4. Refer Ramm pp. 263ff.
5. 2 Corinthians 10:6, 11 – Israel as an example (*tupos*), refer to ch9. n. 2 for a full explanation of types. See also Romans 15:3.
6. *kairos* – Greek word for 'time', which is marked by specific characteristics, as opposed to *chronos* which refers to the general expanse of chronological time.
7. David's stronghold when in hiding as a fugitive from Saul, representing the old order, before his elevation to the kingdom.
8. Quoted by Iain Murray, *The Puritan Hope – Revival and the Interpretation of Prophecy*, p. xiv.
9. *Ibid*, p. 258.

Chapter 12

1. Philip Mauro, *Things Which Must Soon Come To Pass*, p. 180.
2. David Chilton, *The Days of Vengeance – an Exposition of the Book of Revelation*, p. 166.
3. For the full story behind our experiences of intercession in Sydney read, June Coxhead, *Tears of Intercession*, Sovereign World, Chichester, 1990.

Chapter 13

1. Refer to Chapter 5 for a discussion on the 'super-apostles'.
2. For a foundational teaching on the power of the cross over sin and self refer to Paul and Bunty Collins, *Back to the Gospel*, Fountain Gate Christian Foundation, Newcastle, Australia, 1994. www.churchlink.com.au
3. Psalm 51 is the poignant response of David's broken heart when he was confronted by Nathan.
4. *Selah* – occurs 71 times in the Psalms as a musical notation signifying an instrumental interlude – an opportunity for reflection.

Bibliography

Arnold, Clinton E., *Ephesians: Power and Magic*, Baker Book House, Michigan, 1992

Banks, Robert, *Paul's Idea of Community* (Revised Edition), Hendrickson Publishers Inc, Massachusetts, 1994

Cannistraci, David, *The Gift of Apostle*, Regal Books, California, 1996

Chadwick, Henry, *The Early Church*, Penguin Books, London, 1990

Chilton, David, *The Days of Vengeance*, Dominion Press, Texas, 1987

Dowley, Tim (ed.), *The History of Christianity*, A Lion Book, Oxford, 1990

Durkheim, Emile, *The Elementary Forms of Religious Life*, The Free Press, New York, 1995

Elwell, Walter A. (ed.), *Evangelical Dictionary of Theology*, Baker Book House, Michigan, 1984

Fee, Gordon D. and Stuart, Douglas, *How to Read the Bible for all its Worth*, Zondervan, Michigan, 1982

Fromke, DeVern F., *The Ultimate Intention*, Sure Foundation, Mt. Vernon, 1966

Funk and Wagnalls, *Britannica World Language Dictionary*, Encyclopaedia Britannica, Inc., Chicago, 1959

Harris, R. Laird (ed.), *Theological Wordbook of the Old Testament*, Moody Press, Chicago, 1980

Harrison, R.K., *Introduction to the Old Testament*, Inter-Varsity Press, 1969

Hawthorne, Gerald, (Colin Brown, ed.) *The New International Dictionary of New Testament Theology*, Zondervan, Michigan, 1975 (first published 1967)

Hickman, Edward (ed.), *The Works of Jonathan Edwards*, The Banner of Truth Trust, Edinburgh, 1974

Jenson, Robert W., *America's Theologian*, Oxford University Press, New York, 1988

Latourette, Kenneth Scott, *A History of Christianity*, Harper & Row, New York, 1975

Lightfoot, J.B., *St Paul's Epistle to the Philippians*, Hendrickson Publishers, Massachusetts, Third Printing 1987

Mauro, Philip, *Things Which Soon Must Come to Pass*, Reiner Publications, Pennsylvania, 1984

Morris, Henry M., *The Genesis Record*, Baker Book House, Michigan, 1991

Morris, Leon, *The Gospel According to John*, William B. Eerdmans Publishing Co., Michigan, 1987

Murray, Iain H., *Revival and Revivalism*, The Banner of Truth Trust, Edinburgh, 1994

Murray, Iain H., *The Puritan Hope*, The Banner of Truth Trust, Edinburgh, 1991

Neander, Dr August, *General History of the Christian Religion and Church*, George Bell & Sons, London, 1876

Nee, Watchman, *The Church and the Work*, Vols.1, 2, 3, Christian Fellowship Publishers Inc., New York, 1982

Orr, James (ed.), *The International Standard Bible Encyclopaedia*, William B. Eerdmans Publishing Co., Michigan, 1983

Packer, J.I., *A Passion for Faithfulness*, Crossway Books, Illinois, 1995

Ramm, Bernard, *Protestant Biblical Interpretation*, Baker Book House, Michigan, 1970

Renwick, A.M. and Harman, A.M., *The Story of the Church*, Inter-Varsity Press, England, 1985

Rienecker, Fritz, *A Linguistic Key to the Greek New Testament*, Zondervan, Michigan, 1980

Riss, Richard, *Latter Rain – the Latter Rain Movement of 1948 and the Mid-Twentieth Century Evangelical Awakening*, Kingdom Flagships Foundation, Ontario, Canada, 1987

Riss, Richard, *A Survey of 20th Century Revival Movements in North America*, Hendrickson Publishers, Massachusetts, 1988

Rohr, Richard, *Simplicity*, Crossroad, New York, 1992

Schaeffer, Francis A., *The Church at the End of the Twentieth Century*, The Norfolk Press, London, 1970

Schultz, Samuel J., *The Old Testament Speaks* (Third Edition), Harper & Row, San Francisco, 1980

Stott, John R.W., *The Letters of John*, William B. Eerdmans Publishing Company, Michigan, 1988

Strauch, Alexander, *Biblical Eldership – An Urgent Call to Restore Biblical Church Leadership*, (Second Edition), Lewis and Roth Publishers, Littleton, Colorado, 1988

Vine, W.E., *Vine's Expository Dictionary of Old and New Testament Words*, Riverside, Iowa, 1981

Von Campenhausen, Hans, *Ecclesiastical Authority and Spiritual Power in the Church of the First Three Centuries*, Hendrickson Publishers, Massachusetts, 1997

Waugh, Geoff, *Flashpoints of Revival*, Destiny Image Publishers Inc., Shippensburg, 1998

Westcott, B.F., *The Gospel According to St John*, William B. Eerdmans Publishing Company, Michigan, 1981

Biography

David Orton has served as a pastor, teacher and ministry leader for over 30 years. He has recently been a catalytic leader for city-wide pastors prayer summits across Australia, touching hundreds of pastors from more than 20 denominations. He is a prophetic teacher and as the founder of *Lifemessenger* carries a word for breakthrough, particularly in the Western church, communicating through conferences, schools, publishing and electronic media. David is committed to seeing an 'emerging church' across all nations and denominations restored to the apostolic foundation of intimacy with the Father.

He and Jenny are the parents of two young adult children, Daniel and Virginia, and reside on the beautiful Mornington Peninsula, Melbourne, Australia.

Free subscription

You can subscribe to David Orton's free fortnightly e-teaching article *Lifemessage* at www.lifemessenger.org

Contact

David Orton can be contacted by email:

info@lifemessenger.org

or

Lifemessenger Inc.
PO Box 777
Mt Eliza VIC 3930
Australia